Chicagoland Dream Houses

Chicagoland Dream Houses

How a Mid-Century Architecture Competition Reimagined the American Home

SIOBHAN MORONEY

UNIVERSITY OF ILLINOIS PRESS
Urbana, Chicago, and Springfield

© 2024 by the Board of Trustees
of the University of Illinois
All rights reserved
Manufactured in the United States of America
1 2 3 4 5 C P 5 4 3 2 1
∞ This book is printed on acid-free paper.

Library of Congress Cataloging-in-Publication Data
Names: Moroney, Siobhan, 1960– author.
Title: Chicagoland dream houses : how a mid-century
    architecture competition reimagined the American home
    / Siobhan Moroney.
Description: Urbana : University of Illinois Press, [2023] |
    Includes bibliographical references and index.
Identifiers: LCCN 2023021782 (print) | LCCN 2023021783
    (ebook) | ISBN 9780252045516 (cloth) | ISBN
    9780252087622 (paperback) | ISBN 9780252055133
    (ebook)
Subjects: LCSH: Chicagoland Prize Homes Competition,
    1945. | Architecture, Domestic—Illinois—Chicago—
    History—20th century. | Suburban homes—Illinois—
    Chicago—History—20th century. | Middle class—
    Dwellings—Illinois—Chicago—History—20th century. |
    Architecture and society—Illinois—Chicago—History—
    20th century.
Classification: LCC NA2340 .M67 2023 (print) |
    LCC NA2340 (ebook) | DDC 728/.3707977311—dc23/
    eng/20230713
LC record available at https://lccn.loc.gov/2023021782
LC ebook record available at https://lccn.loc.gov/2023021783

For Mama, Daddy, and Tracy,
with whom I shared our own little postwar house.

Contents

Acknowledgments

My journey from political theorist to architectural historian began when co-teaching an American Studies course, American Spaces, at Lake Forest College. Every one of the sixteen students in the course contributed to my first thinking about house design and family relationships. My co-teacher, art historian Miguel De Baca, also provided early consultation when I was first trying to sort the modern from the traditional houses in *Prize Homes*. "They're all modern houses," he said, and that declaration encouraged me to think more critically about what is modern and what we mean by that label.

An early iteration of this work was supported by a Mellon Foundation grant, the Digital Chicago History project. Davis Schneiderman, Emily Mace, and Anne Thomason provided essential guidance on that project, which pushed my research further. Scott MacDougall took the photos of existing houses for that project, and they are reused here.

Don Meyer was my first reader, and I am so grateful for his advice and encouragement. Peter Handler's suggestions and enthusiasm dropped in at just the right moments. Tim Gallagher began listening, most generously, many years ago when I first began thinking about domestic space and how it guides our patterns of living.

Lake Forest College is full of excellent students, and I am lucky to have had a string of research assistants who, over the years, contributed to this project: Téa Thaning, Asimwe Oben-Nyarko, Zachary Hines, Krista Wickramasakera, Leslie Tenerio, Madison Stevens, Delaney Trail, Yaneli Guajardo, and Rumbidzaishe Marufu. I am very grateful for Gabriel Anzeze's dedicated attention to the images in the book, for it was he who digitized, organized, and converted all the photos and images, liberating me to think about other things.

Archivists and librarians can never receive enough recognition for what they do. Much of this research was done during the COVID-19 shutdown of 2020 and 2021. When libraries and archives were closed, librarians and archivists still responded to my emails and queries, and either found what I was looking for or suggested where else to look. Librarians and archivists at Chicago Public Libraries, Milwaukee Public Libraries, the Newberry Library, Syracuse University Libraries, the Cranbrook Archives, and Ryerson and Burnham Libraries at the Art Institute of Chicago contributed. Highland Park archivist and librarian Nancy Webster helped me many times. Local historical societies responded to my queries and sent materials. USModernist, a digital archive of architectural history, is an extraordinary resource; digital access to its library of architectural and design periodicals was crucial to this book.

Without the librarians at Lake Forest College, I never could have completed this work. Cory Stevens, Kim Hazlett, and Nancy Sosna Bohm helped in ways they might not even realize. Michael Karsten can make any book, no matter how obscure, magically appear, and did so many times. I ask forgiveness for all my many, and very late, returns.

Many people provided encouragement when I was not sure that this project could be a book or that I was the right person to write it. Thank you, Tracy Moroney, Rian Thomas, Tracy McCabe, Scott Schappe, Liz Meyer, Don Meyer, Peter Handler, Mary Beth Sova, Andreas Gallus, Lisa Disch, Tim Gallagher, Davis Schneiderman, and Dan Lemahieu for support over the years.

Anonymous reviewers provided constructive feedback and were astonishingly speedy. I thank them, and Martha Bayne, Mariah Schaefer, and Allison Syring at the University of Illinois Press, whose encouragement, quick responses, and suggestions kept the project humming along.

Our homes are intimate spaces, and we quite rightly do not invite many people to breach that intimacy. I am grateful for past and current Prize Homes residents for their openness and generosity. My trepidation about tracking them down—through Facebook groups, Google searches, cold-calling, and door-knocking—was almost always met with consent to be interviewed, but many of them went much further. I thank those who have welcomed my interview questions, invited me into their houses, shared photographs, and given me Prize Homes memorabilia. Their stories are a compelling part of this book.

My own home figures in here, too. In 2020, my two adult children moved back home because of the pandemic; that arrangement, unexpected for all of us, turned out to be a joy. Thank you, Melody and Adam, for the dinnertime conversations about my work, and making many of those dinners, too. Francis Greene, my husband, has been my partner in all things, including this book, which he read word for word, line by line. Thank you, Francis, for everything.

Chicagoland Dream Houses

Introduction

Chicago has a rich and complex architectural history. Balloon-frame house construction, a technique used to this day, is credited as a Chicago invention.[1] Rebuilding itself after the Great Chicago Fire of 1871, the city pioneered fireproof construction techniques that changed the way buildings were erected across the country. Its downtown skyline is dotted with iconic buildings, including two that have, at one time, each held the title of the tallest building in the world: the John Hancock Building and the Sears/Willis Tower. Chicago is home to the self-proclaimed "most beautiful building in the world," the Tribune Tower. And, arguably, it is home to more distinctive skyscrapers than any other city, at least any other American city. As for its residential buildings, the city and its suburbs boast of opulent lakefront mansions, high-rise glass boxes with city and water views, and some of Frank Lloyd Wright's most famous houses. At the other end of the spectrum, Chicago's history of public housing for the poor, particularly in high-rise buildings, has been rightly considered infamous. The names for two such housing units, Robert Taylor Homes and Cabrini Green, became shorthand terms for the methodical clustering of poor, mostly Black, residents into badly maintained and unsafe buildings that jeopardized their inhabitants' emotional, economic, and physical health. Both the highs and lows of Chicago architecture come in for celebration and condemnation, but they are never ignored.

Most Chicago residences, however, are neither unique, showy houses nor bleak slums, but they are vernacular housing, what Thomas Hubka calls the "common houses," for people who are neither rich nor poor.[2] Americans largely dwell in ordinary homes for the middle classes with middle incomes and, because young adults and the elderly have distinctive residential patterns, perhaps for the middle-aged. Housing for regular people lacks the grandeur of the majestic, multi-roomed homes or the shameful, shabby housing for the poor, but it still warrants our attention. The 1945 *Chicago Tribune*–sponsored Chicagoland Prize Homes house design competition sits right in that middle, generating houses that were designed largely by workaday architects who gained little fame during their careers and that, when built, were lived in by ordinary residents of the city or its suburbs. Ordinary, too, is Chicago's history of racial segregation. The ideal of home ownership was, by and large, an aspiration for White people only, whether that would take place in a suburb or within the city limits. The racial element of the midcentury American dream remained unspoken and inexplicit but ever present.

In the midcentury, other small house competitions, sponsored by architectural publications, and other house plan catalogs existed, and the Chicagoland Prize Homes competitions and catalogs can be compared to them, revealing the ways the *Tribune* competition was both similar to and different from its contemporaries. Despite the many architectural competitions in American history, the story presented here is the only full-length treatment of a small house architectural competition. The narrative is based on the *Chicago Tribune's* own extensive coverage of the Prize Homes competition, reporting from other American newspapers, archival materials from the Art Institute of Chicago, personal archives of some architects, public building records, and United States census data. Interviews with past and current residents of Prize Homes provide much important detail on how they use or used their houses, and how they adapted them to meet their needs over the years.

Chapter 1 documents the housing crisis of the Depression and World War II and provides a brief history of the small house competition. The backdrop of the Prize Homes competition was the serious housing shortage Americans faced during the Depression and World War II, which only worsened at the war's end. Concerns about how to house Americans were not unique to Chicago, but the city had special concerns because of its large and racially, ethnically, and economically diverse population, which was also true of its surrounding suburbs. House competitions had been used in previous years to drum up publicity for those who sponsored them, and the *Tribune* was no stranger to that process, having embarked on two in the 1920s. Chapters 2 and 3 mine the contest itself. *Tribune* editors brought together prominent Chicago builders and architects to serve as competition jurors, a combination that kept a focus on practicality and common tastes. Cataloging the submissions to the competition—incomplete as it is—sheds light on the architectural profession and who among architects submitted to competitions. The newspaper devoted significant resources to publicizing the contest and covering the winners, dedicating a great deal of its newsprint—sometimes on the front page—to the competition. Chicago-area residents flocked to a month-long Art Institute of Chicago exhibit of 172 Prize Homes designs in March 1946, and a series of nationwide exhibits exposed the designs to millions of others. The publicity kept the contest in the public eye for several years, as did the paper's 1948 publication of a book, *Prize Homes* (the subject of chapter 4), that joined the twenty-four winning designs with sixty-eight others. That book is the most complete and lasting record of the competition, which largely disappeared from view otherwise.

House designs rest on social norms and aspirations of domestic life. In chapter 5, the floor plans, plot plans, and elevation sketches are analyzed through the lens of how families—at least White, middle-class ones—were expected to live. The competition's parameters and the designs they generated showed Americans who should share a home, which parts of the house were dedicated to which residents, and how they should use their houses. Because the house designs really were adapted to 1945 housing and living standards, every house was a modern one, regardless of the aesthetic style. The following chapter, however, does look at style and the architectural elements that lead us to label a house as a "modern" one. The love that twenty-first-century Americans have today for midcentury modern design was not found among middle-class home buyers, who had many reasons to be wary of a new, unproven modern aesthetic. After that, chapter 7 compares the Prize Homes competition with other architectural competitions and catalogs, where we can see just how unique the *Tribune*'s project was. Prize Homes houses offered the public a middle ground between traditional, colonial styles that were well-established, familiar architecture and the steel and glass boxes favored by the architectural elite.

What truly set the competition apart from other competitions and catalogs, however, was the building project. Chapter 8 tells the story of the postwar housing crisis as it played out in Chicago. Over 100,000 Chicago veterans lacked a home, a situation disproportionately worse for Black veterans. Against that backdrop, the *Tribune* managed to get at least a couple dozen houses moved from paper to reality. When finished, many were furnished and decorated and open to the public in month-long open houses. Most of those houses still exist, albeit many with alterations; chapter 9 looks at how American housing needs and standards have evolved over the decades and how the existing Prize Homes have been altered to meet them. Reviewing the racial and ethnic housing patterns in Chicago history, the chapter focuses particularly on ten houses built in a single West Rogers Park neighborhood of Chicago. That neighborhood, predominantly Jewish then and now, nevertheless has experienced demographic changes to its population that are reflected, significantly, in architectural changes to the houses. The conclusion summarizes the significance of the Prize Homes competition in American architectural history.

Because the *Tribune*'s enterprise resulted in houses that both can be identified and have endured, it is perhaps the most successful competition for middle-class house design of the century. Still, the competition's story has never been told. Neither historians of midcentury American architecture nor the *Chicago Tribune*, nor even the City of Chicago includes this chapter in the history of American vernacular architecture.[3] Yet the story of the Prize Homes competition documents the post–World War II housing crisis, sheds light on the architectural profession, and helps document the built environment of the Chicagoland area. It confirms the centrality of the American single-family house in the midcentury, memorializing the vernacular house in Chicago's history, and it certainly presented middle-class Americans, at least the White ones, with a template for domestic life.

The competition is now beyond the memory of any original participants: *Tribune* employees, the jury, submitting architects, builders, or original purchasers of the newly built homes. But children of those original buyers, residents through the years, and current residents have been included, when possible, allowing them to tell their own stories of living in Prize Homes houses. They lived in what the competition advisor, Boyd Hill, called a "design not merely a dream house on paper" but one that would be built. The Chicagoland Prize Homes competition promoted beautiful and practical dream houses for average Americans, and that is the story told here.

1

Shortages

The Postwar Housing Crisis and Architectural Competitions

The American Depression and World War II contributed to a significant housing shortage in the United States.[1] Unemployment and underemployment left even those with some resources unable to move; lack of basic utilities, like water, sewer, and electricity, kept many Americans in nineteenth-century housing without improvements; decaying urban housing and discrimination relegated and confined much of the Black population to substandard housing. Despite government calls for action, between the crash of 1929 and the 1945 peace with Japan, the United States went fifteen years without building many single-family houses other than custom-designed houses for people who had managed to hold onto wealth, leaving behind not only the poor but even the middle-class house buyer. *Architectural Forum*, a monthly architectural publication, published in 1936 and 1938 two books of small houses built from what they considered exemplary designs. While the houses are small, each was built for a specific client, and not always as a primary dwelling but as guest house, summer home, or studio.[2] Those custom houses could not be a solution to the housing crisis.

Widespread unemployment during the Depression discouraged the construction of new single-family houses or even apartment buildings, as few American households could afford to upgrade their existing housing or move to better homes. By the late 1930s and early 1940s, when the economy improved, entry into World War II continued the stall. War requisition commandeered building materials that could have gone into housing construction, while the military drafted the workers who could have otherwise supplied the skilled labor to improve the housing stock. What little new housing the country did manage to build was mostly apartments rather than single-family houses, and virtually all rentals rather than for purchase, which better accommodated military and war industry workers' housing needs. Much of the housing built during the war was intended to be transitory. The famous Quonset hut, for example, a prefabricated, simple building, served as both dwelling and workspace for military installations across the county. It was expected to be dismantled after the war, and it housed postwar civilians only due to the housing crisis. A drop in the birth rate during the Depression slightly mitigated the housing crisis; a poor and uncertain economic outlook discouraged marriage and childbearing. During both the Depression and the war, householders made do and "doubled up" by sharing accommodations with other family members and sometimes friends. Young people, for whom marriage and parenthood once would have spurred moving out of their parents' homes and into their own, stayed put.

The war's end in 1945, however, brought about changes that both necessitated more housing and created opportunities to build it. Millions of soldiers discharged from the armed services returned home to fianceés and spouses, eager to start or resume family life. Peacetime employment with good wages created the means to move out of parents' homes and into one's own, or to upgrade from inadequate dwellings to more suitable ones. Veterans' benefits (collectively known as the G. I. Bill) included college tuition, work training, and, especially, mortgage assistance that granted loans with attractive interest rates and did not require a down payment. Virtually any White, male vet with a good, steady paycheck might qualify.[3] Steel, lumber, and other materials that had been devoted to the war effort became available for private use, as did workers with the know-how to construct high-quality houses. Need and resources converged to create the largest concentration of housing construction in U.S. history.[4] American culture encouraged ownership of a single-family house, "a concept, an aspiration, and an expectation," according to Archer, "so well known it seldom seems to need explaining."[5] Renting or apartment living could be only a temporary fix.

While the sudden jump in marriage and procreation gets the most attention as a postwar cultural phenomenon, the housing boom preceded it, not the other way around. One narrative suggests that a spike in births drove Americans to new housing, that returning veterans quickly married and immediately began to reproduce, and thus, the Levittown-style suburb, with street after street of nearly identical houses, solved the problem. Returning veterans and their burgeoning families, however, worsened rather than created the housing shortage. Even before the increase in marriage and procreation that Americans eventually labeled "the baby boom," housing specialists—builders, sociologists, demographers, and government officials—knew of and remarked on the lack of adequate housing, looking forward to post-Depression, and then postwar, building. (Conversely, the explosive postwar population growth appears to have been completely unforeseen.[6]) Concerns about inadequate housing increased as Americans anticipated the war's end. An accepted and often repeated data point came from the National Housing Agency, which estimated over twelve million new dwelling units would be needed in the decade after the war.[7] Throughout the war, the *Chicago Tribune* warned of the need to plan for postwar housing. Housing need, the paper cautioned in January 1943, would be "vast," a "boom"; retail stores, builders, and suppliers of building materials ought to plan for postwar demand.[8] Louise Bargelt, a *Tribune* reporter covering the real estate beat, offered several articles during the war about postwar housing needs, especially highlighting new materials and practical developments in house design; all her advice appeared against the backdrop of the building boom to come.[9] The *Tribune* could not be more clear: once the War ended, Americans could anticipate the building of over one million dwelling units (mostly in the form of single-family houses) per year for several years, and the Chicagoland area would see a disproportionate share of that building boom.[10]

The *Tribune* was not a singular voice.[11] *Pencil Points/Progressive Architecture*, a trade publication for architects and builders, also signaled the expected explosion in housing construction. A house architectural contest advertised in the December 1944 issue directed entrants to assume that "the war is finally over and that the reunited family is determined to have its own home."[12] A January 1945 editorial in that publication drew attention to the lessons learned from wartime construction but looked forward to the "progressive postwar buildings [architects] are already designing."[13] And although the August 1945 issue was most likely in press before the official end of the war (three advertisements reminded readers to buy war bonds, and one manufacturer noted its new windows would not be "available until our wartime obligations are fulfilled"[14]), other advertisers presciently offered products for postwar building.[15] One advertiser pointedly asked architects, designers, and draftsmen: "Are YOU ready for the POSTWAR BUILDING BOOM?"[16]

Throughout the war, advertisers had reminded readers in architectural publications that postwar buildings would rely on their products: freon for air conditioners, coal tar roofing, plate glass, plastic screening, and fireproof gypsum board.[17] Builders were standing by: the City of Chicago hosted the March 1944 National Conference on Postwar Housing, which drew over 600 attendees for the three-day event.[18]

In addition to the housing shortage, the economy faced looming changes. The United States was already coming out of the Depression when it entered World War II at the end of 1941, and the war improved the economy even more, bringing the country to full employment. With millions

Rheinhold Publishing Corporation, purveyors of drawing and rendering instruction books, was one of many businesses anticipating the building boom to come. (*Progressive Architecture*, August 1945, 151.)

of American men drafted into the military and thousands more men and women employed in civil service support positions, American manufacturers famously had to hire women even for factory jobs. Rosie the Riveter went to work; so did hundreds of thousands of immigrants and African Americans moving from South to the North and Midwest, attracted to the good manufacturing jobs in Chicago and other upper midwestern cities. Many industries, especially those providing basic materials the U.S. military needed for armaments and machinery, like rubber and steel, shifted from civilian peacetime production to contributing to the war effort, leading to national shortages and rationing. Rosie earned a paycheck—individual and household incomes went up during the war, and unemployment was low— but had fewer things to spend her money on when the country rationed goods. Pent-up demand—for housing, clothing, automobiles, and household items—would explode in peacetime; consumers were expecting to see the shops and shelves full. Business and civic leaders had to think about how to get Americans back to work in private-sector jobs. Those looking to put American men into consistent employment and address a housing shortage would certainly want to get busy building houses.

Chicago was not immune to the housing crisis. *Housing Goals for Chicago*, a report from the Chicago Plan Commission published in June 1946, detailed the impact of the Depression and the war on families' ability to secure housing in the greater Chicago metropolitan area, a region including suburbs in surrounding counties, even in Indiana.[19] The commission had begun its assessment even before the war's onset. During the war, Chicago's already inadequate housing stock became an even greater problem. The hundreds of thousands of servicemen leaving their homes had minimal impact on housing; younger soldiers moved from their parents' dwellings, and the married men left wives and children who stayed, by and large, in the family home. Rather, other demographic changes exacerbated the prewar housing shortage. Marriages in Chicago went up 20 percent during the war, and those couples wanted their own homes. At the same time, divorce increased, too, and those separating couples needed additional housing. War workers flocking to Chicago brought their families. Well-paying jobs, coupled with fewer things to buy, resulted in significantly high savings; Chicagoans had the resources to buy single-family residences, rather than "doubling" with relatives and other families.[20] But the housing market could not meet the demand; too many houses and apartments were inadequate, and many were too big for the smaller families of the time.[21] Vacancies were rare.[22] Three hundred thousand veterans returning to the Chicago area would add even more to the demand; the married vets would return to their homes, but as their family sizes increased, they would need larger quarters. Single people who had left the family home would marry and want places of their own. In addition to addressing the housing shortage, the commission recommended when housing became available that veterans "be extended preference in the purchase and rental of all dwelling units—both new and existing."[23] The problem was not just Chicago's; it was a national emergency. After the war, some national policy-makers wanted to halt construction of federal buildings, factories, and recreational buildings ("night clubs and bowling alleys"), freeing the material and labor that would have gone into those facilities for housing construction.[24]

A popular architectural contest to jump-start home building made sense in this context, especially given the long history of similar enterprises. Architectural competitions go back at least to the Renaissance and possibly back to ancient Greece.[25] Our historical and scholarly knowledge of such competitions, however, is largely confined to initiatives involving significant public or private buildings or public memorials. Submissions for such designs in the last few hundred years come from established designers and international architectural firms with significant resources.[26] Architectural historians focus on high-status sponsors: clerics and devout patrons with immortality and divinity on their minds; municipal, state, or federal governments seeking designs for public buildings, parks, or memorials; philanthropists or philanthropic organizations seeking distinctive museums or memorials; colleges and universities ready to embrace the distinctive; and corporations and businesses eager for noteworthy facilities or office buildings. Contests have usually been site-specific, indicating that a structure would be erected in a location the designer could see in advance. Sponsors invited or screened firms and designers for application eligibility and sometimes financially supported serious applicants through the design process. No matter how many second or third places, or honorable mentions, a jury awarded, only one design could win. But that winning design would usually come to fruition, as the sponsor committed to building the cathedral, the parliamentary building, or the skyscraper. For a submission to be considered, it would need to not only appeal to its audience but also be practical and buildable. The United States' most visible residence arose from a 1792 competition for a president's house, a structure we now know as the White House.[27] Competitions for public structures brought Americans the St. Louis arch and the Vietnam Veterans Memorial on the National Mall, just two examples of highly visible sites that hundreds of thousands of tourists visit each year.

The best example of this is the Tribune Company's own experience in 1922 when, in search of a distinctive high-rise to mark the paper's seventy-fifth anniversary, it solicited entries for the "most beautiful office building in the world." Typical of such grand contests, the *Tribune* asked that submitted designs include working plans, not just sketches. Among the submissions from around the globe, architects Howells and Hood won with a distinctive neo-Gothic building that the Tribune Company built in downtown Chicago, a city internationally renowned for its architecture.[28]

Even losing entries drew praise, with the second-place winner, by Eliel Saarinen, favored by so many that the architect capitalized on the publicity

The neo-Gothic Tribune Tower even today is a striking element among Chicago's distinctive skyscrapers; the building was recently converted into luxury condominiums. (Photo by Gabriel Anzeze.)

by leaving his native Finland and setting up shop in the United States.[29] A non-winning design by Walter Gropius enhanced his international reputation. Their Tribune Tower enterprise was so successful that the *Tribune* corporation continued to sponsor competitions for its buildings. In November 1934, it awarded E. A. Grunsfeld $2,500 for a theater design for a new building adjacent to the Tribune Tower.[30] Twenty-five of the best of the 189 entries received went on display in the *Tribune* want ad office.[31] A 1945 competition for a studio design granted $5,000 to the co-designers who created a 2,000-seat theater for Tribune Company–owned radio station WGN.[32]

In contrast to competitions for notable buildings, house competitions have been more modest affairs, as Jennings shows in a comprehensive treatment of the trade publication *Carpentry & Building,* which ushered the American small house contest into being.[33] These competitions were sometimes labeled "ideas competitions" and might have promoted building materials specified by a business or industry; ideas competitions also created free content for architectural publications looking to fill pages and served as good practice for newly established architects or architectural firms. Such competitions did not require working blueprints but only sketches of floor plans and elevations. Spreiregen defines these contests for "projects that are *not* to be built," citing the 1951 *Architectural Forum* small house competition as an example. He reveals his preference: an open contest for a specific building, like the Tribune Tower, "is a real design competition."[34] Strong admits to intentionally omitting ideas competitions in her work, which effectively relegates small house competitions to footnote status.[35] Lipstadt, in a rare mention of the Prize Homes competition, specifically—and erroneously—labels it an ideas competition.[36] As the stakes for ideas competitions were much lower than those where a building was expected to come to fruition, sponsors could not promise the winners any tangible outcome other than modest prize money. The *Tribune* offered $50,000, $20,000, and $10,000, respectively, to the top three winners of its Tribune Tower contest in 1922.[37] It invested much more in the tower's construction. Four years later, for its 1926 small house competition, the *Tribune* put up only $7,500 in total reward money, dividing it among nineteen winning entries.[38] Twenty-three years later, it dedicated $24,000 to its 1945 housing contest, spread among twenty-four winning designs. A $1,000 prize was not a trifle but was unlikely to be a life-changing reward; it is worth just under $15,000 in 2020 dollars.[39]

Because ideas competitions required only modest rewards, if any, they supplied inexpensive opportunities for corporate publicity, and in the first half of the twentieth century, many businesses and building suppliers took advantage of that opportunity. Promoters of materials or utilities—white pine, flat glass, concrete, electricity, gas, and tile—held such competitions, either by themselves or often partnering with other organizations, usually architectural and design periodicals. Criteria for winning designs would include, of course, the prominent use of the materials being promoted.[40] Industries publicized their contests hoping to interest the public and home builders in their products; it did not matter whether any of the winning designs were built as long as flat glass or tile or electricity was highlighted. In contrast to competitions for non-residential buildings like skyscrapers and public memorials, sponsors did not specify a site, at most suggesting a house suited to a hot or cold climate, or a lot size. Non-trade sponsors, like architectural publications and popular home magazines, awarded prizes through more objective criteria than favoritism toward a particular building material but rarely followed through with a built house.

Some organizations and popular magazines designed and built "dream" or "model" homes. As Secretary of Commerce in the 1920s, Herbert Hoover spearheaded a Better Homes in America movement, creating a Better Homes agency; the program was meant to improve American housing and promote home ownership. In partnership with the women's magazine *The Delineator*, the Better Homes program in 1923 constructed a house on the National Mall in Washington, D.C.[41] The New York office of Better Homes built a model home, America's Little House, in downtown Manhattan in 1934.[42] Chicago's 1933 Century of Progress Exposition (also known as the

World's Fair) included the House of Tomorrow, a model house designed by George Fred Keck using the most up-to-date building materials and techniques. None of these houses was meant to be permanent; the first two were demolished, and the Keck house—and four others at the 1922 exhibition—were dismantled, moved, and rebuilt on public lands in Indiana at the close of the fair.[43]

Designers and architects participating in these competitions absorbed the time and costs of their design work on their own. Since contest sponsors provided no remuneration to entrants, sponsors surely hoped for as many submissions as possible. Anyone winning or even submitting to these house contests might, however, earn some free publicity, as floor plans and elevations from winning and non-winning designs were frequently published, either in the sponsoring periodicals or by industry in booklets distributed either free of charge or for a small fee. For example, The United States Gypsum Company printed a book with seventy-two designs from an *Architectural Forum*/American Institute of Architects-sponsored competition for fireproof homes; consumers could buy it for $1.00 in 1925.[44] Bloomingdale's

Title page from the United States Gypsum Company catalog, featuring fireproof homes submitted to a competition co-sponsored with *Architectural Forum*. (*Fireproof Homes of Period Design: Seventy-Two Designs for Fireproof Homes from a National Competition among Architects, Draftsmen and Architectural Students* [The United States Gypsum Company, 1925].)

"Suburban Houses for New Yorkers" competition resulted in a forty-page booklet that the department store distributed in 1947, probably for free.[45] Such booklets would have been guides for buyers in the market for houses or merely entertainment for people only aspiring to live in a dream home someday, but in most cases, the booklet houses were modest, middle-class dwellings emphasizing practicality and affordability. The same is true for magazines that advertised and sold house plans; *House Beautiful, House and Garden*, and the *Ladies' Home Journal*, all still in circulation, sponsored house competitions.[46]

Wealthy patrons able to afford a distinctive home would eschew these house booklets and magazines, instead hiring architects to realize their own bespoke home dreams. Average-income homeowners, who could not realistically aspire to own a unique, individualized house, would have to settle for a modest, off-the-rack house. Catalogs and house plan books thus catered to affordability and practicality; their acknowledgement of market forces and public tastes made them choose architecture accordingly. As will be shown later, their moderate and conservative choices reinforced themselves; catalog readers got a taste of what was available to them, and that shaped their sensibilities of what was desirable in a house. Reiff's history of house plans demonstrates this point: the plan books and catalogs influenced the architectural profession and, in turn, the buying public.[47]

Dixon suggests the periodical *Pencil Points*, catering to draftspeople and architects, turned to competitions when professional work and commissions vanished during the Depression.[48] The American Institute of Architects had frowned upon architects advertising their services, only slowly loosening restrictions during the Depression and World War II; publicity-generating competitions might have been viewed as a way around those restrictions.[49] *Architectural Forum*, another prominent architectural publication, also co-sponsored contests during the same period; so did *Arts & Architecture. House Beautiful*, an upscale publication for a general audience, held annual house design competitions during the economic downturn.[50]

Betty Blum's oral interview of Chicago architect Ambrose Richardson confirms the importance of competitions during hard times. "During the depression," he said, "there wasn't much work for architects and so regularly there were competitions to do houses. . . . These competitions really launched a good many careers. Although they weren't architectural commissions, they were notoriety, money, and so on."[51] When the *Tribune* announced Edward Burch as one of the Prize Homes competition winners, he found himself, according to his firm's website, "[s]uddenly, as a result of the publicity [with] 20 other homes on his drawing board," and that new flurry of business allowed him to open his own firm.[52]

2

To the Rescue

The *Chicago Tribune*'s Chicagoland
Prize Homes Competition

Like most newspapers, the *Tribune* had long served its readers' interest
in real estate. Classified ads listing housing for rental or sale had been a
lucrative part of local papers' income, as it was a principal means by which
people seeking to rent or buy could identify and secure housing. In addition to supporting the real estate industry, the *Tribune*'s Home Builders'
Department regularly published articles on house construction, house
design, and interior design and furnishings. Such content surely pleased
local lumberyards, hardware stores, manufacturers, and furniture and home
design stores. Creating more content about housing also fit nicely with the
Tribune's promotion of the city's architecture and the Tribune Company's
history of pursuing remarkable design in its own buildings. The *Tribune*
distinguished itself from other newspapers by sponsoring many architectural and design competitions between its 1922 Tribune Tower competition
and the early 1950s, when other papers sponsored none. A *Detroit Free Press*
competition in 1928 is a rare exception.[1] Another is a 1934 or '35 competition sponsored by a *Tribune* competitor, the *Chicago American*, a Hearst
paper. That paper promised to build three houses from winning designs; the
fate of the program is unknown.[2]

The paper sponsored a small house competition in 1926, publishing the
following year the *Chicago Tribune Book of Homes*, a volume that included
the nineteen winning designs and eighty additional plans.[3] Entries came
from across the country, and the houses could be built for about $7,500,
not inexpensive but affordable for the middle- and upper-class families of
the day. Prospective homeowners could buy a set of working plans for three
of the designs: the first-place winner for the two-bedroom house, and the
first- and second-place winners for the three-bedroom houses.

Although the *Tribune* did not spend much effort in following up on the
building, some houses were built from the winning and honorable mention

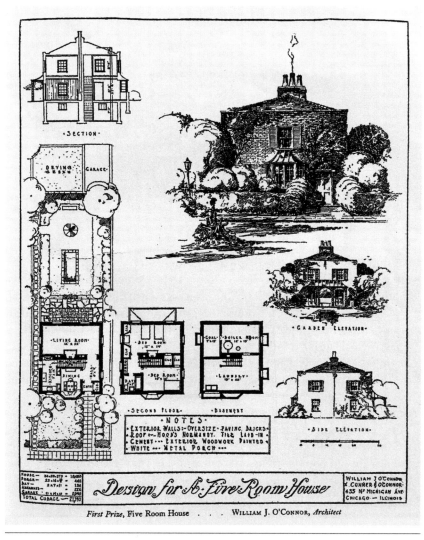

First Prize, Five Room House . . . WILLIAM J. O'CONNOR, *Architect*

William O'Connor's first-place winner from the *Chicago Tribune*'s first small house competition, in 1926. (*Chicago Tribune Book of Homes* [Chicago, 1927], 11.)

designs. People who did not wish to purchase plans directly from the *Tribune* or the architect certainly could have shown the sketches to a builder; Reiff notes the long-standing practice of "borrowing" designs without accreditation or remuneration.[4] Louise Bargelt, *Tribune* real estate reporter, touted in her introduction to the original publication that the book offered an improved small house, one that provided "comfort and convenience," because, where "formerly the attention of skilled architects was seldom given to the house of modest dimensions, we now find trained men of talent incorporating the small home ideas of real worth."[5] The *Tribune* was not alone in promoting small house design; many competitions and catalogs in the 1920s focused on the small house and making it affordable and available to the average-income home buyer.[6]

Just as the 1926 venture occurred amid other, similar competitions, so did its 1945 initiative. In September 1944, the *Tribune* itself featured an article calling for submissions to the Chicago Metropolitan Home Builders Association competition for six categories of dwellings, including "the industrial worker's home, the suburban home, the summer resort home, and the war veteran's home, or 'the home for two.'" First prize would be $1,000, not in cash but given in war bonds.[7] The two additional house categories were for a "city home" and a farmhouse.[8] In December 1944, *Progressive Architecture* rolled out the "Pittsburgh" Architectural Competition, closing in February 1945; that contest anticipated G. I. Joe back from the war, rejoining his wife, ten-year-old son, and six-year-old daughter.[9] An October 1945 issue of *Progressive Architecture* announced a house contest for "the Design of a Realistic House for a Family in Georgia," comprised of "father, mother, and two small children—a boy of five and a girl of two," and a maximum size of 1,350 square feet.[10] The *Tribune*'s competition was not the only opportunity for architects to design modest houses, but it offered the most desirable results: it promised to build some of the houses, and it managed to keep that promise.

The 1945 *Chicago Tribune* competition began with a full-page announcement on page 21 of the Sunday, September 30, edition. "To encourage better home designs, to help launch America's building revival and to create more jobs The Chicago Tribune announces the $24,000.00 Chicagoland Prize Homes Competition." The mission was explicit: "It is the Tribune's hope that the designs produced will combine the best of the old with the best of the new—so that America may be better housed, with greater comfort, convenience and happiness, at costs which will make home ownership attractive and practical to new millions of families."

Neither the war nor its end was mentioned specifically, but text commented on the urgency in both providing housing and getting millions back to work, to "re-establish the nation on a sound economic foundation."[11] President Harry Truman had said as much only weeks before, in a September 6 address to Congress. "The largest single opportunity for the rapid postwar expansion of private investment and employment lies in the field of housing, both urban and rural. The present shortage of decent homes and the enforced widespread use of substandard housing indicate vital

To encourage better home designs, to help launch America's building revival and to create more jobs

THE CHICAGO TRIBUNE ANNOUNCES THE

$24,000.00

CHICAGOLAND PRIZE

HOMES COMPETITION

offering 24 cash prizes of $1,000.00 each for
designs of single family houses

Chicago Tribune
THE WORLD'S GREATEST NEWSPAPER

The full-page competition announcement. (*Chicago Tribune*, September 30, 1945, 21.)

unfulfilled needs of the Nation. These needs will become more marked as veterans begin to come back and look for places to live."[12] Truman further reminded his audience that the war's abrupt cessation had created immediate unemployment for people producing war goods. Getting Americans back to work was imperative.

Submissions needed only to include floor plans, a plot plan, a main perspective (with suggested landscaping), and two elevations. The competition encouraged designs from amateurs and those without formal architectural training, although all the winning designs came from practicing architects, experienced designers, or architecture students. Houses were to be designed for three different categories of families, the differences based on the number, age, and sex of the families' children. The call for submissions had no style constraints; submissions could be contemporary or traditional, borrow from colonial or Spanish or French or Italian architectural styles, or any blend of them. The *Tribune* sought the "attractive, practical and economical" suited to the climate within a 300-mile radius of Chicago. Whatever the style, the paper put designers on notice that anything too extreme would be rejected. The jury was looking for "dwellings which are marketable to the public and attractive as investments to builders and lending agencies."[13] Savvy architects and designers knew in advance they had to had to cater to average consumers, not the rarified tastes of a single client who might be open to a more distinctive architectural style.

Nine jurors, both architects and builders, were empaneled to evaluate the submissions. The paper appointed architect Boyd Hill, member of the American Institute of Architects (AIA), the accrediting institution for professional architects, as a non-voting *Tribune* advisor to the contest; he remained a major face of the competition in subsequent years. An Illinois native, Hill practiced in Chicago, and his connection with the *Tribune* was a long one. Hill's own architectural practice was wide-ranging; in partnership or as a solo architect, he designed hotels and public spaces, as well as luxury homes and apartment buildings, but also contributed designs for a postwar builder's subdivision.[14] He maintained offices in the Tribune Tower, which presumably facilitated his long service as architectural advisor to the Tribune Company; in that capacity, he both took on architectural projects for the Tribune properties and served as architectural advisor to many design competitions.[15]

Nominally, the five architects represented a majority on the Chicagoland Prize Homes jury, with builders having four seats at the table of nine. Chairman Paul Gerhardt Jr., who was president of the Chicago chapter of the AIA in 1945, by the time of his death in 1966 had served thirty-seven years as the architect for the City of Chicago, a civil service position. He designed bridges, public libraries, police and fire stations, and other public buildings.[16] His career did not focus on private residences. But co-chairman Philip Maher's architectural practice did; one of his most prominently publicized projects was a cooperative apartment building in Evanston. Maher is known for his apartment and co-op residences, and, like Gerhardt, public buildings. Both Gerhardt and Maher were sons of prominent Chicago architects. John Merrill, founding partner of the influential Skidmore, Owings and Merrill architectural firm, had been the head architect for the Federal Housing Administration Midwestern States division, before the creation of his firm. His reputation, too, rested on the creation of public buildings, rather than residences.[17]

Architect A. N. Rebori had a long-standing relationship with the *Tribune* and its publisher/editor Colonel McCormick. McCormick owned property in Wheaton, Illinois, which abutted the family farm of Rebori's in-laws, and this connection proved fruitful. Rebori was one of the ten architects or architectural firms who was given a $2,000 stipend to facilitate submission to the 1922 Tribune Tower competition, and he designed the memorial structure at McCormick's burial place.[18] Upon his death, Rebori earned a front-page obituary in the *Tribune*.[19] Although John Park was described in all the *Tribune* publicity, and the subsequent *Prize Homes* book, as an architect, that label was a bit of misdirection. Park joined the Tribune company in 1919 and had been its production manager since 1926, a position he still held in 1945.[20] Nothing suggests Park ever had more than scant, if any, working experience as an architect. Rather than representing the architectural profession, Park represented the newspaper.

Builders on the jury owned construction companies in the Chicago area, and some held significant positions in trade organizations. Irvin Blietz, a founder of the National Association of Home Builders (NAHB), established a successful residential construction company, known especially for upper-income housing in Chicago's affluent north shore suburbs.[21] As president of the NAHB, Joseph Merrion served as spokesperson for the industry in addition to heading his own construction agency. *Tribune* real estate editor Al Chase often consulted Merrion, and juror Arthur Fossier, when reporting on the Chicago building and housing markets, featuring their photos and commentary. Fossier served as president of the Chicago Metropolitan Home Builder's Association.[22] Less information is available about builder John R. O'Connor's career, suggesting his reputation was more modest than that of his fellow jurors. The presence of builders who had their fingers on the pulse of public tastes signaled this would not be a mere ideas

Competition advisor Boyd Hill and seven of the nine jurists for the competition. (*Chicago Tribune*, September 30, 1945, 22.)

competition. Architects would have to submit designs for buildable—and sellable—houses.

The deadline for submissions was December 10, 1945. The bottom right-hand corner of the announcement page was a box with a border design of a perforated line (thus indicating it was to be clipped) containing a coupon inviting interested parties to write to the *Tribune* for copies of more specific contest rules.[23] Opposite that coupon, on the left-hand corner, the paper announced another feature of its enterprise, one that would make the competition different from others.

Watch for Prize Home Construction! When the winners have been selected, it is the Tribune's intention, conditions permitting, to sponsor the actual construction, in Chicago and suburbs and in cities and towns thruout [*sic*] the middle west, of a number of homes based on prize-winning designs produced by the competition. Watch the Tribune for complete details.

The plan to build not one but several houses, and not only in Chicago but throughout the Midwest region, made the competition different from those sponsored by other publications and organizations. Winners could not only take home a cash prize but also see their designs built, the latter perhaps even more valuable than the former. This would be no mere ideas competition.

Facing the full-page advertisement on page 21, an article on page 22 repeated information from the announcement but added a photo: seven of the nine jurors (minus Merrion and Park) and advisor Boyd Hill.[24] On October 3, a very short article reminded readers to send off for contest rules (erroneously listing the deadline as December 15 instead of December 10), and included the clippable coupon; editors placed the piece on page 12 underneath the popular comic strips *Orphan Annie* and *Gasoline Alley*.[25] On October 7, the coupon appeared alongside an article with more substantive information.[26] Although the official kickoff had been only one week earlier, the *Tribune* noted on page 25 that the competition rules had already been mailed to over 3,000 recipients. For the first time, readers learned of three different family groups, or "problems," architects should address:

1. A dwelling designed for a family of father, mother and a son aged 6. The dwelling shall not exceed 1,100 square feet of floor area disposed on one or two stories.
2. A dwelling for a family of father, mother, son, aged 12, and daughter, 8. The floor area maximum is 1,400 square feet.
3. A dwelling for a family of father, mother, two daughters, aged 16 and 6, and a son, aged 12. The floor area maximum is 1,700 square feet.[27]

The newspaper re-emphasized its plan to build: "To help the pubic visualize, locally and at close range, the value offered by the architectural profession, the builder, and the manufacturer, it is THE TRIBUNE'S intention, conditions permitting, to sponsor, on sites in Chicago and suburbs and thruout [*sic*] the middle west, the construction of a number of homes demonstrating the full potential of prize winning designs produced by this competition." The clippable coupon reappeared October 8, 11, 15, and 16.[28] On November 18, the *Tribune* noted it had already received many submissions, and advisor Boyd Hill announced the contest had already achieved its purpose: to "stimulate the development of home designs so attractive, practical and economical that thousands of families can have the kind of homes they want at prices they can afford."[29] The article reminded readers that over the winter, the winning entries would appear with color illustrations in Sunday papers.

A November 25 update touted feedback from readers, who apparently applauded the *Tribune*'s attention to housing.[30] On the eve of the December 10 deadline, the *Tribune* reminded its readers that entries had to be received by 5:00 p.m. at the Tribune Tower, also revealing the first information about the judging process: the jury would meet daily until it had reviewed all submissions and chosen winners. This December 9 alert to applicants would be the only front-page coverage before the contest closed.[31]

By 1945, the American Institute of Architects (AIA) had a long-established history of overseeing architectural competitions. In the nineteenth century, accusations of unfair judging, plagiarism, and competition sponsors appropriating the designs of unpaid architects led to regulations. The *Tribune* followed AIA competition rules: it appointed Boyd Hill as a non-judging professional advisor and manager to the contest and clarified the specific submission rules in a fourteen-page booklet sent to anyone who had registered an intent to enter a design. Submitting—although not winning—architects Marcel Breuer and Ralph Rapson each saved their copies of this important ephemera.

The booklet, following AIA guidelines, supplied would-be entrants with details well beyond the three problems and requirements described within the *Tribune*'s pages: lot sizes, house placement on the lot, confirmation of standard land grade, requirements relating to drawings, scale of drawings, labeling, measures for preserving anonymity, deadlines, jury criteria, and instructions for returning submissions.[32] With names and addresses on file, Hill sent out at least two supplemental letters—preserved among Breuer's papers—to all registrants, providing more detailed information about the contest. As was true of most other competitions, winning entries would become the exclusive property of the sponsor: the *Tribune* also reserved the right to claim ownership of non-winning entries for a $250 fee. Should

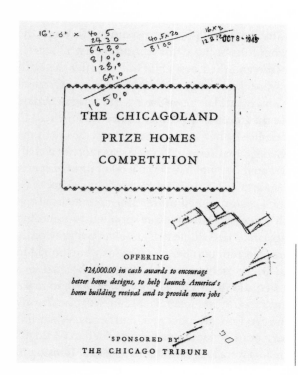

THE CHICAGOLAND

PRIZE HOMES

COMPETITION

OFFERING

$24,000.00 *in cash awards to encourage
better home designs, to help launch America's
home building revival and to provide more jobs*

'SPONSORED BY
THE CHICAGO TRIBUNE

Marcel Breuer saved his copy of the competition program. The front page has what appears to be square footage calculations, presumably in his handwriting. (Marcel Breuer Papers, Special Collection Research Center, Syracuse University Libraries.)

anyone want to build one of the *Tribune*-owned designs, however, the *Tribune* would compensate the designer for a full set of working drawings.[33] Decades later, Coder Taylor, designer of a two-bedroom winner that was built at least once, recalled developing a fuller set of plans at the *Tribune*'s request. He thought he charged the newspaper between $600 and $1,200.[34]

The jury worked quickly. By December 27, a *Tribune* article suggested that despite receiving more than 900 submissions, jurors had already reviewed all designs for problem one, the family with one child, which comprised half of all entries.[35] Designers' focus on small houses lacked prescience in light of the coming baby boom, but Depression-era birth rates were low; many families did have only one child. *Housing Goals for Chicago* expected household size to *decrease* after the war, predicting a 1947 mean family size (including adults) to be 3.4 people, slightly less than the 3.53 mean from 1940.[36] Such a family constellation meant two parents and, most of the time, one or two children. Neither the *Tribune*, which established the three problems, nor the designers anticipated the postwar baby boom that would increase household size; in 1957, the fertility rate for American women was 3.7 children.[37] A family, after purchasing a home, still might need to move to a larger house if they had more children and wanted them to have private bedrooms, increasingly a housing standard through the twentieth century.[38] This would make the two-bedroom house a "starter home": big enough for a couple and their first child but not after the birth of their second unless they were close in age and of the same sex. Original owners of one Prize Home, the Finks, left a two-bedroom house in Skokie because they wanted to have a third child.[39] Winner Coder Taylor chose to design the smallest house because he had only a brief time to devote to the project, but he also acknowledged that the small house was more of a challenge to design well.[40] Small houses cannot have even a bit of unused space; bathroom fixtures, closets, hallways, kitchen layouts, and entries must be precisely arranged. The article also supplied more information about the lot sizes specified for each category, information supplied to potential entrants through the Chicagoland Prize Home rules booklet but previously unknown to *Tribune* readers. Problem number one designs were limited to lots of no more than 150 by 30 feet; problem two houses could be sited on a lot no more than 150 by 50 feet; and the third category would have to make do with no larger than 150 by 75 feet.[41] The smallest specified lot size already increased the lot size for Chicago working-class neighborhoods, which was usually 25 by 125 feet.[42] Restrictions on lot dimensions nodded to Chicago's urban neighborhoods where lots were long and skinny; postwar housing in the suburbs had more squarish lots.

Sources vary about the number of submissions, and the *Tribune*'s lack of an archive leaves a precise number unknown. The *Tribune* reported receiving over 900, while the 1948 publication *Prize Homes*, which briefly described the contest and includes ninety-two of the submissions, including the twenty-four winners, indicated there were 967 entries.[43] In a February 1946 notification about the contest winners, the *Journal of the American Institute of Architects* numbered the submissions as 938.[44] Potentially limiting the number of entries was the short time the *Tribune* gave between the September 30 announcement and the December 10 deadline, and none of the articles announcing the contest merited front-page coverage. On the other hand, given the promotion—even if inside the paper—in Chicago's newspaper of record and that the jury asked for floor plans and elevations but did not require professional blueprints and specifications, many people without any professional architectural or design experience may well have sent in designs, inflating the number of entries.

The *Tribune* had advertised its 1922 Tribune Tower contest in other American and European papers, plus some architectural journals.[45] The paper used the journals again with the 1945 competition, taking out a full-page ad in the October 1945 issue of *Architectural Forum*, including the coupon to send for the rules booklet.[46] *Architectural Forum*, plus two other trade publications, *Architectural Record* and the *Journal of the American Institute of Architects*, published notices about the contest in their November issues.[47] The October 1945 *FAA Bulletin*, a publication from the Florida Association of Architects, published a notice of the competition and indicated that the association secretary had copies of the rules booklet and would share them on request. (This notice advised, "We do not personally believe that an architect should sell his ideas to organizations who will so publicize them that other people, both competent and incompetent, can use them free of charge" but suggested that "you can use your own judgment.")[48] Individual subscribers to these periodicals, as well as architects and draftsmen working in offices that subscribed to them, would have learned of the *Tribune*'s offering. Architect Ambrose Richardson, speaking about that period, commented that "competitions were a way of life." While he was at Skidmore, Owings and Merrill, work came to a halt when deadlines loomed. "I had to declare a holiday. Everybody called in sick at Skidmore when those things were due."[49] (As Richardson himself won an honorable mention in a 1951 *Architectural Forum* small house competition, one wonders whether he, too, submitted to the Prize Homes competition.)

In many ways, the *Tribune*'s 1945 competition mirrored its 1926 version, as the earlier contest also began with a full-page Sunday ad, giving contestants about ten weeks until the contest closed. Requirements for the earlier competition specified houses must have a dining room, or dining area, and a garage, and further delineated two sub-categories of house size: two-bedroom and three-bedroom houses. Cash prizes would be awarded to first through tenth-place winners in each category. Those interested in entering would need to write to the *Tribune* for specific rules, and judging would be anonymous, under the direction of professional advisor and AIA member Earl H. Reed. However, the 1926 jury lacked the prestige—and professional detachment—of the 1945 jury. While Tribune Tower architects John Howells and Raymond Hood headed the 1926 jury, the other three jurors were long-standing *Tribune* employees: real estate editors Louise Bargelt and Al Chase (who were still writing for the *Tribune* in 1945) and Holmes Onderdonk, manager of Tribune Properties. No builders sat on the 1926 jury.[50] Architects were clearly interested; despite a restriction allowing submissions of only one entry per house class, the *Tribune* received 841 entries.[51] Winning designs did come to fruition, including ten houses built all at once in Highland Park, Illinois, in 1927, but the newspaper did not partner with builders or publicize building projects except in a cursory way.[52]

Unless an unknown archive or papers from any of the participants surfaces, a complete list of entrants to the 1945 Prize Homes competition cannot be compiled. Upon request of the entrants, the *Tribune* appears to have returned the submitted sketches to their owners; what few extant entries exist in archives show signs of having been received by the *Tribune* through the attachment of a small, numbered sticker, used to preserve anonymity. Richard Y. Mine's entry, which did not win but was included in the *Prize Homes* book, is archived at the Art Institute of Chicago, and it displays the number 374.[53] Robert Arnold's winning design is entry number 667,[54] and Curtis Wray Besinger's entry is 875.[55] If the numbers indicate entries as they were logged in by the contest administrators, beginning with number 1, or even if the first number assigned were 100, Besinger's number 875 makes 967 entries entirely plausible. National competitions sponsored by architectural publications regularly drew hundreds of submissions: a General Electric/*Pencil Points* 1935 competition for an electric home drew over 2,000 entries, while the *Pencil Points* competition for a concrete house in 1936 collected 1,500 submissions.[56] *The Ladies Home Journal* small house competition brought in 700 designs in 1938.[57] *Pencil Points*' 1944 call for submissions for the Pittsburgh competition for a small house attracted more than 900 entries.[58]

A partial list of submissions to the Prize Homes competition, however, can be compiled from various sources. The twenty-four winners (eight in each category) plus sixty-eight others can be found in the *Tribune*'s 1948 book on the contest, *Prize Homes*. Pamela Hill's research on Marion Mahony Griffin analyzes her submission to the contest.[59] Personal archives indicate Marcel Breuer, Curtis Wray Besinger, L. Morgan Yost, and Richard E. Bishop submitted non-winning entries.[60] When the Art Institute displayed 172 entries in a month-long exhibition in February 1946, the *Tribune* listed the names of local designers whose work could be seen there, supplying an additional twenty-four names.[61] (Art Institute records do not list the 172 exhibitors.) The *Beatrice Daily Sun* of Beatrice, Nebraska, noted local resident Burket Graf's entry was displayed at the Art Institute; Dietrich A. Neyland's hometown paper in Shreveport did the same.[62] *Tribune* journalist Edward Barry wrote a series of twenty articles featuring houses that did not win but that he—or someone affiliated with the paper or the competition—deemed architecturally excellent, and this adds a few more names, among them Ralph Rapson and John Van der Meulen, Eileen and I. M. Pei, and William Hajjar. Presumably, investigation of prominent architects, architects practicing in the Chicago area, and those known to submit to other competitions would likely turn up additional names to a list that now numbers about 120 individuals. Without *Tribune* archives of the competition, it is impossible to draw definitive conclusions about the hundreds of submissions now lost to history. We can, however, reasonably assume a few things about those who submitted and their designs, especially when we compare the *Tribune* contest to other contemporaneous house design competitions.

Given the publicity the *Tribune* gave the contest and number of submissions received, it is highly likely that some entries came from non-professionals, despite the high praise the *Tribune* repeated about the quality of submissions. The competition booklet invited anyone "who wished to come forward with ideas."[63] Boyd Hill said as much in November 1945, indicating that some had sent in "simple drawings, showing their ideas of the home of their dreams." One entry came from a man who sent in drawings of his own home.[64] Keep in mind that the *Tribune* did not insist on working blueprints but asked only for floor plans and elevations. Admitting a few unprofessional designs would be a small price to pay for encouraging enthusiasm about the competition among *Tribune* readers and eventual home buyers.

Submissions by non-professionals could not have been a huge number. Would-be submitters had to register in advance, and upon receiving the rules booklet, they would have encountered competition regulations familiar to architects and designers but foreign to the untrained. If formal training were not a disqualifying requirement, the rules stipulated lot sizes, distance from lot lines, and calculation of square footage, and submissions had to be on particular paper, of a particular size, on a 1/8 scale, and lettering of no more than 3/16 inch.[65] These and other specifications would have tempered the enthusiasm of many amateurs. Some *Tribune* readers surely bypassed the registration system and mailed in their own sketches and doodles. Perhaps the *Tribune* included in its 967 number even the entries disqualified from consideration due to noncompliance with program rules.

Some submissions came from people with art or design backgrounds instead of formal architectural training. This is particularly the case for the eight women known to have submitted. Madge Buckley and Elizabeth Kimball Nedved were architects in practice with their husbands; Marion Mahony Griffin also partnered with her husband, Walter Griffin, although she earned considerable fame on her own. Winner Lucille McKirahan studied architecture, according to her *Tribune* biography, but whether she ever practiced is unknown. Connie Weibezahl submitted her design while still an undergraduate. Entrant Eileen Pei submitted, with her husband, a co-designed house, but she did not hold an architectural degree. Millie Goldsholl's background was design and filmmaking. Artist Miriam Story Hurford submitted a design included in the *Prize Homes* book. She was perhaps one of the most established of the submitters, having a long career as a magazine and book illustrator; readers of the original Dick and Jane primers or Little Golden Books for children regularly saw her artwork. Barry included her design in his *Tribune* series of twenty non-winning houses. Other submissions must have come from talented individuals who had a good eye for design but who lacked architectural credentials. Given barriers preventing women and people of color from architecture schools and practice, they might be disproportionately represented among those who were neither amateurs nor trained architects but nevertheless designers eager to gain recognition for their talents.

Winners' biographies included their architectural degrees, and past and/ or future architectural practices and employment. The *Tribune* described Joseph Gora of Boston as having "handled engineering and planning for the Massachusetts committee on public safety as a member of its technical advisory staff," which does not preclude his having studied architecture. Eric Wenstrand's biography is less ambiguous: he was a commercial artist, not an architect.[66] His plan was something, the *Tribune* noted, "that he and his wife dreamed up for themselves and their 8 year old daughter."[67] Lack of training clearly did not impede the success of his submission; in addition to the prize Wenstrand won, his house was built at least five times.

Some entrants surely fell short in meeting the specific design requirements. Even the more professional competitions hosted by architectural associations and publications discarded entries that did not meet minimum specifications. Especially for the untrained, square footage maximums and placement along lot lines may have proved unachievable technical requirements. A 1937 *Pencil Points* house design contest drew 347 entrants, and nearly all of them likely had formal architectural training. However, jurors eliminated thirty-five—10 percent—from consideration for not conforming to program rules.[68] With the *Tribune* contest nearing a thousand submissions, even a 10-percent disqualification from non-professional or non-qualifying entries would have been a significant number.

One non-winning design included in the *Prize Homes* book came from Erling H. Bugge. His c/o address was Sears, Roebuck & Co., Department 712, in Kansas City, Missouri. Bugge worked as the head of the real estate division of Sears.[69] House catalogs flourished between 1900 and 1940; Reiff describes the demand of that period as "insatiable" and notes that no fewer than seventy-five separate companies published house plan books and catalogs.[70] Sears and Montgomery Ward made fortunes selling house plans and even house kits, and they might be the most recognizable, but other companies also had thriving catalog businesses. The house catalog industry very rarely credited its architects, and its employees—anonymous architects, draftspeople, and designers—may well have submitted designs, like Bugge.

The competition booklet invited entries from "architects, architectural draftsmen, architectural students," and students certainly did apply.[71]

Connie Weibezahl would not graduate from Syracuse University until 1948, but as a twenty-one-year-old undergraduate, she submitted a design for a modern house that merited a spot in the *Prize Homes* book. The address listed for Weibezahl was her Syracuse dormitory, Slocum Hall. Louisiana native Patrick Gallaugher was nineteen years old and in an officer training program at the University of Notre Dame when he teamed with fellow student Bernard James Slater to submit a design included in the *Prize Homes* book. Notre Dame's Walsh Hall was Gallaugher's official address. His partner, Slater, earned a 1946 degree from the undergraduate architectural program at Notre Dame; by the time the *Prize Homes* book was published, Slater's address was at the Iowa State University in Ames, Iowa, where he attended graduate school.[72] It is likely that other architectural students also submitted. Chicago's Institute of Design, founded in 1937 as the New Bauhaus, had a thriving architectural program, headed in 1945 by Ralph Rapson, who entered two designs co-created with John Van der Meulen. The School of the Art Institute of Chicago also had an architectural program. The University of Illinois architectural program, downstate in Champaign-Urbana, was large and prestigious. An assistant professor in that program, F. D. Miles, submitted a drawing with former student O. J. Baker; their listed address was a campus building.[73] Miles's students likely would have known about the competition. A $1,000 cash prize would have been a good sum for students, and because of their coursework or internships, they may well have had house designs already at hand.

Thirty percent of architects licensed to practice during World War II were in military service, and many submissions came from those still performing or winding down wartime duties.[74] The *Tribune* noted this in its early announcement of winners: submissions by Captain Jack Sackville-West, Lieutenant Curtis S. Woolford and Ensign Ralph DeLos Peterson, Lieutenant Ray Stuermer, and Lieutenant W. R. Burns included those architects' military titles, and their photographs, along with Frederick Sloan's, showed them in uniform. Stuermer, the *Tribune* reported, "sketched out solutions to the competition's problem No. 1 and 3 during his ship's last trip to the South Pacific to pick up homeward bound service personnel."[75] During spare evening hours while on duty in the Navy, Lieutenant Charles Berg worked on his drawings.[76] Coder Taylor, released from the Navy but on public works service on the East Coast, had written in for competition rules. On his way west to join his pregnant wife, he stopped one night at his parents' home in Pittsburgh. Learning there that his wife had given birth earlier than expected, Taylor stayed up all night to design and draw. Before taking off the next morning to see his wife and newborn, he asked his father to mail it in for him.[77] Taylor forgot about the contest and was surprised when he learned he had won.[78]

Some of the house plans designed by professionals, if technically conforming to the competition parameters, must have been knocked out of consideration due to their design's lack of appeal or practicality. Marion Mahony Griffin's solution to problem two (which, when modified, could also address problems one and three), presented, in Hill's assessment, "severe impracticalities," including accessing the son's room through a kitchen or bathroom, or a bathroom directly off the living room.[79] Jurors in the Pittsburgh competition expressed discouragement about the 900-plus drawings they received, even though almost half came from registered architects. Designs lacked "good taste and sound realism."[80] Kenneth Reid, commenting on submissions to the 1945 Georgia house competition sponsored by *Pencil Points/Progressive Architecture*, found "a disappointingly large number of designs that missed the boat." Hoping for brilliance, architects ended up instead with pretentious, overly complex designs. In the future, he urged competitors, stick to simple plans.[81] As will be discussed later, Prize Homes jurors selected relatively conventional house designs, rejecting anything terribly unusual.

We can surmise that the pool included repeat applicants. Far from prohibiting one entry per designer, the original announcement and the rules booklet invited designers to submit as many designs to as many of the three problems as they wished.[82] Clearly, several took the *Tribune* up on that offer. Ray Stuermer won in categories one and three; Merwin Freeman's entry in category three won him a prize, but Edward Barry highlighted a non-winning entry for problem one. The *Prize Homes* book indicates the team of Ralph DeLos Peterson and Curtis Woolford submitted at least two designs for category number one, winning for one of them; the same is true of Floyd Yewell. R. W. Tempest won no prizes, but *Prize Homes* included four of his designs across all three categories, and Barry featured three of his houses in the *Tribune*. Robert Arnold submitted in categories two and three. Comparisons to other competitions proves fruitful; in many others, architects submitted multiple drawings in the same and/or different categories. The *Tribune*'s own 1926 contest, which resulted in a published book of winning and additional designs, indicates a few architects submitted drawings for both the five-room and the six-room categories.[83] A 1936 competition for designing a concrete house, specifying categories for northern and southern climates, indicates multiple submissions within and across the divisions.[84] *Pencil Points* 1945 and 1946 house competitions indicate multiple submissions.[85] Architects and designers with plenty of ideas had nothing to lose but the time spent making drawings and mailing them in.

Some architects never, or rarely, entered competitions. Bertrand Goldberg, practicing in Chicago, declared he had only entered one competition ever (and for a European opera house, at that).[86] Comparing the *Tribune* entries to other competitions, however, reveals that many architects repeatedly—even frequently—entered architectural competitions. Chicago architect L. Morgan Yost, who submitted to the Prize Homes competition, admitted in an oral interview to entering a few.[87] Between a 1916 White Pine Association contest for a suburban house and a small house competition sponsored by *Architectural Forum* in 1951, fifteen house contests over that thirty-five-year period indicate a consistent roster of applicants.[88] Some winners and mentions in the White Pine Association competition won or earned mentions five years later in the 1921 Own Your Own Home Exposition. Four years after that, some of those earlier designers gained mentions or wins in a competition for fireproof homes. The *Tribune*'s earlier design competition, in 1926, shows many repeating names. Names do change over time, as architects retired or fell behind in style and new architects started their careers. But scanning the winners and mentions from one contest to another one reflects a clear repetition of names over decades of competitions: Alfred Cookman Cass, J. Ivan Dise, and Royal Barry Wills eventually made way for Hugh Stubbins, Richard Neutra, and John Hironimus.

Among the known Prize Homes entrants, Kazumi Adachi, Stephen J. Alling, Elmer Babb, C. N. Chau and Leon Hyzen, Oliver Lundquist, I. M. Pei, Ralph Rapson and John Van der Meulen, Paul Schweikher, Frederick Sloan and Walter Thies earned prizes or mentions elsewhere. Rapson and Van der Meulen's *Tribune* submission did not make it into the *Prize Homes* book, but their design for the Ladies' Home Journal Small House competition in 1938 won a $50 prize, and Rapson's submission to *Progressive Architecture*'s Pittsburgh Architectural Competition took third prize just a few months earlier, in April 1945.[89] Hyzen and Chau, whose Prize Homes designs went on display at the Art Institute, earned mentions in the Pittsburgh contest. Lundquist and Babb, non-winners included in *Prize Homes*, earned mentions in the Pittsburgh contest.[90] A few Prize Homes entrants had success in earlier *Tribune* competitions. Richard E. Bishop's six-room house won the first-place award in the *Tribune*'s 1926 Homes Competition, although his submission to the 1945 Prize Homes competition did not generate any attention.[91] Paul Kilp of Minnesota earned an honorable mention in the *Tribune*'s 1934 W-G-N theater competition, and William Boedefeld earned an honorable mention a decade later, in a second W-G-N theater competition.[92]

J. (John) Floyd Yewell warrants special attention for turning up in at least a dozen house competitions over a thirty-year span. Born in 1885, he and co-designer Lewis Welch took third prize in the 1916 White Pine Association contest.[93] His second-place award in the American Face Brick design

America's Most Popular Small House Plan

As built in Atlanta, Ga.
Burge, Stevens & Candin, Supervising Architects

DINING ROOM 12'-6" x 11

PORCH 12'-6" x 8'-6"

LIVING ROOM 16 x 12

KITCHEN 3' x 10'-6"

HALL

PANTRY

First Floor

BED ROOM 12'-6" x 10'

BATH

HALL

BED ROOM 12 x 16

BED ROOM 3' x 9'-6"

CL

CL

Second Floor

First Floor—Living room with fireplace and built-in window seat, living porch or glassed-in sun parlor, vestibule hall with coat closet, dining room, separate breakfast nook, kitchen with built-in cabinets, 2 closets, service vestibule with ice box recess.

Second Floor—3 bedrooms, fireplace in master bedroom as shown, 6 closets, tiled bathroom, trap door in ceiling providing access to storage space above. A detailed description of this plan will be found on the opposite page.

As designed by John Floyd Yewell, Architect

Plan No. 216   JOHN FLOYD YEWELL, Architect   20,500 Cubic Feet

J. Floyd Yewell's house in a popular house plan book; the design was widely copied. (Henry Atterbury Smith, ed., *Books of a Thousand Homes*, vol. 1. [New York: Home Owners Service Institute, 1923], 7.)

competition of 1919 was the first house featured in Smith's *Books of a Thousand Homes*; Reiff's research indicates it was widely copied.[94]

Two Yewell designs won group mentions and one a singular mention in a 1921 Own Your Own Home competition.[95] An English-style fireproof home won a first prize in a 1925 contest. He earned mentions for entries in the *Tribune*'s 1926 contest; a *Pencil Points* 1930 competition for an eight-room house; another *Pencil Points*/Flat Glass industry contest in 1934; a 1936 design for a concrete house suitable in a southern climate; the *Pencil Points* "Suntile" 1937 contest for a doctor's house; and a 1946 "Georgia" contest by *Pencil Points*. Bloomingdale's department store sponsored a competition for houses for New Yorkers; Yewell's design for a three-bedroom home earned a second-place prize and inclusion in the 1947 booklet of winning designs.[96] His two-bedroom entry in the Prize Homes contest won and was included in an *Architectural Forum* article about the contest. A brief biography of

Yewell in the *Tribune*, appearing when Prize Home winners were first announced and likely based on information he gave to the paper, mentions his interest in small house design and notes, modestly, his awards in "various competitions in that field."[97] (Yewell was also one of the five painters the *Tribune* commissioned to render the winning designs in watercolor.)

Yewell's story is perhaps atypical. Not only did he frequently enter competitions, but he also did not discriminate among them, entering competitions sponsored by industry associations (White Pine), established architectural publications (*Pencil Points*), and newspapers (twice for the *Chicago Tribune*). Some architects may have considered it good practice to toss in a design when possible, and thus regularly entered competitions like Yewell did. Ralph Rapson, whose co-entry to the Prize Homes competition neither won nor merited inclusion in the *Prize Homes* book, submitted to over thirty architectural and design competitions in his career, beginning in his student days.[98]

Because so many architects entered so many competitions, at least some architects probably reused or revised previously drawn house designs. (This research leaves aside the possibility that some submitted others' designs, though Reiff's history of architectural catalogs thoroughly describes how homage easily turned into piracy.) At least one winning Prize Homes design reflects this practice. Walter Thies's first prize design for the 1936 *Pencil Points*/Portland Cement Association bears remarkable resemblance to his 1945 brick Prize Homes winner.[99] The former house is large, with three bedrooms, two-and-a-half bathrooms, and a sewing room, compared to the modest two-bedroom, one-and-a-half bathrooms of the latter submission, and the rooms in the cement house are larger overall. The attached garage is at the side of the 1936 house, but as the 1945 competition required a smaller lot, the garage juts from the front of the latter house. The cement house is flat roofed, while the Prize Homes house is traditionally roofed. But the façades of the houses are immediately identifiable as coming from the same architect. Window and front door placements, especially on the front elevation, are nearly identical, as is corner brick detail. The first-floor plan is reversed, but living room, dining alcove, kitchen, powder room, study, laundry, and stairway placements are virtually identical. Thies's thumbnail biography in the *Tribune* includes the fact that he "recently won a prize in a competition for home design sponsored by a cement company," clearly referring to the 1936 contest, which was not very recent. Also unmentioned is the striking similarity between the two designs.[100]

The jury for the *Pencil Points* 1936 competition even then complained "there were a considerable number of competitors whose designs were painfully reminiscent of prize-winning drawings in other competitions of recent

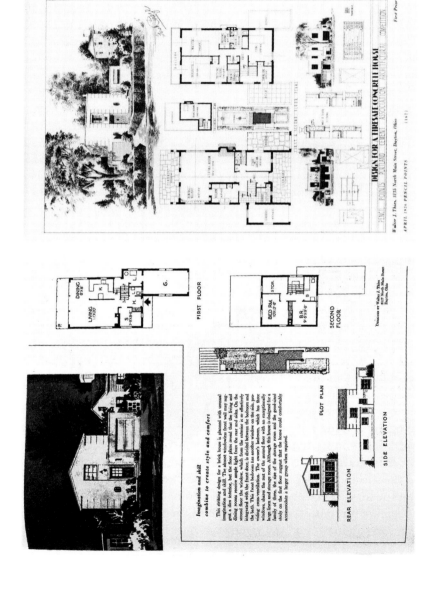

Two winning designs by Walter Thies bear striking resemblance to each other. One is his Prize Homes submission; the other is for the 1935 *Pencil Points*/Portland Cement Association competition. (*Prize Homes*, 11; "Report of the Jury Award," *Pencil Points*, April 1936, 165.)

years, even to the reproduction of the trees, bushes, porch furniture, and clouds," although it is not clear whether they objected to architects replicating their own designs or stealing others' work.[101]

Architect R. W. Tempest submitted at least four designs to the competition. One four-bedroom, one-story modern house for problem three created a U shape around an interior courtyard; another, more traditional "cottage" for problem three blended elements of modern and traditional houses.[102] But two designs, for problems one and two, share many features. Both are two-story, flat-roofed, with a front snout garage. Projected corner windows (this is remarked upon in the *Prize Homes* book text for both houses) are nearly identical. Each has a "hidden" entrance, behind the garage or on the side. Despite being for two different family constellations, each has three bedrooms on the second floor. The stairway is differently shaped but in the same place. They are remarkably similar.[103] Reiff suggests it would have been easy and economical for architects to minimally revise designs already on hand, even if already subsidized by previous clients.[104] Ralph Rapson's papers indicate he saved the *Tribune* article featuring one of the co-designs he submitted with John Van der Meulen. Handwritten at the top of the newspaper is this commentary: "An early house done for a Chicago Competition. We had several small ones of this nature."[105] If we interpret the "small ones" as houses already designed, that suggests that, at least for this particular team, they did not wholly create new work but reused or repurposed existing creations.

Plenty of the architects submitting designs either never practiced architecture or had undistinguished careers. But others were or would become quite renowned for their talents. By 1945, Marcel Breuer had an established international career as a designer and, with his mentor and partner Walter Gropius, an architect. Paul Schweikher and Winston Elting submitted a co-designed house; each already had significant reputations as modernists in the Midwest. Kazumi Adachi and Stewart Williams contributed to the midcentury boom of Palm Springs modernist houses, still in high demand. I. M. Pei in 1945 was finishing a master's degree in architecture but would in time become world renowned, his pyramid addition to Paris's Louvre but one example of his international work. Tucker's review of small house architecture in the interwar period suggests many dismissed the work of plan book architecture, focusing on small houses, as unworthy of established architects.[106] Perhaps some thought that architectural competitions were beneath them, but even the limited list of Prize Homes architects does not support that conclusion.

Some Chicago-area architects and designers competing in other national contests surely must have competed in their local, hometown contest.

Chicagoans Stanley Kazdailis and Pat Marshall earned, respectively, special mention and mention for their *Pencil Points*/Pittsburgh designs submitted in December 1944.[107] The Chicago Metropolitan Builders held an expo in Chicago in February 1945 and displayed plans from its architectural competition. That included designs by Chicago-area architects Charles Schreiber, Charles Nixon, Earl Carruthers, and E. C. Mahoney.[108] Charles D. Wiley earned a mention for the *Pencil Points* Georgia contest, held nearly simultaneously with the *Tribune* competition; that submission listed a Chicago address.[109] Wiley won first place in the *Arts and Architecture* 1945 competition sponsored by the United States Plywood Corporation. Chicago architect Harry Weese, who eventually designed some of Chicago's most iconic buildings, earned an honorable mention.[110] George Matsumoto, fourth-place winner of the Home Design Competition of 1951, lived only one year in Chicago, but that year was 1945.[111] The New Bauhaus, a school of design now known as the Illinois Institute of Technology, had reopened in 1939; during the *Tribune* contest, Ralph Rapson headed the school and prominent architect George Fred Keck taught there. Keck's brother and architectural partner, William, reported having submitted to the Plywood competition and a few others, but he complained "we have never won any of them because they're [Kecks' submissions] too good."[112] Perhaps either or both of the Kecks submitted one of their "too good" houses to the Chicagoland Prize Homes competition.

Twelve of the twenty-four Prize Homes winners came from architects practicing in Chicago or its suburbs. If we are confident in the anonymity of the judging process (and there is no reason not to be), the competition probably drew disproportionately from those living in the Chicagoland area. Of 172 designs displayed in the Art Institute show, at least fifty-five are known to have been from local designers.[113] Edward Barry's twenty features of additional designers included eight from Chicago. Twenty-seven of the ninety-two collected in the *Prize Homes* book came from local designers. A Chicagoland contest, for houses built for Chicago-area weather conditions, heavily publicized in Chicago, surely attracted most of its entries from Chicago-area architects. Other contests indicate a disproportionate number of submissions from New York and Los Angeles, arguably the centers of midcentury American architectural innovation. The contest parameters insisted that judging would be anonymous, and prizes would be awarded regardless of the creators' residence. But selections of which houses to include in the Art Institute show, which additional houses Barry featured, which houses to build, and which to include in the subsequent *Prize Homes* book certainly could have been influenced by hometown pride. It was, after all, the *Chicago Tribune*.

The foreword to the *Prize Homes* book indicates entries came from "architects and designers throughout the North American continent and many foreign countries."[114] Only one design is confirmed in that category, from Canadian architects R. Hugh Crawford and Henry Fliess, who submitted a jointly designed house for problem two.[115] World War I, anti-Semitism, and resistance to "radical" art forms displaced a good many European architects and designers, even before the outbreak of World War II. Walter Gropius and Marcel Breuer were among those who sought refuge in the United States. Many of those who submitted to Prize Homes had established practices in the United States but were not born, or perhaps trained, in the United States.

Anonymity of judging potentially created opportunities for designers otherwise facing social and legal discrimination. The 1918 White Pine architectural competition, for example, awarded Paul R. Williams one of its four prizes and included his design in their annual monograph. An African American who eventually developed a robust practice, Williams famously learned to draw and draft upside down as White clients preferred to sit across from rather than next to him. But he also established a storied, decades-long career, building modern houses for celebrities in Los Angeles and shaping California architecture for generations.[116] Already noted is the number of women whose designs were included in the *Prize Homes* book. Reviewing the history of house competitions indicates that, while there were few women winners, and even fewer women as solo designers, some did win or earn mentions.[117] Despite the United States' recent completion of a war against Germans, Italians, and Japanese, the *Prize Homes* book included numerous designs by people with Germanic, Italian, or Japanese surnames. Richard Y(oshihiro) Mine, a Japanese-born architect who also earned an honorable mention in the Tribune Tower competition of 1922, is included *Prize Homes*. So is Tohzo Nishiseki, who submitted from a New York City address. Three years earlier, he had been confined to the Tule Lake Relocation Center, an American concentration camp for Japanese Americans. While there, according to a weekly newspaper by and for detainees, he designed a landscape plan for an administration building.[118]

3

Spreading the News

Putting the Competition before the Public

After the *Tribune*'s steady but modest promotion of the contest, upon announcing the winners, the paper pulled out all the stops for the next year and a half, heralding the competition and its tangible impact when construction began on prizewinning house designs. Sunday front-page announcements, color pages, partnership with its radio station, WGN, and ties with advertisers combined to keep the contest in readers' view. Patriotic, economic, and hometown boosterism coincided with the *Tribune*'s interest in selling papers.

When ready to announce contest winners, the *Tribune* finally began using its Sunday front page. On January 6, 1946, the Sunday edition unveiled the list of winning designers, awarding eight winners in each problem category. The front-page article featured two of the twenty-eight designers: Ray Stuermer and Lucille McKirahan. Stuermer won awards in both problems one and three. As notable as his double prize was his Navy service—he had sketched his designs onboard a ship in the South Pacific—although the paper did not highlight his Chicago connection, going no further than including his Chicago address. McKirahan's prize generated comment due to her sex; the wife of an architect serving in Japan, she "utilized her own extensive knowledge of design to win one of the prizes in the competition's problem No. 2." Inside the paper, readers could see thumbnail photos and brief biographies of each winner.

No more than three or four sentences, biographies included addresses for Chicago and Chicago suburban architects and city of residence for others. Most of the biographies included information about wartime service activities in the military or private sector, and many indicated their rank and service branch. Five of the photos show winners in uniform. The *Tribune* took out full-page ads in the *Architectural Record* and *Architectural Forum*

Winners in The Tribune's $24,000 Chicagoland Prize Homes Competition

The first announcement of winners featured their pictures and short biographies. Several were pictured in uniform. ("Brief Sketches of Winners of Tribune Prizes," *Chicago Tribune*, January 6, 1946, 4.)

February issues, announcing the winners.[1] The following month, duplicating the information, the *Record* ran a brief announcement of the winners. As that article also featured McKirahan and double winner Stuermer, the *Architectural Record* piece appears to have come straight from the *Tribune*'s own January 6 announcement.[2]

After that first promotion, the *Tribune* featured the contest for the next couple of years. It celebrated with ten winners at a January 9 lunch at the Palmer House hotel.[3] Alerting readers that winning drawings would soon be published, the paper reminded them to "be sure to start your collection of prize home designs on Sunday so that you will have the facts about all 24 designs developed in this nationwide project" and that the color pictures would be found in the Sunday Color Graphics section of the paper.[4] Designs appeared in five successive Sunday editions: February 3, 10, 17, 24, and March 3.[5] At the bottom of each full-page article on the front page of the C section, the *Tribune* urged readers to save that day's page and those

On Sunday, February 3, 1946, the *Tribune* released the first set of winning designs. (Edward Barry, "Winning Designs in the Tribune's Prize Homes Competition," *Chicago Tribune*, February 3, 1946, C1.)

already published. Each week the *Tribune* featured four or five houses, intermingling the different house sizes.

Every winning design included floor plans and a color sketch elevation. On the inside continuation of the story, each house received three or four paragraphs of laudatory copy, sometimes quoting a juror's praise, and a brief biography of the designer. Architect Coder Taylor recalled the weekly features as very colorful.[6]

While none of the 1945 articles about the contest included a byline, the *Tribune* credited reporter Edward Barry in all the Sunday articles featuring the winning houses; he also wrote about plans for building some of the homes, groundbreaking ceremonies, landscaping, and decorating the house interiors. Barry had been hired as a music critic; during the competition period, the paper also published his reviews of film, theater, music, and books.[7] Perhaps the *Tribune* considered architecture to fit within an arts niche, although Barry was not a disinterested reviewer when it came to the Prize Homes coverage. Not once in the pages of the *Tribune* did even a hint of criticism appear about the houses' designs.

Under Barry's byline, the *Tribune* ran articles on twenty additional submissions that had not won prizes. (Eleven of those appeared in the *Prize Homes* book, but nine did not.) Reporting in April 1946, *Architectural Forum* indicated there had been no initial plan to publicize any designs but the winning ones, but the contest proved so successful that the Sunday editor, Ardis Kennedy, elected to bring forward some of the "honorably-mentioned."[8] It is not clear whether jurors, editor Kennedy, Barry, or someone else chose which additional houses would be included in the paper's coverage; unlike other architectural competitions, there was no official category of "special mention," "honorable mention," or "mention." Six of the Barry pieces quote or cite advisor Boyd Hill, who commends particular features; perhaps Hill selected additional houses that the paper might feature.

In contrast with the *Tribune*'s choice to assign a single reporter to cover the contest results, it selected five different artists to provide the presentation renderings, drawings that architects use to show how a building will look when finished. The renderings were published in the paper, displayed in the Art Institute show and, eventually, appeared in the Chicagoland *Prize Homes* book; they also "toured" with the submissions. Five Sundays in a row, the *Tribune* displayed its winners, and for each Sunday's coverage, a different artist was commissioned for the drawings. The *Tribune* most likely had staff artists, but editors elected to draw on other illustrators. The sketches of the first five houses, published February 3, were credited to Chicago artist Charles E. Kemp. His short biography, accompanied by a photo, noted his work as a commercial artist and vacation painter of landscapes.[9] The second cluster to be publicized, on February 10, attributed the drawings George Cooper Rudolph, in an article accompanied by Rudolph's photograph. His biography mentioned that he was a frequent illustrator for magazines featuring home designs; it did not indicate his city of residence.[10] The third group of winners, displayed on February 17, included the most interesting choice: architect/artist J. Floyd Yewell, himself a prizewinner. His own winning design was not among the five he painted, but it would appear the following week, by yet another artist. The note on Yewell also indicated all the artists used watercolor.[11] As noted before, Yewell had entered a significant number of architectural competitions, going back at least thirty years. Today he is known more for his artistic work than his architectural designs.[12]

Howard Raftery drew the four houses in group four, published on February 24. Raftery, in addition to practicing architecture in Chicago, found success as an artist; the National Gallery of Art owns several of his lithographs.[13] Readers learned not only about the medium—again watercolor—but also that he worked from the submitted drawings.[14] It is unknown whether he, like Yewell, submitted a design to the Prize Homes competition, but he did submit a two-bedroom house design to the *Tribune*'s 1926 architectural competition.[15] Ted Kautzky of New York finished the final set of watercolors. Labeled an artist and architectural designer, Kautzky also "designed a number of exhibits for the Century of Progress exposition in 1933," a Chicago event fresh in the minds of many readers.[16] In the first image of this book, one can see his name as author of a book on drafting, for sale in the pages of *Pencil Points* magazine.

Illustrators must have worked quickly; winners were announced on January 6, and the artists faced two deadlines. Foremost, the *Tribune* wanted the color pictures for its planned, expansive coverage in the color section of the Sunday paper. But the Art Institute exhibit required the winning watercolors to be ready for a February 9 opening. Clearly, artists did not meet this latter deadline: only ten watercolors of the twenty-four prizewinners were displayed on February 9, with the other fourteen added as the month-long exhibition continued. Contemporary photos of the exhibit shed little light on how the designs were displayed, but the winning floor plans and elevations appear to have been blown up, perhaps on 2-foot by 4-foot paper or board. The watercolor illustrations for the winners were both matted and framed in white.[17] Renderings contributed color and detail to the houses, adding bright curtains to windows, ivy climbing up trellises, blooming bushes, and mountain backgrounds, occasionally including people in the yards and outdoor spaces.

Chicago architect Coder Taylor, interviewed for the Art Institute's oral history project, commented on the fate of the watercolor renderings. He thought the *Tribune* had given the paintings to the University of Illinois at Navy Pier, site of the university's city architectural program, then headed by Harold McEldowney. One day, McEldowney's secretary called Taylor.

> She just happened to call me one day and say, "These drawings are here—would you care for yours?" I said, "sure I certainly would." Kautzky did it,

and mine was an original Kautzky. It's almost like an original of any good artist. I went down the next day, I think, to get it, and there were a number of other renderings there. I asked, "What are you going to do with these?" She said, "Oh, probably throw them out." I said, "Well not now—would you mind if I have them?" She said, "No fine, take them." I took everything.[18]

Taylor ended up with not only Kautzky's painting of his own design but also six others: Kautzky's rendering of Lucille McKirahan's house, Kemp's depictions of Sloan's and Schroeder's houses, Yewell's painting of Burns's house, Raftery's illustration of Garbe's house, and Rudolph's rendering of Cedarstrand's design. Upon his retirement, Taylor donated all seven paintings to the Art Institute of Chicago. They remain in the collection and have been displayed, although they are not on permanent display.[19] The institute's information about those paintings indicates they are watercolor on illustration board.[20] Unfortunately, three of the paintings are mislabeled in the Art Institute directory. Rudolph's and Raftery's paintings, and Kemp's picture of the Schroeder house, attribute those illustrations to the architects, not the artists.[21] The status of the remaining seventeen paintings is unknown, but Taylor was correct: the watercolors, as viewed from the Art Institute's digital archive, are quite beautiful, and perhaps others of them were saved.[22] Through a third party, reproductions of the Rudolph painting and Kemp's depiction of the Sloan house are available for purchase; they are also misattributed there.[23]

Yewell's watercolor of Eric Wenstrand's house beautifully sets the house in a winter scene, with snow-covered pines behind the house and a snowy lawn. When the *Tribune* covered the Blue Island groundbreaking of the Wenstrand house in June 1946, however, it used a different sketch. The pines were gone, and what was a bare, snowy-branched deciduous tree was now in full leaf.[24] That was probably Wenstrand's original. In a story about the construction of the Sackville-West design, the picture of the house is not identical to the watercolor rendering: some of the background foliage is absent, and a tree in the foreground is in a slightly different place. The caption refers to the "artist's sketch," and the article reminds readers that the *Tribune*'s earlier publication of the winning design came with a "color sketch."[25] This, too, was probably from the original submission. *Tribune* coverage of non-winning entries relied on the architects' original elevation sketches, as the paper commissioned renderings only for the winning designs.

Concurrent with the five-week roll-out of contest winners, the *Tribune* promoted its efforts through a partnership with the Art Institute of Chicago.[26] An exhibit of 172 submission drawings—including the color paintings the *Tribune* published—opened at the institute on February 9. That it opened without the drawn-out fanfare with which the *Tribune* heralded its contest winners could suggest that the exhibit was a last-minute plan, although a precedent existed for this, since the Art Institute also exhibited submissions to the 1922 *Tribune* Tower contest and the 1926 small house competition. The first *Tribune* announcement of the exhibition appeared along with the February 3 publication of the first set of designs, briefly mentioning that an exhibit of about 200 of the best drawings would begin February 9 and close March 8. Only ten of the winners would be ready for review by opening day, with others added until March 2.[27] But exhibit planners worked far enough in advance to send invitations to a private showing on February 7, when the exhibit would display "original sketches of the prize winning and 143 other entries received."[28] Marcel Breuer's copy of that invitation includes a handwritten message at the bottom of the invitation: "Your entry will be among those displayed." On the reverse side of the invitation, the recipients learned of a post-exhibit cocktail party at the Palmer House, located around the corner from the Art Institute.[29] Chicago Mayor Edward J. Kelly attended the preview show.[30] On Sunday, February 10, the *Tribune* again reported on the exhibit, this time listing exhibitors from Chicago or its suburbs; the list includes thirty-four names of entrants not among the roster of winners. On February 15, the newspaper announced that, thus far, fifteen of the twenty-four winning designs already had been added to the exhibit, alongside a photograph of Illinois Governor Dwight Green holding the framed painting of Howard Uebelhack's house.

Illinois Governor Dwight Green at the Art Institute of Chicago, holding a framed watercolor of Howard Uebelhack's winning design for problem three. ("Sees Home Designs," *Chicago Tribune*, February 16, 1946, 3.)

On February 27, the *Tribune* boasted that Art Institute attendance was up by a third from the same time the previous year, and that six-year-old actor Natalie Wood visited the exhibition the day before.[31] At the end of the month-long show, the *Tribune* quoted Chauncey McCormick, president of the Art Institute, who attributed the exhibit's popularity to an overall increase in museum visitors.[32] As entrance to the museum was then free three days a week, including Saturday and Sunday, there were minimal economic barriers to attendance.[33]

The *Tribune* did not mention until April 7 that visitors to the Prize Homes exhibit at the Art Institute had the opportunity to vote for their favorites among the 172 entrants; it is not clear how that voting took place. Museum visitors were free to choose from all the entrants, yet the seven top vote getters came exclusively from prizewinners. (Prizewinning designs were presented with the watercolor paintings, possibly affecting voter preferences.) A Finney and Glidden design and Howard Uebelhack's entry tied for first place, winner Edward Hanson's design took third, with Ray Stuermer's in fourth place and Charles Schroeder's in fifth. W. R. Burns's house earned sixth place, and Arthur "Jack" Sackville-West's placed seventh.[34] Not only did the Art Institute patrons get to vote on favorites, but *Tribune* readers also made their preferences known. Barry, reporting on inquiries to the paper about the houses, noted the most frequently asked about was Sackville-West's, followed by Burns's, Uebelhack's, Frederick Sloan's, and Finney and Glidden's. Designs from Stuermer, Wenstrand, and McKirahan also drew favorable attention.[35]

In addition to the Art Institute show, the *Tribune* eventually arranged for winning drawings to be showcased elsewhere throughout Chicago and the Midwest. Some exhibits were large and some were small, but most seem to have included at least the twenty-four winners. The first exhibition occurred concurrent with the Art Institute show. The National Home Builders' Exposition in Chicago in February 1946 announced even before the paper published the final sets of winning designs that the designs would be on view at the expo.[36] (The expo could not have displayed the renderings hanging in the Art Institute at the same time, since presumably there were no duplicates of the watercolors, but the floor plans and architects' own elevation sketches were easily copied.) In March, all 172 houses displayed at the Art Institute were on view at the Engineering Society in Midland, Michigan.[37] Ten winners went on display in Evanston, Illinois, with plans to move the exhibit to the Illinois cities of Highland Park, Waukegan, and Crystal Lake.[38] A Boyd Hill letter to the 172 exhibitors at the Art Institute show indicated that the Hudson's department store in Detroit wanted to display the entries, so the return of the original submissions would be delayed;

this plan was in place as early as March 21, the date of that letter.[39] Along with Hudson's, Ayers department store in Indianapolis hosted the exhibit for two weeks in the summer of 1946.[40] Both stores advertised the displays in local papers. At the end of the summer, visitors to the Escanaba State Fair, in the upper peninsula of Michigan, could view 148 designs.[41] Attendees at the Midwest Stoker Association and Chicago Coal Merchants Association could see them in 1947.[42] In 1948, Milwaukee residents got their turn, and when announcing that display, the *Tribune* boasted that more than 350,000 people had viewed the exhibit in over thirty cities.[43]

Even in 1950, by which time the *Tribune* had largely dropped its coverage of the contest, at least four Chicagoland banks mounted exhibitions.[44] Each bank exhibited forty-two designs, suggesting that a particular collection traveled throughout the area. In 1951, one hundred of the designs were exhibited at the Culver Military Academy in Indiana, an astonishing venue, as it is a boys' prep school with emphasis on military leadership. The exhibit was brought at the instigation of Warner Williams, the school's

The Detroit branch of Hudson's Department store was one of many venues throughout the country that displayed the Prize Homes collection of winning and worthy designs. ("J. L. Hudson Slates Home Plan Show," *Detroit Free Press*, June 16, 1946, 15.)

You Are Invited to Visit
**Hudson's
Home Planning Show**

- Prize-Winning Designs from The Chicago Tribune's Competition

See 200 up-to-the-minute home designs, including the prize winners in the "Chicagoland Prize Homes Competition."

- See Eight Scale Models from Better Homes and Gardens Exhibit

These models, all completely furnished and landscaped, represent ideas garnered across the nation by Better Homes and Gardens on the conveniences and comforts people want in new homes.

- See a Scale Model of the D.S.R.'s New City Hall Bus Terminal

Interesting to all transportation-minded Detroiters, this model of the new project which will be built as soon as condemnation proceedings, now underway, are completed.

Through June 29

HUDSON'S—Auditorium—Twelfth Floor

artist-in-residence.[45] Geographically, the farthest known exhibit was the 1952 Los Angeles Home Show, which displayed one hundred designs.[46] And in 1953, the Freeport, Illinois, Chamber of Commerce reported that while plans had not been finalized, it had "hopes" that it could exhibit Prize Homes designs. With whom they had to finalize such plans remained unreported.[47]

How many people saw the drawings outside of the *Tribune's* pages cannot be known, other than the Art Institute attendance numbers reported in the paper. Even if nobody made a special trip to view the exhibits, however, bank customers doing ordinary business in their local branch, department store shoppers bustling through the store lobby, and families strolling through the state fair must have been exposed at least briefly. Aside from the hundreds of thousands who viewed the prize homes designs in the *Tribune* or the Art Institute show, thousands more would have seen the traveling exhibitions.

By the end of 1946, *Tribune* Sunday circulation was 1,400,000, and ad revenue was at an all-time high. In October of that year, the Graphic section of the Sunday edition shifted from just another section of the paper to a magazine-sized insert, printed on rotogravure stock in four-color inks.[48] *Tribune* editors and staff must have considered the Prize Homes competition a contributor to the paper's success, for they found a way to repeat the process in the next years, not with an architectural competition but with a room decoration contest. Drawing on Boyd Hill again as professional advisor, the *Tribune* announced a "Better Rooms Competition" in December 1946, asking for interior designs for seven different interior spaces: living room, dining room, combination living and dining room, owners' bedroom, child's bedroom, kitchen, and recreation room. Devoting $26,250 to cash awards, the *Tribune* offered first, second, and third prizes plus honorable mentions, ranging from $1,000 for first prize (the same as the Prize Homes competition) to $100 for honorable mentions; 161 monetary awards would be granted.[49] As before, interested parties had to register and obtain the rules booklet and, as before, the *Tribune* aimed for inclusivity. Edward Barry, whose byline appears for most of the articles regarding the competition, called it "the first contest of its kind to be held on so large a scale, [and] is open to nonprofessionals and professionals alike. Every woman who enjoys redoing and rearranging her home, every man who periodically sketches out the recreation rooms he plans to have someday, now are afforded the chance to win one or more prizes . . . for their original ideas." Further encouragement came from assurance that lack of artistic talent disqualified nobody, as "[t]he value of the ideas themselves, not the artistic excellence of the drawings, will be the basis for judgment." Barry promised the winning designs would be publicized, with color reproductions. In a boon to commerce, he also suggested prospective entrants "may want to crystalize some of their ideas by visiting home furnishings and furniture stores or the sections devoted to this merchandise in department stores."[50]

A three-week exhibit at the Art Institute followed.[51] Local furniture and department stores—among them Marshall Field's and John M. Smyth—created room displays from winning designs; the *Tribune* boasted that "furniture, home furnishings, and appliance dealers thruout [*sic*] the city . . . set aside the period of Sept. 15 to Nov. 15 as Chicagoland Home and Home Furnishings festival."[52] As with architectural competitions, some submitted multiple entries in multiple categories, and several names from the Prize Homes competition reappeared as cash prizewinners: Wenstrand, Hanson, Martorano, Eileen Pei, Alling, Brooks, and Adachi. Renderer George Rudolph won in more than one category.[53]

The *Tribune* must have been pleased with this endeavor, for it ran a Better Rooms competition in five more consecutive years. With some tinkering of minor details, the main formula remained the same: about $25,000 in total prize money, open to everyone except *Tribune* employees, multiple cash prizes across several room categories, a three-week Art Institute display, and winning and worthy designs showcased in Chicagoland furniture and department stores. By 1951, traveling exhibits of winning sketches had been shown at fairs, libraries, stores, schools, and museums in twenty-two states, among them Evansville, Indiana; Wichita Falls, Texas; Missoula and Great Falls, Montana; Cairo, Georgia; and Florence, Alabama.[54] In early 1952, the *Tribune* was advertising the results from the "sixth annual" Better Rooms competition, but in the fall of 1952, when the paper would have begun the call for submissions to a seventh annual competition, the editors dropped the enterprise, and it was never revived.

A More Permanent Legacy

Publishing the *Prize Homes* Book

More than the *Tribune* coverage, the Art Institute show, and the traveling exhibits, the 1948 publication of the *Prize Homes* book generated the greatest publicity for the competition, and that book remains the most expansive and permanent record of the competition. There was precedent for publishing the winning designs, as the *Tribune* had done this after its 1926 competition, when it printed *The Chicago Tribune Book of Homes* the following year. The *Tribune* planned a book early. An April 1946 letter from W. J. Byrnes informed Marcel Breuer that his "design has been chosen for inclusion in a book of home designs selected from entries in the Chicagoland Prize Homes Competition which we plan to have published in response to requests from readers of the Chicago Tribune." (In the end, Breuer's plan was not included in the book.) A first printing would be 100,000 copies, and the paper already had a publisher lined up. The letter asserted that despite the *Tribune*'s sole ownership of all submitted designs, the corporation would share book profits with those whose designs were included but had not won cash awards.[1]

Whether the book made any money or whether profits were shared is unknown. Also unknown is why the publication came three years after the competition, when the *Chicago Tribune Book of Homes* appeared merely one year after the 1926 architectural competition.

Prize Homes combined the twenty-four winning entries plus sixty-eight other house designs in a collection of ninety-two house designs, published by Chicago publishing company Wilcox & Follett. *Prize Homes* credited no author, although it acknowledged that the book was designed by Stanford W. Williamson. He would become, or perhaps already was, the publishing house's art director, and he had an interesting, varied career. He served as book designer for several Wilcox & Follett books during the period that *Prize Homes* was issued, accumulating a significant number of awards for design work.[2] Williamson was also an artist and writer. A painting titled

Chicago Tribune
THE WORLD'S GREATEST NEWSPAPER

TRIBUNE TOWER • CHICAGO

April 23, 1946

Mr. Marcel Breuer
1430 Massachusetts Ave.
Cambridge, Mass.

Dear Mr. Breuer:

Your design has been chosen for inclusion in a book of home designs selected from entries in the Chicagoland Prize Homes Competition which we plan to have published in response to requests from readers of the Chicago Tribune.

We thought you would like to know of this plan particularly in view of the fact that, though the rules of the Competition give us the unqualified right to publish all designs entered in the Competition without payment to the entrants, we have decided to distribute a share of any profits from the sale of the first edition of the book to non-prize-winning entrants in the Competition whose designs are included in the book.

We have no way of telling at this time what the sale of the book will be but the publisher with whom we are working is considering a first edition of over 100,000 copies and feels confident that when published they will sell quite well. When the edition sells out and the figures are all in, we hope to be able to send you our check as an expression of goodwill and appreciation.

Very truly yours,

Manager, Research & Promotion

W J Byrnes-jg

CIRCULATION FOR FIRST QUARTER, 1946: DAILY, OVER 1,040,000; SUNDAY, OVER 1,450,000

Chicago Tribune manager W. J. Byrnes informed architect Marcel Breuer of the *Tribune*'s intention to publish his design in the subsequent book, but Breuer's design did not appear in *Prize Homes*. (Marcel Breuer Papers, Special Collection Research Center, Syracuse University Libraries.)

"Pale Objects" was displayed in a 1958 Art Institute of Chicago exhibit of local artists, and his paintings were held in private collections and exhibited in galleries.[3] A few articles under his byline appeared in the *Chicago Defender*, a daily newspaper for Black Chicagoans; Follett published his children's book, *The No Bark Dog*, in 1962.[4] In 1964, Williamson wrote copy for a well-received book of photographs, *With Grief Acquainted*, featuring photographs of Chicago's Black South Side residents.[5]

The number of houses in the volume—92—is a little odd. The *Tribune*'s 1927 *Book of Homes* included 99 house designs in 110 pages. The 92 houses in *Prize Homes* span 102 pages, but three pages are devoted to photos of built homes, and there are three blank pages, not including endpapers, so the book length is essentially the same. Perhaps the initial plan was to include 99 or 100 houses, similar to the *Tribune*'s earlier venture. The length is roughly comparable to other plan books published in 1946. Williams's *The Small Home of Tomorrow* is 96 pages, Dean and Breines's *The Book of Small Houses* has 145 pages, while Group's *House-of-the-Month Book of Small Houses* has 138.

Explanatory copy provides no clues as to who selected the sixty-eight additional house plans. The number may have been fluid; Breuer was informed in April 1946 that his design had been selected for the book, but it was not. Edward Barry's reporting went beyond the winners when he reviewed additional houses for the *Tribune*. Because not all of them made it into the published volume, it seems unlikely that *Prize Homes* houses stemmed from Barry's preferences. Competition advisor Boyd Hill worked on the competition well past its official conclusion: he commented on the winning designs for the paper's initial coverage, worked closely with developers in choosing the built houses, regularly appeared at the ground-breaking ceremonies, continued to be engaged through decorating and landscaping, and promoted open houses. Perhaps he chose the additional sixty-eight houses.

The book's uncredited foreword recapped the competition: the makeup of the jury, the three problems, the selection process, and the large number of submissions: 967. The foreword included information about the Art Institute exhibit: 90,000 visitors saw 172 designs in February 1946.[6] Despite the absence of a named author, the brief text accompanying each winning house is identical to Edward Barry's descriptions of the houses when first printed in the *Tribune* in February and March 1946. Eleven houses included in *Prize Homes* were among the twenty non-winners Barry featured, but nine were not. It is not clear who chose which non-winning entries to include in the book; if Barry had a hand in the selection for the *Tribune* articles and the book, there would have been a perfect overlap. The five artists who painted the watercolor elevations—Kautzky, Kemp, Raftery, Rudolph, and Yewell—went uncredited, although their illustrations are featured in the book. The artists signed their work; signatures or initials are clearly visible in six of the seven paintings in the Art Institute collection. But editors of the *Prize Homes* book removed artists' names or initials in its reproductions, with one exception. Charles Kemp's full name is visible on the watercolor of Frederick Sloan's design, though without magnification, it looks like landscaping. The same is true in Kemp's painting of the Charles Schroeder house, where one can see "Kemp" nestled in the landscaping, though it is only barely visible with magnification.

Whatever the reason for the delay between the winners' announcement and the book's publication, the lag made it possible for the book to update readers on the project's outcome. Contributing to the narrative of a successful competition are photographs in *Prize Homes* of eight built homes—one each in the Chicago suburbs of Palatine, Highland Park, and Lombard, and five in the Chicago neighborhood of Deer Park—reminding readers that the *Tribune*'s promise to see the contest through to construction was kept. Beyond the brief foreword and photos of the built homes, each of the ninety-two house designs occupies a full page, including the elevation sketch and floor plans published in the *Tribune* in 1946 but also additional elevations and plot plans. Some pages show enlarged detail, such as Miriam Hurford's front door on a two-story, four-bedroom house, Victor Chiljean and Carl Fricke's interior window/door combination, and Erling Bugge's interior of an activities room.[7] Winning designs appeared in full but muted color, while other pages of designs and photos appear in monochromatic blue, black, brown, or green.

Unlike most other house plan books and catalogs, *Prize Homes* has more in common with a coffee-table art book than an industry pamphlet.[8] Its

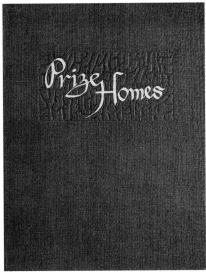

Dust jacket and front cover of *Prize Homes*. (*Prize Homes* [Chicago: Chicago Tribune Company, 1948].)

hardcover is embossed with the title, surrounded by an embossed, abstract pattern. A bright-red dust jacket displays Burns's three-bedroom design; it is clear enough to reveal a human figure, clad in red, standing in front of the house, a feature barely discernible inside the book, where the same picture is darker and less sharp.

The use of color inside also distinguishes it from similar house plan books, which were usually printed in economical black ink. Consumers could buy less expensive house catalogs: in 1946, APS Home Plans cost only fifty cents,[9] *Small Practical Homes* listed a price of $1.50 on its cover,[10] Group's *House-of-the-Month Book of Small Houses* and *Blueprint Plans* each sold for $2.50,[11] Dean and Brienes's *The Book of Houses* did come out in hardcover, with one color added to a book jacket, but still only cost $2.00,[12] and the Scale Model Home Planning Company sold a booklet of house designs in 1948 for only $1.00.[13] *Prize Homes* cost more. Brink's Book Store's advertisement in the *Holland Evening Sun* alerted Michigan readers that the *Prize Homes* book was in stock and available for purchase at $3.50, but book buyers at the Book Mart in Lincoln, Nebraska, would have to pay $4.00.[14]

As the book directed "[i]nquiries concerning working drawings and specifications should be addressed to the designers," *Prize Homes* put the onus on readers to secure working blueprints.[15] Rather than having the Tribune Company facilitate communication between designers and their potential customers, this practice may well have cost some of the designers some business. Group's *House-of-the-Month Book of Small Houses* and Robinson's *Book of Small Home Designs* steered readers to one address to which they could send inquiries.[16] Maintaining a single source for contacting architects permitted catalogs to update addresses and/or telephone numbers. *Prize Homes* contact information contained no telephone numbers, only addresses, and in many cases did not update them from the original, fall 1945 submissions. Students who had listed their dormitories would have moved out by then. Postwar mobility and housing disruptions could have left other addresses out of date. Service members who were just leaving wartime duty at the time of submission certainly would have relocated. Prizewinner W. R. Burns, for example, was in 1945 a decommissioned officer stationed in San Francisco, and his listed address was the San Francisco Ferry Building, which had been commandeered for the war effort. By 1948, that was an inappropriate place to reach him.[17] As the book continued to be for sale and available in libraries for many years, the *Tribune*'s lack of a single address through which to contact architects probably inconvenienced at least a few architects and buyers. On the other hand, including any such information was better than none at all. A 1946 booklet, *Small Practical Homes* (which included designs from Prize Homes submitters Walter Thies and Lawrence Schwall), admitted that one could not buy plans through them. Some of the designs are credited, but readers were encouraged to "[s]ee your builder, building material dealer, or architect and submit to him the ideas that you draw out of this book," confirming Reiff's point that "borrowing" was pervasive.[18]

Because the contest had concluded more than two years before the book's publication, the *Tribune* saw fit to publicize *Prize Homes* within its pages, reminding readers of its good work. Its announcement of the book's publication, in April 1948, proclaimed "we can at last answer that frequent phone call; 'When is The TRIBUNE [*sic*] going to have its prize winning homes published in book form?'" It reminded readers of the project's outcome: seventeen houses built.[19] Although *Prize Homes* appears to have been at least partially and perhaps fully ghostwritten by Edward Barry, Barry reviewed it for the *Tribune*, lauding the contest's high quality and the included designs' practicality, and, once again, reminding readers that "many" of the designs had been built.[20] The *Tribune* reported the following month that publisher Wilcox & Follet considered the book to be "enjoying a heavy sale."[21] Ads for the book appeared in the *Tribune* until December 1949.[22] The book was available in bookstores or directly through mail order from the *Tribune*, but whether the book exceeded the expected 100,000-copy first printing Boyd Hill indicated in correspondence to selected designers is unknown.[23]

With or without *Tribune* endorsement, one Prize Homes house appeared in a house plan book before the *Prize Homes* book was published. Sackville-West's two-bedroom house is Plan No. 917 in the APS Home Plans catalog published in 1946. The architect is not credited, nor is there any reference to the competition. The house is named "the Willis," and the copy calls attention to its suitability for a narrow lot. While the elevation sketch is neither the *Tribune*-commissioned watercolor by George Rudolph nor the architect's submission sketch, the house is unmistakably Sackville-West's. The APS sketch is very similar to the architect's sketch, with only minor alterations in the landscaping, and the floor plan is identical, with one difference: in the APS catalog, the house is two feet longer, which enlarges both the living room and the dining space. The "dinette" on Sackville-West's floor plan upgraded to a "dining room" once it became "the Willis." Copy accompanying the drawings indicates it is "available in three bedroom homes," though it is not clear where a third bedroom would go. The original floor plan also shows stairs to a basement, while the APS version omits the basement but has a thumbnail illustration with an "alternate plan with stair to cellar."[24]

Since the *Tribune* owned the licensing privileges of every Chicagoland Prize Homes competition winner, APS's inclusion of the Sackville-West house rests on questionable legal ground. The architect retained no legal right to license his own design. The *Tribune* could have granted permission,

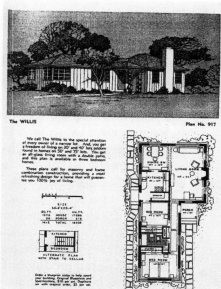

The American Plan Service produced a 1946 catalog containing a Prize Home winner. Sackville-West's house is unmistakable, but his name is removed and the house is merely plan 917, "the Willis." (American Plan Service, *APS Home Plans: 40 Plans for 1, 2 and 3 Bedroom Homes Suitable for Building Anywhere in U.S.A.*, 1946. Plan 917.)

or the APS could have just appropriated the design without attribution. Given the number of plan books in existence, other Prize Homes houses also may have been appropriated for catalogs, with or without permission.

Prize Homes received a good bit of publicity outside of *Tribune* coverage. At the time of the book's publication, public libraries used local newspapers to let community members know which books had been newly added to the libraries' collections. Newspaper archives give a little taste of where the book might have been available to local citizens. The highest exposure to library patrons was in Illinois and the Midwest, with libraries in Michigan, Wisconsin, Iowa, and Ohio adding the book to their collections.[25] But citizens of Waxahachie, Texas; Olean, New York; and Gustine, California, could also pick up the book in their local libraries.[26] The California library notice came late, over five years after the initial publication, indicating the book was still available for purchase at that time.

Significant publicity for the *Prize Homes* book came from a syndicated series of articles on small houses by Dean H. Robinson. A former ad and sales manager in Detroit, Robinson joined in the establishment of Home

Planners, Inc., which provided blueprints and specs to home buyers, in 1946. One unique product on offer was a scale model, giving "prospective home builders a three-dimensional view of their future house instead of a flat picture of only one side."[27] After 1946, Robinson was affiliated with the Scale Model Home Planning Co.; the company published his *Book of Small Home Designs* in 1948, and two more editions of that catalog.

Robinson's newspaper articles appeared around the country. Each article featured a single house, including an elevation sketch and a single floor plan (only a small fraction of the houses had two floors, but those that did omitted second-story plans, and no basements were shown). Robinson emphasized economy, and sometimes expandability for growing families. Houses never had more than three bedrooms, and they rarely had enough square footage for a separate dining room, instead opting for a dining area or alcove. Architects went uncredited. For each house featured, readers could buy full sets of building plans by writing to the newspaper or directly to Home Planners, Inc. Purchasing information could be found either in a clippable form adjacent to the article, or in the body of the article itself. Presumably, Home Planners, Inc., made Robinson's syndicated features available free of charge to newspapers; they appeared across the country in papers with wide and narrow circulations. Between the end of 1948 and early 1952, *The Salt Lake City Tribune*, for example, ran nearly ninety Robinson articles featuring small homes, always on Sundays, and the bulk of them in 1950 and 1951.

While other papers did not put Robinson's articles in the same heavy rotation as the *Salt Lake City Tribune* did, they occasionally printed his pieces. As in the *Salt Lake City Tribune*, the syndicated articles picked up by other papers appeared almost always on Sundays, usually in sections of the paper devoted to real estate news and listings. People who wanted to buy got a good deal: a picture, floor plan, and complete specifications cost $5.00 per set, with only $2.50 per each additional set.[28] Payment could be sent either directly to the newspaper or to Model Home Planning Co. For only $1.00, interested readers could also buy *The Book of Small Home Designs*; the 1948 edition featured twenty-six houses.

Three of Robinson's syndicated pieces featured Prize Homes winners. Winner number 10, designed by Eric Wenstrand (a house built at least five times) appeared as early as June 1949 and at least fourteen more times before September 1952. The elevation illustration is neither Wenstrand's original sketch published in the *Chicago Tribune* nor Yewell's watercolor painting included in *Prize Homes*. The floor plan shows a couple of minor modifications from Wenstrand's original: closets in two bedrooms have been slightly altered, and a utility room is eliminated in favor of stairs to a basement. Robert Gripp, who grew up in a Wenstrand house in Whiting,

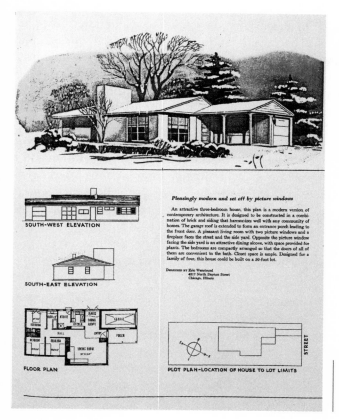

Pleasingly modern and set off by picture windows

An attractive three-bedroom house, this plan is a modern version of contemporary architecture. It is designed to be constructed in a combination of brick and siding that harmonizes well with any community of homes. The garage roof is extended to form an entrance porch leading to the front door. A pleasant living room with two picture windows and a fireplace faces the street and the side yard. Opposite the picture window facing the side yard is an attractive dining alcove, with space provided for plants. The bedrooms are compactly arranged so that the doors of all of them are convenient to the bath. Closet space is ample. Designed for a family of four, this house could be built on a 50-foot lot.

DESIGNED BY Eric Wenstrand
4517 North Dayton Street
Chicago, Illinois

SOUTH-WEST ELEVATION

SOUTH-EAST ELEVATION

FLOOR PLAN

PLOT PLAN-LOCATION OF HOUSE TO LOT LIMITS

Eric Wenstrand's house for problem two was winner #10. (*Prize Homes*, 43.)

Indiana, confirms that his house had a full basement and that the kitchen expanded into the utility room.[29] Despite the lack of credit to his design, it is Wenstrand's house. Robinson colorfully described "finding" the house.

> Have you ever been out driving on Sunday afternoon and passed a little house that made everyone in the car say, "Oh, isn't that lovely, or cute or precious," or some other superlative? That is what happened to us when we drove by the home we are showing today. It was so attractive from the road we drove around the block and back again—and finally got up nerve enough to walk up to the door and ask if we might be shown through. . . . A brand new bride greeted us and was proud to show us her home.[30]

Robinson further describes the house's interior. Did Robinson really happen upon the house accidentally? Most certainly not. The clippable coupon adjacent to the copy or the copy itself, in addition to offering the opportunity to buy house plans for this particular design, offered readers the option to buy "a 'Prize Homes' planbook, containing 92 prizewinning home designs, many in full color," for $3.50, clearly a reference to the *Prize Homes* book.[31]

Since the newspaper stipulated in its competition regulations that "all prize-winning solutions shall become the exclusive property of the sponsor upon payment of the awards" and "any non-prize-winning solution submitted in this competition shall become the exclusive property of the sponsor upon payment to the entrant of the sum of $250.00," the newspaper clearly licensed or sold the designs.[32] None of Robinson's articles on Wenstrand's house mentioned the competition.

Robinson's feature on Sackville-West's two-bedroom house received even more attention. Each article showed Raftery's watercolor elevation and a floor plan. The floor plan shows slight variation from Sackville-West's original, with one bedroom's closet repositioned; perhaps the floor plan reflects the house as actually built in Palatine or Chicago. "A very practical, one story, five room home," Robinson wrote, "which would be easy and inexpensive to construct and which looks much more pretentious than it really is."[33]

His feature on this particular house was reprinted more than thirty times between April 1948 and August 1953. Headlines, presumably written by the

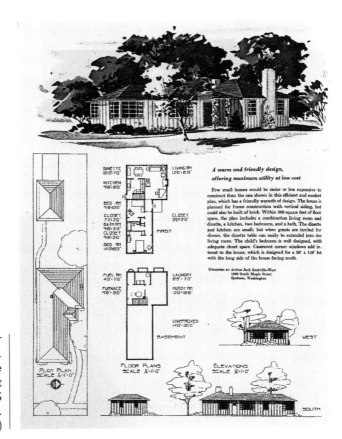

Winner #2, by Arthur "Jack" Sackville-West. Compare the house to the one that appeared in the APS catalog on page 55. (*Prize Homes*, 14.)

local papers, varied, and the articles may or may not have included Robinson's byline. Articles informing readers how they could get the house plans followed the same formula: write to the newspaper or to Scale Model Home Planning Co. The latest newspaper found to have offered up this house was the *Altoona Mirror* of Pennsylvania, which in August 1953 still indicated that plans could be purchased from Scale Model Home Planning.[34] Robinson's copy indicated the house was one of the prizewinners of the "1947" Chicagoland Prize Homes competition.[35] But other articles did not mention the competition. The *Waxahachie Daily Light* was the last newspaper to include the house, in January 1950; beginning with the version in the *San Pedro News-Pilot* in March 1950 and including the fifteen other reprints until August 1953, the syndication omitted any mention of the competition.[36]

Between August 1948 and August 1954, a Dean Robinson–syndicated piece on Coder Taylor's two-bedroom winner appeared at least nineteen times, in newspapers from Maine to California. The article reproduced the Kautzky watercolor elevation, keeping his signature on the painting.

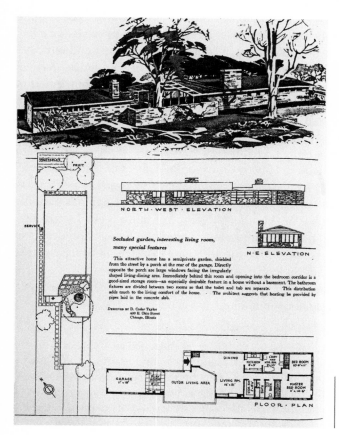

D. Coder Taylor designed winner #1, for problem one. (*Prize Homes*, 16.)

As in the articles featuring the Wenstrand and Sackville-West houses, Taylor was not credited as the architect. But Robinson did indicate, in the first sentence, that this "unusual and distinctive small home was one of the prize winners in the Chicago Tribune's Chicagoland Prize Home Competition in 1945."[37] Because the article added that information, headlines often picked up that detail: "Today's House Plan Is Winner in Contest," "Unusual, Distinctive Home Was Prize Winner at Chicago Home Competition," and "Small Prize-Winning Home Designed for Narrow Lot; Boasts New Features."[38] Unlike the piece on the Sackville-West house, Robinson's article on the Taylor house always included the competition information. In the former article, the information came late in the article and in a discrete paragraph, making it easy to eliminate, but in the latter, the placement of that detail in the first paragraph would have required a rewrite, rather than a mere deletion.

Under Robinson's authorship, the Scale Model Home Planning Co. published three editions of *Book of Small Home Designs*. In the 1948 first edition, each page contained one design, including elevation, floor plan, and descriptive copy. Sackville-West's and Taylor's two-bedroom houses, and Wenstrand's three-bedroom design, were among the twenty-six included. The foreword gives brief bios of each contributing architect and indicates that the architects "submitted" designs, and a board of eight judges deemed these the best. The *Tribune* received acknowledgement, both in the bios of each Prize Homes design winner and on each page devoted to the design, with the notation that "[T]his home was one of the prize winners in the Chicago Tribune Chicagoland Prize Homes competition in 1945."[39] Also, *Book of Small Home Designs* credits the *Prize Homes* book, as each design is "Courtesy of Wilcox & Follett, Chicago, Publishers of 'Prize Homes.'" The elevations are the watercolors commissioned by the *Tribune*; Yewell's name is easily seen on the Wenstrand house; Rudolph's name is partially obscured on Sackville-West's house; but Kautzky's name is eliminated. Taylor indicated he did not come into possession of the Kautzky rendering of his design until years later; Scale Model Home Planning must have gotten access to the paintings directly from the *Tribune* itself.

Robinson's introduction promotes the role of an architect in not only house design but also house building.

> The average American, and by average I mean those of us who don't have $15,000.00 cash to pay for a home, has never consulted an architect to any degree when he decided to build. There is no good reason for this as a good architect can usually save his client his fee, which is from five to ten per cent [sic] of the total cost of the home, by the proper supervision of the construction and the inspection of the materials that go into a home. The layman doesn't know the difference between B and Better Finish and

#1 Common, but there is a difference in the price, and if B and Better is specified, the architect will see to it that that is what goes into the building. . . . But until the real value of an architect's services is implanted in the layman's mind, stock plans by leading architects and designers are the answer to the average man's dream of a home.[40]

A second edition is unavailable, but by the third edition of *Book of Small Home Designs*, in 1951, with two designs per page, the company offered 154 houses. Architects' names, references to the *Chicago Tribune*, the Chicagoland Prize Homes competition, and the *Prize Homes* book vanished. Wenstrand's house is referred to as a "Prize Winning Home" but with no indication of what prize. Original renderings for the Sackville-West and Wenstrand houses were replaced, although, inexplicably, the Kautzky rendering of the Taylor house was not merely preserved but now made Kautzky's signature visible. The *Tribune*-winning house plans had become just three among many house plans for purchase. Readers could buy a full set of building specifications for those three houses, or any of the additional 151 houses, for $7.00 plus $3.50 for each additional set. Robinson's introduction explained how it worked:

> Our aim has been to find good honest small home designs that have proven their worth and that are economical and practical to build. Thousands of plans go through our office each year and we try to choose those we think are the best and will have the most universal appeal. The plans we select are either purchased from the architect or designer for anywhere from $300.00 to $1,000.00, or we enter into a Royalty agreement with the architect. The only way we can sell our plans for only $7.00 a set is because we sell many sets from the original drawings. We have to select good sound plans of popular appeal or we could not stay in business.

Robinson's description of paying for the design comports with Coder Taylor's memory of earning between $600 and $1,200 for the working plans for his design, although Taylor was paid by the *Tribune*, and not Scale Model Homes. Although Robinson was the author of record, the short paragraphs accompanying each design-for-purchase lack the flair of Robinson's multiparagraph series for syndicated publication.[41]

Robinson's business model affirmed that the goal of the house plan books and catalogs was to sell. To make money from a $7.00 set of plans, the company had to sell many of them. With the rise of the housing development and the real estate agent, Americans would rely on catalogs less and less and more on real estate agents to help them buy houses, but Robinson's company still exists as Homeplanners, LLC. Via its website, one can still peruse and buy complete sets of house plans, including vintage ones, although not the Wenstrand, Taylor, or Sackville-West designs.[42]

5

House Design and Domestic Life

Analyzing the Houses

What happens in a residential building—a house? At a minimum, a house functions to provide the cyclical care human bodies require. People sleep every day, and in Western culture, heavy, immovable beds need dedicated space, and it must be determined where those spaces will be and who will occupy and/or share (or not share) them. Humans excrete waste every day; a housing norm since the turn of the twentieth century has been to accommodate that inside the building, with a fixed, flush toilet in its own room. We must eat daily to live, so food must be stored, prepared, and served; under contemporary conditions, these actions require cabinetry for dishes and non-perishable foods, refrigerators and freezers for perishable foods, a water supply for cooking and cleaning, tools and small appliances for preparation, oven and stove for cooking, and surfaces for preparation and eating. Protecting the body means mitigating nature's harsher elements; residents must be kept warm when it is cold and cool when it is hot, but they also need fresh, clean air inside, historically provided through windows. Twentieth-century hygiene standards require regular and frequent cleaning, both of bodies and the clothing and bedding that clad them, and for convenience, that cleaning takes place in the home, through baths and showers and laundry machines.[1] Through most of history, the dwelling has also been a commercial workplace, a location for agriculture, woodworking, metallurgy, and spinning and weaving. Twentieth-century industrial and postindustrial wage work, however, is located apart from the home—sometimes quite far—so there must be some means of transport to that workplace; an automobile must be stored. (In the last decade, however, people have returned to the practice of income-producing work partially or exclusively taking place within the home, not by farmers or manual laborers but those in the clean and indoor service economy, necessitating yet another change in home design: the addition of the home office. Unusual for the time, Charles Hendricks in the 1960s used a spare bedroom to run his construction business in the Wenstrand house in Blue Island.[2])

In the twentieth century, we no longer expect a home to care only for the body. The assumption that the best life includes personal development and fulfillment has meant we use our homes for that, too. Children's intellectual and psychological development necessitates play, reading, development of social skills by interacting with other children, and the extension of school activities through homework and science and art projects, for example. A child's habitat should have room both for those activities and the material objects—toys, books, and games—used during them. Even adults will seek enrichment and satisfaction through recreation, hobbies, and media consumption. Increased leisure time for children and adults across the twentieth century has created opportunities for new, non-income-producing activities, many of which occur at home.

But humans are social animals, and the house is also a place for community. First, the residents are in relationships with each other. Adults in a romantic and sexual relationship seek privacy to affirm that bond, in a dedicated room that we usually designate as the home's primary bedroom. Residents want to spend time with each other in conversation, perhaps along with making and consuming food, perhaps without the distractions of cooking and eating. Shared leisure activities need dedicated space. But social and familial relationships go beyond the dwelling; residents want to maintain ties to family who do not share the residence and to create and maintain bonds with non-kin. Living rooms, dining rooms, rec rooms, backyard decks: these provide spaces where nonresidents can temporarily join the residents' activities. Cultural and religious rituals and rites of passage occur in community: a baby's first birthday party in the living room, Thanksgiving dinner in the dining room, Independence Day barbecue in the backyard. Sociologists, psychologists, and historians have devoted attention to space usage, but it does not take deep investigation to understand the basic ways people use their homes. Samuel Glaser's 1946 plan book, *Designs for 60 Small Homes*, broke down six categories for its readers: general living activities, dining activities, culinary activities, relaxation activities (which meant sleep), storage, and recreational activities.[3] He omitted only cleaning and waste.

"Domestic architecture," Gwendolyn Wright insisted, "illuminates norms concerning family life, sex roles, community life . . . associations a culture establishes at any particular time between a 'model' or typical house and a notion of the model family to encourage certain roles and assumptions."[4] Kenneth Jackson proffered a similar sentiment: our homes set up "living patterns that condition our behavior."[5] How we live determines what we want in a dwelling, but that dwelling also informs how we live. The study of vernacular architecture focuses on the common dwellings lived in by most people—the ordinary, everyday folks who make up the bulk of the world. Certainly few people have ever actually lived in a Prize Homes house, but the ninety-two houses collected in the *Prize Homes* book offer an opportunity to view how Americans in the midcentury might have wanted to live or were expected to live. It is a snapshot of midcentury aspiration.

Thus, through the parameters of the contest's rules and the three "problems," the *Chicago Tribune* both reflected and confirmed a set of social norms for the proper American family constellation. Designers' choices about which rooms to put where, and how big or small to make those rooms, or even to suggest outdoor usage on the plot plan, reflect assumptions and create, if not mandate, cultural expectations about how middle-class Americans ought to live. As discussed earlier, Edward Barry wrote the short copy that accompanied the winning designs when first publicized in the *Tribune*. Those house descriptions, and one for each of the non-winning houses in *Prize Homes*, whether written by Barry or someone else, highlighted house features. And in promoting specific advantages, they signaled what home buyers did or ought to want.

Architectural historians have demonstrated the challenges of classifying houses by type, based on either their interior layouts or exterior elements. Labels have changed over time, architects and builders mix elements from different styles, and homeowners adding to and removing from their houses over the years have edited their homes' styles and room arrangements. As this review of house plans focuses more on family constellation and house usage, it does not rely on any particular classification system. Whether the kitchen is in the back or the side, or where the chimney and stairs are placed, or whether there is a side hall is less important.[6] This analysis will also bypass the technical aspects of house building and the materials used in construction, instead focusing on interior arrangement of rooms and dedication of spaces for specific activities, privacy, and efficiency. When possible, analysis will be coupled with the experiences of people who did or do live in the houses, illustrating how they used their homes.

Most essentially, the competition's call for a single-family house indicated that is where American families should reside: in a house detached from other buildings and on a separate lot, and this should be a home that they (and, only for a while, their lending institution) own. This housing standard emphasized private ownership, autonomy, and privacy. Jackson documents the American pull of home and land ownership as beginning in the early nineteenth century.[7] Owning a single-family home had been the aspiration for Americans for quite some time but particularly in the early twentieth century; the Own Your Own Home movement of the 1920s stressed the moral, political, and economic benefits of building equity in ownership over renting, and that meant a separate house rather than a unit in a multi-family building.[8] A single-family home had long been viewed as a well-earned retreat for hardworking families, so for Depression-era and post-WWII households with too many people in them, subjected to the sounds, smells, and strife of shared walls and common hallways, the separation from neighbors would have been welcome relief. A kitchen to call your own, unshared space for outdoor recreation, plenty of room for kids to play: these amenities appealed to families, especially those who had or expected children. Builders make more money, too, in putting up single-family houses over multi-family dwellings, and when people spread out rather than cluster, manufacturers sell more goods, such as household appliances, cars, and lawn mowers.

For an area as densely populated as Chicago, home to iconic two- and three-flats, perhaps duplexes and smaller multi-family units might have made more sense as a solution to the housing shortage. Architects Smith and Mielke submitted a design for an affordable, detached row house; it was not included in *Prize Homes*, but Edward Barry featured the plan in a *Tribune* article. Barry noted that the usual problems with such row houses are the monotony of design (the *Tribune* article included a street-view photo of a row of identical bungalows) and the lack of privacy, as the buildings' closeness leads residents to look directly onto neighbors. Smith and Mielke staggered two designs so that the second-floor bedrooms and bath are alternately placed in the front or back of the house, keeping the private rooms away from peeping neighbors. The houses are modest, affordable, and attractive solutions to an urban/suburban housing crisis, but not at all what the competition planners had in mind.[9]

Vernacular house competitions usually specified the size of the house in either overall square footage or the number of bedrooms, or both. The *Tribune*'s small house competition in 1926 named two categories of judging criteria: two-bedroom houses and three-bedroom houses. Nineteen years later, the newspaper did not specify the number of bedrooms but made the needs of the occupying families clear: each of the three problems specified a heterosexual, married couple with, respectively, one, two, or three school-aged children living at home. Instructions defined child residents by sex and age. The *Tribune*'s choice of problems, the description of the *hypothetical* occupants of the house designs, reflected the familial norms and aspirations of the time, and these assumptions guided the designs. The houses were to be for families, not boarders, cohabiting couples, paying guests, unrelated housemates, nor any non-familial residents at all. Beyond that, the competition constrained even which family members would reside there. Grandparents, aunts or uncles, nieces or nephews or cousins, or grandchildren went unmentioned, as did parents without children. Architects designed houses for exactly two specific generations, not one or three generations, and certainly not four. The married couple at the center of the family would not be newlyweds, either, with an infant or a baby on the way; the youngest age specified was six, though copy accompanying Baker and Miles's problem one house notes: "One side of the owners' bedroom can be shut off with a folding partition. This portion may be used for a baby's bedroom and later converted into a study."[10] In 1945, six-year-olds would have been conceived before the war, not during; perhaps this problem concedes that the youngest couples, newlyweds with the wage-earning husband just beginning a career, lacked the income to purchase a house. Nor was the resident family an older couple, with children grown and out of the house, although Esther and Charles Hendricks bought their three-bedroom house in Blue Island when they were already grandparents, with no adult children living at home.[11] These houses were not, at least nominally, for aging parents to move into, nor for adult children to come back to. The single exception is Merwin Freeman's four-bedroom house for problem three. Copy on the page points out that by placing two bedrooms and one bath on the second floor, and two bedrooms and a bath on the first floor, the "plan will appeal to the family with a married son or daughter living at home or for the owner whose parents live with him. When the family grows smaller, the second floor can be shut off, leaving a complete five-room house on the first floor."[12] It is the only admission that families might not be merely parents and minor children.[13]

Yet Freeman's design acknowledges housing practices quite common for the time. First, adult children do not always permanently "age out" of the family home. Friedman and Krawitz report that even during World War II, when servicemen and -women were sent to training camps and deployed for long stretches of time, a third of adult children who had left their parents' home returned to it to live for several months.[14] Second, and more significant, many people residing in the United States, particularly but not exclusively recent immigrants and their children, assumed and even desired multiple-generation residency. A couple moving into a house with their one or two children, as the Prize Homes competition mandated, meant that each set of that couple's parents would have to have housing of their own, paid for by their own resources. Those elders would have to navigate the world without their children, an extra burden if their language and customs were far outside standard American practices. Grandparents and grandchildren living together, for mutual care and transmission of language and culture, was a lower priority than nuclear family residence. An adult child's obligation to care for parents would not include making room in the family home for them. Ironically, multiple incomes from a multigenerational and/or extended family makes home ownership more viable for more American

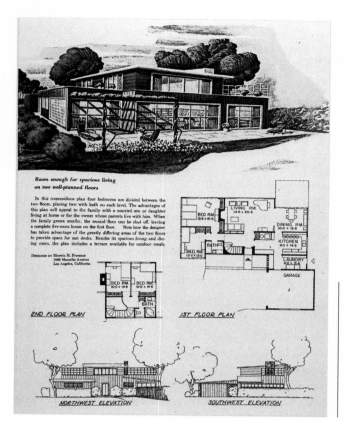

Room enough for spacious living
on two well-planned floors

In this commodious plan four bedrooms are divided between the two floors, placing two with bath on each level. The advantages of this plan will appeal to the family with a married son or daughter living at home or for the owner whose parents live with him. When the family grows smaller, the second floor can be shut off, leaving a complete five-room house on the first floor. Note how the designer has taken advantage of the greatly differing areas of the two floors to provide space for sun decks. Besides its spacious living and dining room, the plan includes a terrace available for outdoor meals.

Designed by Merwin H. Freeman
1066 Manella Avenue
Los Angeles, California

BED RM 12·6 × 13·6
LIVING RM. 14·0 × 20·6
BATH
DINING RM. 10·0 × 13·6
KITCHEN 9·0 × 14·6
BED RM 10·0 × 13·0
LAUNDRY 6·0 × 15·6
GARAGE

BED RM 10·0 × 14·6   BED RM 10·0 × 14·6
BATH

2ND FLOOR PLAN   1ST FLOOR PLAN

NORTHWEST ELEVATION   SOUTHWEST ELEVATION

Merwin Freeman's house was highlighted for its possibilities for intergenerational living, the only house among ninety-two to mention that familial arrangement. (*Prize Homes*, 79.)

households. Freeman's two-story arrangement, separating two generations of adults, would have suited thousands of Chicago-area families. Many Prize Homes families had multigenerational living arrangements: before moving into a Prize Home, the three-generation Gripp family lived in a two-bedroom flat, with the young son sharing a bedroom with his grandmother while his parents occupied the other. Moving to a three-bedroom Wenstrand house in Indiana gave each generation its own bedroom, and the grandmother lived with the family until she passed away.[15] Multigenerational living, while rarer in the twenty-first century, is not unheard of. Dan Creinin reports that when he and his wife bought a Wenstrand house in 2008, having had one child and another on the way, they specifically chose a single-story house anticipating that his wife's grandfather would eventually share their home.[16] A third Wenstrand house, in Blue Island, has housed three generations of the Black family, with Jo-Ellen Black living there in 2022 with her grandson.[17] Generational changes also occur over a family's tenure in a house. 1950 census data indicates Benjamin and Bernice Kramer resided in a four-bedroom Prize Homes house with their three children; the two older children were sixteen and twelve. But at the end of the decade, a 1959 obituary of Henry Gimpel, Bernice's father, gave the address as his home.[18] One can surmise that the older kids had left home by then but the elder parent had moved in. The Finks' grandfather lived with them in summers.[19] Marilyn Domsky, widowed, lives alone in her four-bedroom, two-and-a-half-bathroom house; even so, extra beds in the basement accommodate children, grandchildren, and great-grandchildren when needed. Next door, the Kanters, on the cusp of becoming empty nesters, view their five-bedroom, three-and-a-half-bathroom house as essential for accommodating visits from their married children, their children's in-laws, and their grandchildren.[20] Avrum Weinfeld reports that since his grown children, with children of their own, live nearby, their Burch-designed house is visited "literally every day" by family.[21]

Without specifying the exact number of bedrooms, mandating the age and sex of the children in each of the three problems guided designers. Houses for the smallest families—to be occupied by two parents and their six-year-old son—garnered the most attention; the *Tribune* reported that at least half of all submissions were for problem one. A minimum requirement for those families would be two bedrooms. It had been a long time since it was acceptable for children to share bedrooms with adults. In these households, the young boy would not sleep in a Murphy bed, a pullout couch, or a cot in a dining room; such an arrangement was what the new house was supposed to eliminate. A separate bedroom, with a door, was not an aspiration but a requirement. But several entries for problem one went beyond the two-bedroom minimum. Eight of the thirty-one added an additional room that, while labeled for guests, a study, or a playroom, could clearly be used as an additional bedroom for a second child.[22]

Families the next size up, with a twelve-year-old son and an eight-year-old daughter, needed even more space. By 1945, it was also no longer acceptable for opposite-sex children to share a bedroom; a contemporary circular distributed by the newly constituted University of Illinois Small Homes Council affirmed this, warning prospective home buyers that "[s]mall children of opposite sex will need *two bedrooms* when they grow older" (emphasis in original).[23] A two-bedroom house would not suffice. All the proposals for problem two accommodated that norm, giving each child a separate bedroom, with five designs going beyond the minimal three bedrooms to add a den, study, or guest room.[24] Especially interesting is the response to problem three, which would be for a family of five, who would have a twelve-year-old son and two daughters, one six and one sixteen. Sisters *could* share a room without violating social norms. But of those thirty houses, only six contain only three bedrooms. Twenty-two of them show

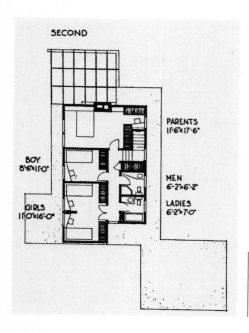

SECOND

PARENTS
11'-6"x17'-6"

BOY
8'-6"x11'-0"

MEN
6'-2"x6'-2"

GIRLS
11'-0"x16'-0"

LADIES
6'-2"x7'-0"

Robert Pierce's design shows the sisters sharing a room, but it uses a partial wall or divider to give each child some privacy. (*Prize Homes*, 95.)

four bedrooms, and one more floor plan contains three bedrooms but includes a study that could be used as a fourth bedroom.

One of the four-bedroom houses even adds a study, and another notes that attic space over the garage could be converted to an additional bedroom.[25] Only seven of the thirty houses indicate the daughters would share a room. Although more than half the competition submissions were for problem one, a family of parents and one child, *Prize Homes* reflects a disinterest in two-bedroom houses, making the three- or four-bedroom house the norm. Seventy-eight of the ninety-two houses have three or more bedrooms.

While the owners' suite—bedroom with attached bathroom for the married couple—as a housing norm was in its early days, mostly available in bigger, more expensive houses, even the small houses managed to convey the special quality of the parents' exclusive space. In *Prize Homes*, designers usually clarified which bedroom belonged to whom, with labels for "masters," "parents," or light-hearted designations: "Mr. & Mrs.," "Mom & Dad," and "Pa & Ma."[26] Floor plans without specific delineations nevertheless cued the viewer: the putative owners' room is bigger than the others, might have more closets, or show twin beds or a larger bed. In case of confusion, accompanying copy might signal which is the owners' bedroom.

If the owners' suite was not yet standard, many problem three houses nevertheless offered that amenity to buyers who could afford a larger, more

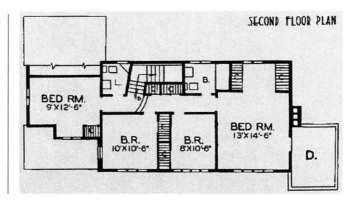

Though bedrooms are undesignated, and even lack furniture cues, Edward Hanson's design signals which is the owner's bedroom, the one much larger than the other three bedrooms and with two closets. (*Prize Homes*, 78.)

expensive house. William Pfeufer's design uniquely shows four bedrooms of equal size, a feature not only clearly visible on the floor plan but also noted in the text.[27] Equality in bedroom size was otherwise nonexistent; marital couples always got the bigger room, even when the two daughters of problem three were going to share a room.

Dedicating a specific room for the parents had been an established practice, but the importance and meaning of that room has changed over time. Victorian-era designs placed the room at the front of the house on the second floor, above the parlor, as parents could be counted on to preserve quiet, while children's rooms, and their accompanying noises, would be at the back of the house, above the smelly and hot kitchen and where guests (and even some family members) would never go. With the death of the parlor, and the rise of the kitchen as a cleaner, more hospitable space, the couple's space moved to the back of the house, the most private spot. This privacy cements the centrality of marital intimacy—including but not limited to sexual intimacy—as a goal of marriage and ongoing element of family life. The most privacy-enhancing designs separated parents from children altogether, using corridors or bathrooms to prevent shared walls, or at least placing closets along shared walls. *Prize Homes* houses follow the practice of making parents' rooms as separate from the rest of the house as they can: they are usually in the back, in a house corner, and they share as few walls with other rooms as possible.

After designating which room belonged to parents, designers could have left the remaining bedrooms unassigned; readers would know they were for the children. Plans for problem one were the least likely to indicate the child's room, since it would be obvious for whom the second bedroom was intended in a two-bedroom house for a one-child family. But many in that category did provide room assignments, through labeling a bedroom for child, son, or boy. Olen Puckett shows where "Junior" would sleep, while

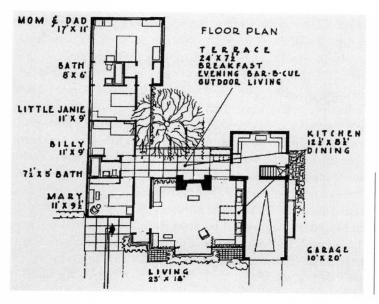

FLOOR PLAN

MOM & DAD 17' X 11'

BATH 8 X 6'

LITTLE JANIE 11' X 9'

BILLY 11' X 9'

7½' X 5' BATH

MARY 11' X 9½'

TERRACE 24' X 7½'
BREAKFAST
EVENING BAR-B-CUE
OUTDOOR LIVING

KITCHEN 12½' X 8½'
DINING

LIVING 23' X 18'

GARAGE 10' X 20'

"Mom & Dad" share a Jack-and-Jill bathroom with "Little Janie" in Edward Burch's floor plan. (*Prize Homes*, 73.)

John Davis's two-bedroom shows "Sonny's Bed-Rm."[28] Houses for problems two and three, which had to accommodate more than one child, often designated which child would go in which room, and those room assignments reveal a significant pattern. In the problem two category, when designers indicated which rooms were for whom, in those thirteen houses where one bedroom was closer to the parents' room than another, girls were assigned that room ten times; only three times did the boy get the bedroom closer to his parents.

Problem three house designs reflected a less stark, though similar pattern: the six-year-old girl or the girls together were placed closer to parents than the boy, eight to three. Two two-story designs indicate sharp contrast: one puts the sixteen-year-old girl on the first floor, while parents and her two younger siblings occupy second-floor bedrooms.[29] But another plan with the same bedroom arrangement clusters daughters and parents, leaving the twelve-year-old boy on his own downstairs. A few houses anticipate the late-twentieth-century trend of separating adults and children altogether, placing the parents' bedroom at one end of a one-story house or on the first floor while all children occupy the upstairs bedrooms.[30] Overall, the younger and female children were positioned closer to their parents, while the older and male children were farther away.

Despite differing room assignments for daughters and sons, *Prize Homes* designs rarely delineate other gender expectations. Darkrooms and workspaces are not labeled for dads; sewing rooms are not specifically assigned to moms. Pierce's problem three house provides two full bathrooms on the second floor, site of all the bedrooms; the bathrooms are labeled for "men" and "ladies."[31] While many catalogs used copy to explicitly place women as main users of kitchens, laundry rooms, closets, and storage spaces, and men as main users of hobby rooms and work spaces, *Prize Homes* does so only twice: when promoting a partition between kitchen and dining room as "a desirable feature to any housewife serving meals from the kitchen." A headline for a four-bedroom house with area for "quiet living" promotes the house as "[f]or the man who wants a den of his own."[32] Gender norms for particular house spaces were so standard in 1945 that perhaps no explanation would be necessary, but overall, *Prize Homes* does not explicitly suggest that only women cooked and only men pursued a photography hobby.

Designers placed bedrooms and bathrooms mostly within a separate zone in the house, and clustered together. Two-story houses contained bedrooms upstairs, although the larger houses might have a bedroom on the first floor (or a den or study that could be used as a bedroom). Richard Y. Mine's submission for problem one uniquely separates the bedrooms, with parents at one end of the long one-story building and the son at the other end, but the accompanying copy notes that oddity: "Numerous features not often found in the average five-room house give this plan special distinction. Its bedrooms are at opposite ends of the house, with living, dining, and kitchen areas between."[33] It is markedly unusual; the door to the boy's bedroom is right off the living room. Americans had become accustomed to the buffering hallway in a single-story dwelling, and Mine's design is an exception that highlights the norm.

FLOOR PLAN

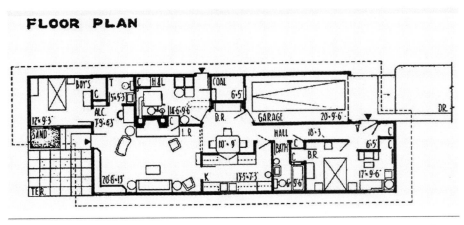

The child's bedroom is accessible only through the living room in Richard Mine's plan. (*Prize Homes*, 25.)

When bedrooms were placed along a corridor, owners' bedrooms tended to be at the end of that hallway, not in the middle or at the start. Parents' rooms were destinations, not meant to be passed along the way to another place; such placement preserved the marital room as the most private space in the house.[34]

In addition to attending to children's sleeping arrangements, *Prize Homes* designers made room for children in other ways. Resident children would need space to play, and the house plans accommodated that requirement. Designers included various ways to describe and specify outdoor space, giving homeowners terraces, porches, decks, and barbecues. Every house had a garden, yard, or lawn, usually explicitly labeled on the plot plan. Designers frequently specified the yard as a place for children; twenty-seven designs indicate sections of the yard for play or games. Erling Bugge's design indicated a paved play area would be for, specifically, basketball, handball, skating, and badminton; Mel Ensign's design showed where families would play croquet, tennis, and volleyball; and Charles Koch added a badminton court.[35]

Three houses give special attention to adult supervision of children's play; Ray Stuermer's problem one house included a court, where "a child playing there can be constantly under the parental eye"; Harold Zook's problem three house also includes "a large enclosed outside play area, which can

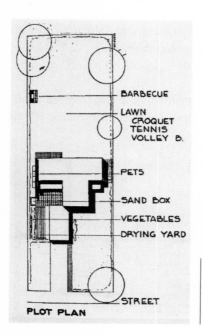

Mel Ensign's plot plan indicated all the activities to take place in the yard: barbecuing, croquet, tennis, volleyball, sandbox play, a vegetable garden, and a drying yard. (*Prize Homes*, 65.)

easily be supervised from the kitchen."[36] Woolford and Peterson did not need a copywriter to state it; their floor plan included an outdoor "supervised play" area.[37]

Space for play is also accommodated within the houses. Nine houses indicated play or game space inside the house, either through a designated play area or a playroom, while another fourteen marked a part of the basement for rumpus, play, or recreation. Jonathan Taylor's house designated a basement area for play, and his arrangement makes the space more inviting. One staircase in the main part of the house, connecting the first and second floors, leads directly to the basement play area. A second stairway, located outside next to the side door and garage, heads down to the laundry room; a doorway separates the laundry from play area.[38]

Americans had begun to learn the importance of play to children's intellectual and emotional development. Not only the materials they played with—toys and books should be educational as well as fun—but the space they played in also drew attention. Ogata shows how play space in postwar homes captured the attention of designers and women's magazines.[39] Bright and airy rooms invited creativity more than dark ones, and rooms big enough to accommodate doll houses, toy trains, and cities built of construction blocks let imagination run free. Not all houses could include a dedicated playroom, however, nor could it always be above ground with constant sunshine. But even a corner of the kitchen or a play area in the utility or laundry room just outside the kitchen could keep the creative child under surveillance. With a dedicated play space came the ability to contain not just the creative and developing children but their things: dolls, blocks, games, and paints. This kept clutter out of sight, a positive reflection on the housekeeper's ability to keep a tidy home.

Less often but still noticeable, adult recreational time also received attention. Space for a workshop or a hobby appears a dozen times, usually in

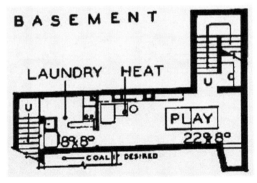

Two interior stairways lead to the basement, one to the play area and the other to the laundry, in Jonathan Taylor's design. (*Prize Homes*, 63.)

Considering that *Prize Homes* designs were meant to be affordable, the designs are generous with bathrooms. Throughout the twentieth century, Americans expanded the activities taking place in bathrooms, going beyond basic bodily functions to skin and nail care; applying and removing makeup; washing, drying, and styling hair; and daily shaving, showering, and bathing. The increase in time spent in that spot created competition for the room that could be alleviated only through proliferation. Nineteen of the thirty-one problem one houses have a single, shared bath, but twelve have an additional lavatory. Only ten of the problem two houses have a single, shared bath, and among the problem three houses, only one design has a single, shared bathroom.[52] Problem one houses did not include owners' bathrooms, but eight of the thirty-one problem two houses did, and twelve of the thirty problem three houses did. Jack-and-Jill bathrooms—bathrooms with two doors, usually accessible through bedrooms—were popular. They occasionally linked an owners' bedroom to a child's room, more often connecting two children's bedrooms. Some owners' bedrooms had half-baths attached, too, missing a bath or shower. Two-story houses without first-floor bedrooms included lavatories on the first floor, in a two-to-one ratio, as providing a bathroom for guests there meant they did not need to breach the privacy of the second floor.

Suburban life required automobile ownership, and *Prize Homes* delivered on the garages needed to house those cars. Ninety houses had garages, most of the time attached to the house, although not always with a connecting door. Occasionally the garage is a separate building, indicated on the plot plan. Some garages were accessed from the back, perhaps a nod to Chicago's alleys, but most garages were visible from the street and accessed through driveways up to the front of the house. Ten houses sported garages accommodating two cars, one each for problems one and two, and eight in the larger problem three houses. Cars were mandatory in 1945 suburban life, but American middle-class families were still a few years away from being the two-car households they would become; designers making room for two were prescient.[53] Robert Shields's plan had a car shelter, rather than a full garage. His address was Seattle, where perhaps an enclosed garage could be discretionary, unlike in the snowy Midwest.[54] Only Hugh Garden's small two-bedroom house had no indication of a garage, although the lot certainly could accommodate one if accessed through a back alley.[55]

House designers used the same small house design techniques that had come into play even at the end of the nineteenth century, when bay or large windows and widened interior doorways expanded domestic space.[56] To expand the market for house purchases, to make a house affordable for working and lower-middle-class households, it needed to be smaller and thus considerably less expensive than the Victorian styles of the nineteenth century.[57] At the same time, houses required some space-hogging things earlier vernacular architecture lacked: fixed bathrooms, water and toilet pipes, hot water heaters, heating units, and duct work. To keep the house small in spite of these new requirements, architects eliminated anything nonessential. Rooms and staircases for servants could go; small house purchasers did their own cooking and housework. Sewing rooms and dens largely disappeared. While nineteenth-century dining and living rooms may or may not have been adjacent rooms, in twentieth-century small houses, they nearly always were, with the barriers between them diminished: doors became double doorways, often without doors at all, and many walls became half walls.[58] Dining rooms and living rooms flowed into each other, and some designs eliminated the dining "room" in favor of a dining alcove, dining ell, or just an "area" designated on the floor plan in an otherwise large living room. Eliminating walls—or shrinking them to demi-walls—allowed light to flow from room to room. A longer sightline made rooms feel larger. Entry halls and foyers can take up a lot of space; in small houses, front doors open into very small vestibules or, in the more space-saving design, directly into living rooms.

Prize Homes houses followed those patterns. A minority of plans reflected a front door opening directly into living space with no hallway at all. But entry halls tended to be quite small, a place to access a coat closet or a lavatory and not usually large enough for even a table or small chair. The Shiels, living in the popular Wenstrand house, removed the walls around the tiny entry to make their dining and living rooms larger and flow into each other, and they moved a doorway to the kitchen that is more visible from the living room; their added skylights brighten the space, too.[59] While not always clear on the floor plans, some entryways may have been separated by screen or divider rather than a solid wall, or half wall, visually opening the space to living areas. Burns's prizewinning house combined living and dining space in a 16-by-29-foot space. The Bryant daughters, whose family lived in the Lombard house for twenty-five years, found the large room a magnet for friends, as the huge room could accommodate a television, stereo, and a throng of teenagers. A design so friendly to visitors, however, was ill-adapted to the other family needs. When their mother returned to college, she needed a quiet place to study, and the girls, who once had separate rooms, began to share a room when the third bedroom was converted to a study.[60]

Perhaps the biggest twentieth-century alteration in vernacular architecture involves the dining room. Large houses for the wealthy had long devoted space just for eating; indeed, the larger the house, the more specific that eating could be, with rooms for breakfast, family dining, and guests.

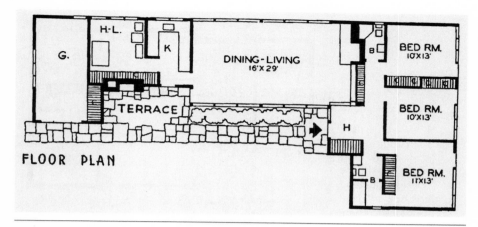

A winning design for problem two, W. R. Burns's plan combined living and dining into one large space. (*Prize Homes*, 41.)

In nineteenth-century vernacular houses, however, for all but the upper-middle and upper classes, as Thomas Hubka has pointed out, families ate where they cooked, in the kitchen. As kitchens are historically hot, greasy, and smelly, they have not been pleasant places to linger, so housing for the working classes improved when, among other developments, they were able to move dining from the kitchen to a different room.[61] *Prize Homes* largely keep families from having to eat exclusively in the kitchen. That does not necessarily mean that a dining room would be a separate room, though, because single-use rooms, separated by closed doors, are expensive real estate and indefensible in a modest house. Cromley argues that the move away from separate rooms also reflected the loss of servants; closed doors hid the maids and cooks, but the resident homemaker needed no isolation—indeed, she rejected it.[62] Small houses in the teens and twenties had designated a room for dining but without the exclusivity of a dining room in an upper-class Victorian home; perhaps it could be used for homework, sewing, reading, or family activities. *Prize Homes* houses continued that trend. Floor plans indicated, usually, where people would eat, with a label like "dinette" or various nouns to follow the modifier "dining": room, area, alcove, space, or gallery. Among ninety-two house plans, fewer than ten have a designated dining space that can really be called a separate room. A few designers eschewed it altogether in favor of eating in the kitchen, but that infrequency was commented upon: In Charles Clinton's house, the "kitchen is planned for family meals, and the dining room has been eliminated," and even a large, four-bedroom house by Charles Koch combines kitchen and dining (although it also has an outdoor dining porch).[63]

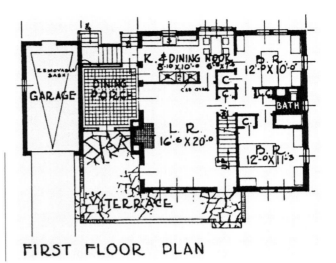

Charles Koch's fairly conventional house design locates a dining nook adjacent to the kitchen. There is otherwise no designated dining area. (*Prize Homes*, 88.)

FIRST FLOOR PLAN

One modern design separated activities into two categories—quiet or conversational against bustling, general activities—and placed dining in the latter category.[64]

But more than half of the houses—forty-eight of ninety-two—created a dining area, room, or alcove, placing it adjacent to the living room. Usually, this was accomplished through an architectural ell, without walls, doors, or even room dividers, although sometimes furniture placement showed readers the division between living and dining areas.

Almost always, designers created a living room that easily flows into the dining area by turning a corner. From a dining room one continues to the

A typical dining ell, open to the living room, is found in this house by Edward A. Dwyer. (*Prize Homes*, 52.)

FIRST

kitchen, although kitchens and dining rooms have more barriers between them than dining rooms and living rooms. A third of the designs, however—thirty-two of them—put dining activity in the same large room, with no architectural distinction. A floor plan that included furniture placement would put the dining tables and chairs close to kitchens but otherwise, with one large room, occupants had no architectural signals about where to eat other than proximity to the kitchen. Clearly, the combination room presented design challenges. When the *Tribune* began its "Better Rooms Competition" in 1947, one of the categories of room design was the "living-dining room," and that design problem received the plurality of submissions across all seven room problems.[65] Such multipurpose rooms, if they had a label, merely indicated the space was devoted to "living-dining" (and always in that order). Diagramming of space could have been useful: Ann Moran, who lived in the Coder Taylor–designed house in Highland Park, found one drawback of the house to be the lack of eating space. Having never seen Taylor's sketch of the floor plan, the Morans kept their television in the area he had marked for dining, as that is where the previous residents had kept their television. The Morans improvised dining in their very small kitchen by pulling out a kitchen drawer and putting a board over it.[66] The Fink family, first owners of a large prize home that lacked any place to eat in the kitchen, found it irritating to always have to eat in the dining room; there was a pass-through from kitchen to dining room, but it was awkwardly placed and inconvenient.[67] Hubka's persuasive argument that the dining room upgraded the living conditions of the working classes neither acknowledges the convenience of kitchen dining nor anticipates that the need for, size of, and uses of dining rooms would continue to be debated through the century and even into the next, with many people finding it to be completely superfluous and others insisting on its presence.[68]

Copy in *Prize Homes* promoted conveniences in the kitchen. Ample storage and cupboard space, proximity to laundry facilities, convenient layout: such features would make the kitchen experience more pleasant and time saving. While dining rooms had not disappeared, kitchens were places not only to prepare food but also to eat it. Ten house descriptions noted the inclusion of a snack bar, breakfast nook, or space for "family meals." Two others referred to "pickup meals" and yet another to "quick family meals," suggesting an informality to the family dining experience.[69] By 1945, daily domestic day labor for middle-class households had been long gone (with the exception of White families in southern states). Most American women did their own washing, cooking, and cleaning, so *Prize Homes* houses made no concession to servants. A kitchen where people could also eat—even if only breakfast, snacks, and children's lunches—saved the housekeeper time and steps.

Perhaps more than any other single appliance, washing machines revolutionized domestic labor.[70] Instead of devoting an entire day (or multiple days) to washing, drying, and ironing clothes and linens, the owner of a machine could forgo heating the water, agitating the clothes and linens by hand, rinsing out the soap, and wringing out the water, activities that required enormous physical labor and many, many hours. While sixteen *Prize Homes* designs left laundry facilities off the floor plans, most of those houses had basements, and presumably, the washing machine would be located there (basement floor plans were not always shown, even when floor plans indicated stairs in a one-story house). Addressing homemakers' concern, however, seventy-six designs specifically included "laundry" or "utilities" somewhere on the floor plans. Fifteen of those put laundries in the basement, an arrangement that makes sense when a designer is trying to use every bit of a limited amount of square footage for living space (competition rules stipulated that basement space need not count toward the total square footage). Nearly two-thirds put laundries on the first floor, however, and nearly all of those in rooms right off the kitchen. Six designers located laundry facilities in the kitchen itself, but the rest created a separate room, marked for utilities or laundry or both (this room often contained the hot water heater and/or heater, hence the "utilities" label).[71] Copy accompanying twenty-five of the houses featured the laundry facilities, either their convenience to the kitchen or their ample size. This benefit was spelled out: one of the rare split-level houses promised residents that "[o]nly six steps down from the living-room level floor of this house, and you are in the basement play area and laundry."[72] A mother could keep tabs on her children and her washing.

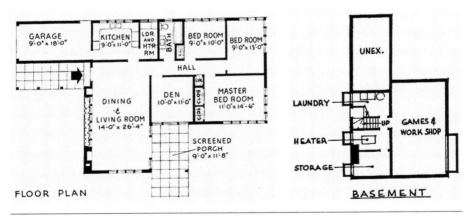

Lucille McKirahan's basement-less house, on the left, located the laundry right next to the kitchen; the room also houses the heater. All utilities, including the laundry, are in the basement of Lester J. Jorge's design on the right. (*Prize Homes*, 46, 58.)

In addition to housing people, a home needs to provide space for things, so house buyers and especially homemakers cared about storage. Copy frequently—twenty-two times—highlighted "ample" closet size and extra storage, with many more houses described as having "adequate" closets. Connie Weibezahl's three-bedroom house for problem three does contain a remarkable amount of closet space, and the description promoted that feature from the very first sentence: "What family ever finds itself adequately provided with storage and closet space? It can be seen in the plan that this house has an unusual amount of such space, actually about double the amount ordinarily included in designs of this size."[73] Even after four years of relative consumer deprivation caused by the war, Americans owned many objects, and the management of those objects required some deliberate planning. Clothes, toys, sports equipment, holiday decorations, special dishes for entertaining, materials for hobbies: these things were welcome markers of middle-class living but required space. Sufficient closets could keep winter boots and coats out of sight until needed. Basement and attic space housed Christmas ornaments pulled out only once a year. A dedicated laundry room kept drying items, ironing boards, mending baskets, and loads of washing out of guests' sight; the most popular place for a laundry room was off the kitchen, right near a back or side door or garage door, convenient to the housekeeper but also well away from the front door and living room. A ringing doorbell did not have to mean a flurry of picking up before opening the home to a guest or a stranger. The homemaker who could keep a tidy, organized home would be free from disapproval. And as the person at home all day, while the husband worked and children played or went to school, she could also be free herself from unsightly messes of daily living. Tidiness was for her, too.

Sufficient storage did not always mean attics or basements. Attics were never shown and never mentioned in copy, though small houses certainly could make use of overhead space to stash infrequently used items. A house with a flat or low-pitched roof could not have an attic; a *Boston Globe* article about one of the entrants' design announced it in the headline: "Joseph C. Gora's Plan Eliminates Both the Cellar and Attic."[74] Many *Prize Homes* roofs, however, had enough pitch to use at least some of that overhead space. Basements could add living and storage space; according to the competition rules, basements and attics did not need to be added to the square footage but were "free" space. But fifty-nine of the designs neither show basements on the house plans nor mention them in the copy, while three designs are specifically described as to be built on a slab.[75] Burns's design, built twice, sat on a slab, with a pull-down stairway to an attic that, according to resident Kathy Bryant, did not hold much.[76] Thirty-two houses did include basements, and if the floor plan were included and the designer labeled rooms and their uses, designers expected the basement to serve many purposes. As shown earlier, basements could be used for recreation and play, as thirteen floor plans indicate, and they could be used for adult hobbies, as another thirteen floor plans indicate. Two houses have toilets in the basement; at one time, basement toilets kept domestic help from using family facilities, but in a servantless home, a basement lavatory was convenient for residents who were working or recreating down there.[77] When laundry facilities and utility areas that were labeled were not on the first floor, they were in the basement. More than any named usage, basements contained storage. Thirteen floor plans labeled space for storage, and some clarified what kind of storage. A few designs revealed needs harking back to days before refrigeration. Two plans indicated where fruit could be stored, one more indicating vegetables.[78] One differentiated between storage and cold storage, the latter certainly for food.[79] Another specifically showed where food could be stored.[80] The Finks had an ample pantry in the basement of their Prize Home.[81]

Unlike other room uses, storage space could be fungible. Bedrooms could not be swapped for kitchens, and living rooms could not be exchanged with bathrooms. Garages were not intended for entertaining guests. But holiday decorations, winter boots, and baby keepsakes could go in the attic, a hall or bedroom closet, the garage, or the basement.

Built-in cabinetry, outside of the kitchen, helped keep items stowed away. Linen closets in bathrooms or near them conveniently kept sheets, towels, and toiletries near where they would be most needed. But people also wanted bookshelves or places to display decorative objects. Myhrum's house had built-in shelves and cabinets below the living room windows; current

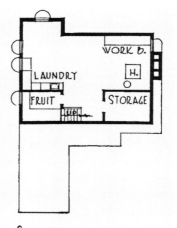

Fruit earned a specific location in Paul A. Kilp's basement. (*Prize Homes*, 60.)

· BASEMENT ·

owners added glass sliding doors to the shelving. When they took occupancy, there was still a built-in radio and stereo.[82]

Any assistance in housekeeping was welcome. Despite the labor-reducing devices available to homemakers in 1945—easily regulated ovens/stoves, refrigerators with freezers, washing machines, coffee pots, mixers, blenders, electric irons, and vacuum cleaners—and grocery stores full of prepared and semi-prepared foods, housekeeping still required many hours a day. Over the next decades, additional time-saving appliances would become standard in middle-class dwellings, but dishwashers and dryers were expensive luxuries at the time, and microwave ovens were years away. Only Bernard Bradley's house for problem one indicated the presence of a clothes dryer.[83] Time-savers available at the time also needed space: a room for a washing machine, counter space for the electric coffee pot, closet to stow the vacuum, and a basement spot for the chest freezer.

A modern house meant efficiency not merely in the appliances but also in the arrangement of rooms, and *Prize Homes* reminded readers of the ways its houses provided convenience, usually when touting the short distances to get from room to room. Service/side entrances and garages conveniently located near the kitchen saved labor when bringing in groceries. Already noted is dining rooms' proximity to kitchens, reducing distance and time in serving a meal and then clearing up after. "Efficient" and "practical" were the U-shaped kitchens where everything a cook needed was steps away, "convenient" and "compact" described the closeness of the laundry to the kitchen, or the ability to get directly from the garage into the house. Domestic work is rarely one single task after another but hours spent multitasking, so a mother who needed to pull the clean clothes from the washer and get them outside on the line, while monitoring her children, and making sure the pot on the stove did not boil over, and answer the telephone, had an easier time of it when all those endeavors were merely steps away from each other. Small houses, after all, had limitations, so promoting compactness turned a potential liability into a desirable feature.

Prize Homes houses emphasized privacy, not so much within the house but from outside the house. One element was the drying yard. Before the ubiquity of dryers, when homeowners had to dry their clothes on an outdoor clothesline, neighbors and passers-by would have seen family laundry, including undergarments and bedlinens. A dedicated drying yard, away from prying eyes, preserved family privacy. Thirty-seven designers indicated where families should hang their clothes; three more placed symbols that perhaps stood for a square or hexagonal drying rack. Using the labels of "drying," "service," or "utility," sometimes coupled with the noun "yard"—with one referring to a "laundry court"—navigated an inherent conflict between privacy and convenience, for a modern house should also save the housewife steps. Placing the drying at the very back of the lot line—as fourteen designers did—kept the laundry farthest from the street and the house, and even the next-door neighbors, but closer to the back fence neighbor. Ann Moran recalled hearing from her aunt, who rode the commuter train that ran right behind the Morans' Highland Park house, that when the diapers from the Morans' three children hung at the back of the yard, riders laughingly wondered whether the house was a day care center.[84] Wet laundry had to be transported to the back of the lot, and dry laundry had to come back, a process not exactly comporting with the step-saving convenience promoted in a modern house. Charles Koch's house for problem three does not indicate a drying yard, but the copy boasts that the house has two stairways from the basement, one with "direct access from the laundry to the yard."[85] Twelve designers placed a drying spot on the side of the house; given the rectangular lots, the space would have been more

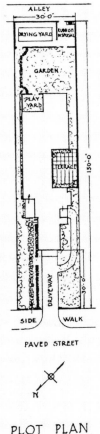

The drying yard sits at the back of the yard in Charles Kenneth Clinton's house, next to the garbage bins. (*Prize Homes*, 18.)

PLOT PLAN

compact than what was available in a backyard, but it provided the greatest privacy if there was a high enough fence between the lots. Thies's side elevation includes a charming detail of clothing on a line.[86] Nine more designed a place in the back but near the house; a housewife needed fewer steps, and it was the farthest from the back neighbors, but it put drying clothes close to the family's own windows. The three designers who placed a drying yard at the front of the house provided an architectural screen.[87]

Open spaces—without walls or closable doors—make it difficult for members of the household to find privacy. Freeman's house, the only one to acknowledge the possibility of multiple adult generations, separates the elders from the younger ones by floor.[88] Copy describing Zook's house promotes both separation between generations and supervision of the elder over the young: "There are three separate wings. One wing contains the owner's bedroom and bath. In another wing are the [three] children's rooms. . . . Off the children's rooms is a large enclosed outside play area, which can easily be supervised from the kitchen."[89] A house by Bugge placed a "living room" all by itself, with three unshared walls and the fourth adjacent to the entry hall, far from the "activities" area, which occupied the center of the house. Accompanying text likened the arrangement to "front and back parlors" of our grandmother's era; like the front parlor, the living room offered a "quiet retreat from the rest of the house."[90] As noted earlier, the absence of space for multiple generations other than parents and minor children kept to a minimum the number of residents. Beyond that, architectural elements like a dedicated marital bedroom, separate children's bedrooms, and as many bathrooms as could be afforded, helped keep even people residing in the house from each other. Emphasis on quiet spaces indicate that sometimes residents needed to be alone.

By far the greater concern about privacy, however, was exposure to neighbors. House design needed to navigate the narrow path between a house that was open, airy, and light-filled and one that maintained privacy. A window overlooking a natural vista—such as a mountain, valley, forest, desert scene, or water—might bring repose or connection to nature. A house might highlight a distant urban landscape, with city lights twinkling in the night or a horizon dotted by skyscrapers. Those house buyers, however, had to pay a premium for the view.[91] Buyers of modest houses on predetermined lots knew that their views would be of the street and their neighbors. Those neighbors presented a challenge: vernacular small house design had long used big windows, bay windows, bowed windows, and picture windows to bring in light and make rooms seem bigger. But the same windows that let in sunshine and air opened the family business to the neighbors and the street. And modern-style houses, with window walls and expansive use of glass, compromised privacy further. Privacy landscaping and, with a big enough lot, distance from the lot line could keep neighbors at bay, but *Prize Homes* houses were designed for modest lots, and neighbors would be close by. Their presence had to be acknowledged. Descriptive copy directly addressed this in a dozen houses. High windows let in light but not views. For one house with a large picture window in the living room, copy recommended two sets of curtains: "a transparent set for light diffusion and a heavier set for privacy."[92] The Weber family, living in a Prize Homes house with two large banks of windows in the living room, always had sheer curtains to moderate the incoming light, plus drapes.[93] Storako's two-bedroom, two-story home accompanied this headline: "An attractive small house, with a maximum of privacy." The privacy is available by "putting all the glass area of the living and dining space to the rear. Windows on the lot-line sides have been avoided as much as possible. The only points at which the owner of this house would look directly into his neighbor's house are in the kitchen and at one corner of the owner's bedroom."[94] Using glass block helped the process; Pfeufer's use of that material in a dining room "causes the area to be flooded with light and at the same time affords privacy."[95] Street privacy gained the highest praise; *Prize Homes* notes seven times when a house is shielded from street views.[96] Valerie Kanter was dismayed when her back fence neighbors removed trees that provided a barrier between the two lots. "I don't want to look in their windows," she said, and when trees were added to the Kanter property a few years ago, she had them strategically placed to block the sightline between her bedrooms and theirs.[97]

A few interiors are markedly distinct, and none of them were prizewinners. Mine's design, putting the child's room at the other end of the house from the parents' room and having the child's bedroom accessible directly from the living room, is unusual enough. But even more remarkably, it places the front door right next to the parents' bedroom. Residents and, more important, visitors, would have to walk down a long bedroom corridor and pass through the dining room to get to the living room.[98] Genchek's problem two house gives the boy and girl built-in berth beds on the shared wall between their two bedrooms; the son gets the upper berth in his room, and the lower berth is on the daughter's side. Saving space in their very small bedrooms provides an opportunity to create a common "all purpose" room for study and play, but the built-in beds might be problematic for older children or guests, so it is hard to see how the space would accommodate the family in a few more years.[99] Owners may have preferred to skip the play space in favor of two separate but larger bedrooms. A few designers created different spaces for quiet life, like visits from guests or for conversation, and activities that would create more noise and clutter: Wares's problem two house opened the layout to an extreme, as the "small kitchen is treated as part of the general living-dining area."[100] Ensign's design marks two first-floor common spaces: one is "visitors' niche" and the other is "rumpus" for "play, toys, movies, hobbies and dining." Such designations anticipate what would be known in a few years as the formal living room and the family room.[101] Huboi's house also contains a first-floor "rumpus," and the copy notes this "unusual feature," which is nevertheless "an extremely practical arrangement for many families."[102]

No floor plan is more unusual than Raymond Clouse's for problem three; accompanying copy acknowledges the distinctiveness.

> Present-day trends toward informal living are reflected in this unusual contemporary design. All the bedrooms are extremely small by the usual standards, and it is the intent of the designer that they are to be used as sleeping rooms only. The big feature of the house is the 20' x 25' activity room, with provision at one end for eating and at the other for a fireplace group. The actual living center of the house is called the kitchen-living area, which measures approximately 11' x 24'. Here most of the furniture is built in, the dining table being an extension of the kitchen countertop.

The three children's bedrooms are indeed quite small, with room for a bed but not much more, and even the parents' room is small, although it adjoins a study that is also accessible from the activity room. What the copy does not mention is the strange bathrooms. The floor plan is somewhat difficult to read; Clouse appears to have provided two toilets but in rooms with no sinks. It is not clear where the family would bathe, and it is difficult to imagine a family would find such an arrangement appealing.[103]

As the houses were specifically intended for middle-class dwellers, it is no surprise designers provided elements of respectability and propriety. Kelly's history of Levittown indicates the community's restrictions on hanging laundry were intended to demarcate the suburb from urban areas, where laundry hanging in windows, across alleys, or on porches would have been a regular practice.[104] *Prize Homes* houses keep the laundry out of sight. Vegetable gardens would be for residents to have a healthy or patriotic hobby, not for harvesting produce for sale. Backyards were for playing and socializing, not businesses. If Dad worked on the car, it was safely tucked back in the garage at night, rather than left, hood open, in the front yard. Family animals were pets, not livestock. Whether darkrooms and woodworking benches, basement space dedicated to furniture making, or sunroom easels for oil painting, such spaces were for recreational activities rather than commercial ones.

Overall, the *Prize Homes* interiors adhered to a consistent pattern of nuclear family living. Residents would be parents and children but not members of an extended or multigenerational family. Bedrooms and family bathrooms were separated from the rest of the house. If that could not occur easily through placing them all on a second floor, they could be clustered on one side of a single-story house. Either way, designers distinguished between common, public rooms for group activities and visitors and private, individual spaces for residents. Children nearly always got their own bedrooms, and the bedroom placement was based on age and sex. Children also had other assigned places—indoors and out—for their play. Open interiors dominated where entries, living rooms, and dining rooms were concerned, but kitchens still were separate rooms, although they were more open to the house than in earlier times. Designers devoted generous attention to outdoor living by adding terraces and courtyards (the word "patio" is not used), perhaps more generous than warranted in Chicagoland's relatively cold climate. Garages were obligatory, often big enough to include a workbench. These houses had plenty of closets and cupboards. Nobody wanted to live in a dark house, so *Prize Homes* promoted big windows, banks of windows, window walls, at least twenty-five times specifically pointing out how much light was available to make the house cheery and bright.

Every house, then, would be a "modern" house with as many conveniences and as much spaciousness as could be packed into a modest home on a small footprint. All the houses were designed for modern living in 1945, when the workplace for wage earners was away from the family home, and the residents of the household had time for leisure. Midcentury families played games together, barbecued in the backyard and worked on their hobbies after school and on the weekends, ate simple and quick meals, and casually entertained friends inside and outside their homes. They used modern appliances and owned a car. They maintained intra-house privacy through clustering bedrooms and bathrooms in separate areas. Borrman observes that twentieth-century house footprints had quietly and by default become standardized, with the layout of public rooms (living-dining) at the front of the home, and the "work spaces" at the back.[105] *Prize Homes* houses largely adhere to this pattern. *Prize Homes* architects anticipated a few architectural standards of the coming decades: kitchens' increased openness to living areas, en suite owners' bedrooms, and two-car garages. They failed to predict the architectural revolution required by the availability and ubiquitous adoption of television in the American home, which in less than a decade helped make the "family room"—a place for that television—a significant part of middle-class vernacular houses.[106] By 1952, the *Tribune's* Better Rooms competition promoted designs that integrated the television into the modern home.[107]

6

Modernism Skepticism
Contemporaneous Views of the Modern Aesthetic

Twenty-first-century Americans are mad about midcentury modern design. Furniture, lamps, fabric patterns, dishware, bar sets: slap on the phrase "midcentury modern" or even just the initials MCM, and manufacturers have a dedicated market. Wedding gifts to a couple marrying in 2020 look quite a bit like what a couple might have received in 1960, and furniture stores and catalogs are filled with reproductions of midcentury couches, chairs, and lamps. What defines the "middle" of the century is fluid, but any definition certainly includes the houses built in the housing boom after World War II. The term "modern" turns out to be fluid, as well, and the question of what makes a house modern persists. Analysis of the houses must include an assessment of their modernism, both in substance and in style, considering both the interior floor plan and the exterior façade.

"Modern" as an architectural or design term means different things to different people. As discussed in the previous chapter, it means at a minimum the infrastructural elements basic to twentieth-century American living: protection from the elements, a reliable power source, running cold and hot water, heating and/or cooling (depending on the climate), and a system to remove human waste. Without those amenities, we would not qualify a dwelling fit for permanent human habitation. It must have enough space for residents to store, prepare, and eat food; sleep; excrete; and receive guests. Thomas Hubka's social history of the evolution of house design defines a modern house as containing a minimum standard of "domestic technologies," including "kitchens with contemporary, labor-saving appliances; three-fixture bathrooms; heating systems and electricity." He also sees the modern home as providing comfort through personal space, room for recreation and relaxation, and ease of domestic labor.[1] And he explicitly cautions that modernity in a house must be determined regardless of "style."[2]

Ford and Ford's 1940 *The Modern House in America*, a defense and celebration of new design, defined the modern house: "The essence of the new residential architecture is revealed in its twofold purpose: to base its plans upon the organized life of the family to be housed, and to make logical use of the products of invention. . . . Thus human need comes first." Residents, the Fords pointed out, no longer do wage work from their homes, modern appliances reduce the space required for domestic labor, education and socializing often take place outside the home, family size has declined, multigenerational living has declined, and reduced housework increases leisure for women and children alike.[3] A modern house reflects those social conditions. (Nearly all the residences featured in *The Modern House in America*, however, are far too large and expensive for the average 1940 home buyer; most of them include rooms for one or even two live-in servants, despite the Fords' understanding of the modern house as one where the occupants do their own domestic labor.)

If we view a modern house as one that accommodates the differing needs of its residents—nuclear families comprised of parents and children, cooks and hobbyists, those whose wage labor occurs somewhere else, commuters who depend on automobiles, their proliferation of consumer goods—*Prize Homes* houses reflect life as lived in the 1940s. No clearer example can be found than in the lack of accommodation for servants. Even middle-class families had domestic servants in the early twentieth century, so houses had to be large enough to include bedrooms and bathrooms for live-in help, service entrances, and back stairways for maids to use. When a housewife began to do all her own housework and care for children without nannies, those space-hogging necessities could be eliminated. Another concession to modern living is the automobile. Nineteenth-century houses for even the middle classes would have had coach houses for the horses and/or early autos, but their placement was meant to keep the dirt and smells of these conveyances, animal or mechanical, as far from the house as possible. Modern house design acknowledges the reality of the everyday, frequent use of cars for the middle-class household, conveniently connecting the garage to the house. Housing the car is not an afterthought but integral to the home and thus its design.[4]

Although modern homes reduced the number of doors or walls in the public areas of the house, they continued the practice of separating the private, familial places where individuals might retreat (bathrooms and bedrooms with closable doors) from more open, public spaces where the family could gather and even welcome nonresidents—with few exceptions. And except for the adult couple who have and are expected to share a room and bathroom, the bedrooms (and increasingly the bathrooms) for the other residents are private and unshared; not only do residents need dedicated space away from the public areas of the house, but they also require some respite from each other. A modern house gives children, at least in an average-sized family, their own bedrooms. Storage space and garages accommodated the twentieth-century ability of even the middle and lower-middle class to afford *things*: clothes, toys and board games, bicycles, automobiles, books, appliances, and dishes. Anyone touring a nineteenth-century house for an upper-class or wealthy family has been surprised by the very small—or complete lack of—bedroom closets, a sensible allocation of space, since wardrobes of a well-off family would have been only somewhat larger than those of the middle classes. As the global economy made clothing and accessories less expensive, Americans have responded by buying more; twenty-first-century houses sometimes contain closets the size of rooms. The rise of affordable consumer goods in bulk is one reason many Americans cannot park their cars in their large garages.

As Smiley points out, a house does not have to look modern in style to be modern.[5] The traditional Cape Cod can have a U-shaped kitchen that saves steps for the housewife. A Dutch colonial with a center hallway and staircase that architecturally divides the first floor can still include plenty of closets, while a Tudor cottage can attach a backyard patio or an accessible garage. Two-story four-squares certainly can give each child a private bedroom and accommodate an owners' room with private bathroom. As has been shown, all *Prize Homes* houses adhered to this understanding of modern. Above all, the built *Prize Homes* houses would be modern because they were *new*.[6] The plumbing and wiring were state of the art. Appliances were fresh off the factory floor. Brand-new windows and doors opened and closed properly. Cabinets were newly constructed, tile and grout were clean and unchipped, the paint was fresh, and the carpets were pristine.

But what twenty-first-century Americans love about midcentury modern houses is their aesthetic, the house features that set them apart as distinctive from other vernacular styles, not only the U-shaped kitchen, ample closets, or attached garage. Considering this leads to questions of modern style or modern aesthetic, and how modern house architecture style was received at the time. The twenty-four Prize Homes winners, and the sixty-eight others included in *Prize Homes*, reflected what the jury thought the public wanted: some houses had modern-style features but none too extreme or distinctive. This was foreshadowed, a bit, in the *Tribune*'s prewar coverage of what it expected to find in the postwar housing boom. Real estate reporter Al Chase indicated the concerns of the building industry as early as January 1944: builders worried consumers would want a "magic house," a "dream cottage" they could not deliver.[7] Reporting on a trade group, another

Tribune writer remarked that the "disappearing dining room" was met with resistance, and "not all post-war homes will be ultramodern, streamlined, or prefabricated dwellings."[8] Another trade representative, noting that "Joe" on the front lines could not speak now for his home preferences, spoke for him: "chances are that Joe, in his foxhole, is not dreaming about any ultra-modern, streamlined house with 'posture-perfect' chairs, but is fondly remembering the living room he left, with its corner what-not, its comfortable rocking chair and its other well-loved, tho [*sic*] strictly nonperiod pieces. When he comes back he'll be wanting something he's used to, something he can find relaxation and comfort in."[9] Bargelt reported more starkly: despite improvements in building materials, postwar home design will pick up where it left off at the start of the war.

> One fact is certain—the average person has no real urge to pioneer in new treatments in his home. House features and designs are not as changeable as cars. People who build want to be sure before they start that their homes, which in many cases are a lifelong investment, remain as permanently in style as possible. For those who are planning and saving for a home of their own with the coming of peace it will be wise to keep informed on the best of ideas adopted before the war and to retain an open mind as to ideas born of the war.[10]

Competition jurors selecting winners, and whoever chose the non-winning designs included in *Prize Homes*, heeded Bargelt's advice and mostly selected houses without "pioneering" features.

Architectural choices presented to the buying public usually provided labels in some form or another. A catalog might name a design in a way that could cue the viewer: a house called the Essex would not look like one called the Tuscan or the Lombard, although names frequently bore little connection to a style. Copy accompanying house plans frequently referred to a house as a colonial or a Cape Cod, a traditional or a modern. *Architectural Forum*'s 1925 competition for design of fireproof homes conveniently awarded prizes for different categories of exterior style: Spanish, colonial, Italian, and English. Those four vernaculars contained enough distinctive elements, at least some of the time, to render the styles identifiable, although there was sufficient overlap that it was helpful when the house was labeled the "Palermo," which indicated it was Italian, or the "Chiquita," giving it away as Spanish.[11] Some stylistic elements are more readily available to the lay public, who can identify English Tudor through its half-timbers, the Dutch colonial by the distinctive roof line, or a Cape Cod through the boxy shape and dormer windows.

What gives away a house as a modern one? For some, it is the absence of certain elements. Lewis Storrs's 1946 *The Key to Your New Home: A Primer of Liveable* [*sic*] *and Practical Houses* includes, among its advice on exterior and interior design, fifty-two house plans and their corresponding photographed elevations. He devotes virtually no effort to labeling a house as "Cape Cod" or a "French style," although the houses are largely traditional. But his descriptions of the few modern houses provide a clue: a modern house is known by what it leaves out. A Neutra design "attempts no picturesque revival of the horse-and-buggy days." Another modern house, by William Wurster, "has not been influenced by any historic style," and the architect of a third house has made "no attempt to follow any stylistic precedent." Storrs suggests that it is the absence of the colonial or traditional features, rather than their presence, that makes a house distinctive in style.[12] Whatever modern is, it does not include dormer windows, mansard roofs, wrap-around porches, gingerbread trim, window shutters, or any elements that alert the viewer to a particular regional or period style.

"What makes a single-family house modern?" asked Sabatino in 2020. "Does a house need to be built of glass and steel or glass, brick, and wood with an open plan to be modern or can it combine tradition with innovation?"[13] Sabatino's question divides the house style between interior layout (open plan) and mostly exterior building materials (glass and steel). Although the use of building materials is not covered in this research, the modern house in the midcentury used technological advances in plate and reinforced glass, steel, concrete, and plastics, both inside and outside, while house builders traditionally relied primarily on wood, brick, or stucco. Again, it is not primarily the materials that help us identify, when we drive down a street today and cannot see a building's interior layout, which house embodies a modern style. As Supreme Court Justice Potter Stewart once claimed of pornography that was difficult to define: "I know it when I see it." Just as we can pick out the Tudor by its visible half-timbers or the Dutch colonial by the gambrel roof, we can point to the elements of modern style. *Prize Homes* provided assistance when describing one of Merwin Freeman's designs: "Big windows, sun decks, and front garages are some of the aspects of contemporary home design."[14] *Architectural Forum* editors George Nelson and Henry Wright wrote in 1945 that the large window was "modern architecture's most important contribution to house design."[15] Other elements include not just big windows but window styles, rooflines, and placement of main entries and garages.

No single architectural feature drew more attention than windows in *Prize Homes* copy, likely because, as Isenstadt has shown, improvements in glass technology and window manufacturing had a profound impact on vernacular architecture.[16] Windows, uniquely, are architectural elements visible from both the outside and the inside. Twenty-seven house descriptions did not directly mention windows, although they still promoted the airiness and light available in the house, and references to cross-ventilation always implicitly affirmed the presence of windows on at least two walls in a room, usually a bedroom. But more than two-thirds of the house descriptions explicitly praised the design's use of windows. Whether large, big, picture, clerestory, corner, casement, high, strip, bay, skylight, French, found in banks or walls, protected from the elements, or facing south—windows drew the spotlight. Window style, especially, signaled a modern or traditional house. Jurors in the Portland Cement–sponsored competition of 1936 complained that some architects thought all one needed for a modern house was to add corner windows; apparently the jurors found this detail insufficient in making a house truly modern.[17] But corner windows were and are an element of modern style, as are strip windows, high windows, sliding glass, clerestory windows, and window walls. Modern windows are frequently found in *Prize Homes* houses. At least a third of the houses have corner windows. More than twenty have high strip windows or clerestory windows.

A few implement glass brick, especially in garages. A traditionally styled house would have windows of roughly equal size placed on all sides of the house, with perhaps bathroom windows smaller for privacy and kitchen

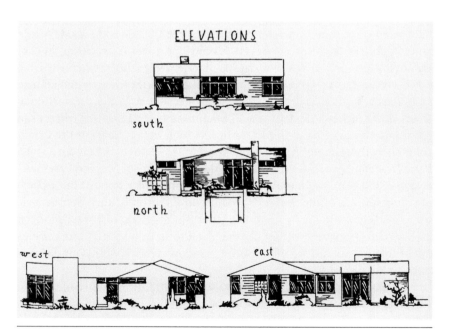

Copy emphasized the strip windows for privacy in the bathroom of Robert A. Genchek's design for problem two. (*Prize Homes*, 51.)

windows smaller because of built-in cabinetry. Many modern houses eschewed such regularity, keeping windows to a minimum on the street side of the house. *Prize Homes* designers sometimes indicated in their lot siting plans that the back of the house should be facing south, and they put their window walls there to take advantage of greater sunlight, as well as to maximize privacy.

Placement of the house's main entrance can be a distinguishing feature of modern style. A "front" door in a traditional design, on a relatively flat front façade, up a few steps, is easily identified as the place for a nonresident seeking admission to the home. A little more than half of the *Prize Homes* houses comport with this style, with a front door easily visible from the street or sidewalk. But that leaves many houses with a main entrance that is less visible, or even hidden, and there are two differing reasons for this. One is the desire for a house more closed to the outside world. Combined with a front porch, even if only a small slab, an easily seen and accessible front door invites visitors and guests. As shown earlier, Americans wanted plenty of light and air but also sought to keep neighbors and passers-by from getting a close view of their home's interior and their activities there. Entrances farther from the street, off to the side, accessible only through a courtyard or side terrace, mean your visitors are nobody else's business. It discourages drop-in guests, and certainly the unwelcome canvassers or solicitors. Your comings and goings are less visible to your neighbors. A twentieth-century shift from front porches to backyard terraces began with the rise of street noise generated by cars, eventually leaving the front porch little more than a minimal entry.[18] The Kanters, bucking the trend, extended their Prize Homes porch slab to accommodate some furniture.[19] A modern-styled house by Tempest has a nominal "front" door in that it faces the street. But the door is behind the garage and thus unseen.[20] His house for problem two features "a pleasant walk along the side of the garage" to reach the side entry.[21] Ensign's problem two house requires walking along the side of the full garage, making a right turn to cross a sidewalk in front of the kitchen, and then a left turn and walk along the side of the kitchen before getting to the main entry.[22] Another Tempest house and one by Stein placed entries on the side, tucked into the house.[23]

A Myhrum modern house left open space between the garage and the house, but the second floor traversed the two first-floor units. Visitors had to walk well into the covered area to reach the main entrance, which was perpendicular to the street; one could not see that door until one was right in front of it. At least before 1968, one of the homeowners of the built version closed up the open space, creating a conventional, street-facing entrance.

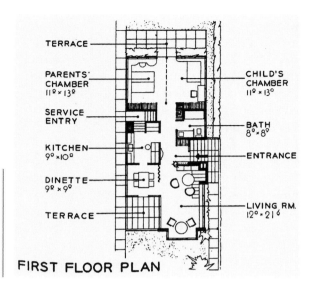

TERRACE

PARENTS'
CHAMBER
11⁹ × 13⁹

SERVICE
ENTRY

KITCHEN
9⁹ × 10⁹

DINETTE
9⁹ × 9⁹

TERRACE

CHILD'S
CHAMBER
11⁹ × 13⁰

BATH
8⁰ × 8⁹

ENTRANCE

LIVING RM.
12⁰ × 21⁶

FIRST FLOOR PLAN

One enters the house only after traversing half the house's footprint in Benjamin H. Stein's design. Even then, the door is not visible until the visitor turns the corner. (*Prize Homes*, 37.)

Door placement might have been chosen for another reason, however, and that is the garage. *Prize Homes* copy affirmed that "front garages" are part of modern design, and most of the garages in the book are in the front of the house. Back alleys—and Chicago, like many other cities, has plenty of those—accommodate a backyard garage, and this was true of large, spacious lots and small ones. Not every neighborhood had alleyways, however, and suburban lots in new subdivisions would not. Competition rules stipulated that submissions to problem one could include an alley at the designer's discretion, and twelve of the thirty-one houses in that category made use of a back alley for automobile access to a garage.

Houses for problems two and three had to concede to the alley-less suburban practice; a garage could be accessed only from the front.[24] Only two of the known built homes back up to alleys.[25] (Initially, an alley ran between some of the ten built houses in the Deer Park subdivision in Chicago, but the garages were in front; in any case, the alley eventually disappeared. The backyards of the *Prize Homes* houses just extended back over the alley space, and now only fences separate the lots.) Driveways that came through the street front could snake all the way to the back of the lot, if an architect still wanted to hide the garage from street view, but then an enormous part of the lot would be sacrificed to the driveway, rendering both the house footprint and the lawn smaller.[26] Placing the garage in front, with a short driveway, proved to be the practical solution for a modest or small lot, and if the "snout house" is excoriated (or even prohibited) today, it addresses the need for a garage *and* maximizes a house's square footage on a

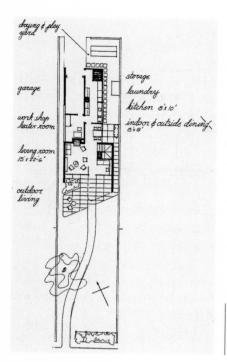

The handwritten labels on the plan read:

drying & play yard

garage

work shop heater room

living room 15' x 22'-6"

outdoor living

storage
laundry
kitchen 8' x 10'
indoor & outside dining 8' x 9'

Stephen J. Alling used an alley driveway to access the garage, but this is a rare solution to the garage placement problem. (*Prize Homes*, 28.)

small piece of land. Plenty of houses in the decades before the Prize Homes competition included front-facing garages, but when a garage is set back, the house's living spaces and front door remain prominent. Koch's house features a front-facing but set-back garage; Edward Dwyer's house has a garage flush with the front façade.[27] But a garage protruding from the house makes the garage door the most prominent feature of the front façade. While many houses had side doors that seemed intentionally designed to be hidden from passersby, other houses had doors that were front facing but still deep into the lot. How deep depended on how much of that snout jutted from the house. Sometimes the protuberance was relatively small, when the back of the garage was integrated into the house overall. In those cases, the main entry still could be seen easily. But sometimes it protruded the entire length of the garage, and sometimes that garage included storage or hobby space, further deepening the distance. Anyone seeking entrance would have to take many steps alongside the garage to get to the front door. This was sometimes extended farther when other rooms were placed behind the garage but before the entry; in that case, the visitor might walk past bedroom or kitchen windows to enter. In Coder Taylor's two-bedroom house, one passes the detached garage, with a playroom at the back, and an open courtyard before reaching the entrance.[28] Glidden and Finney's house

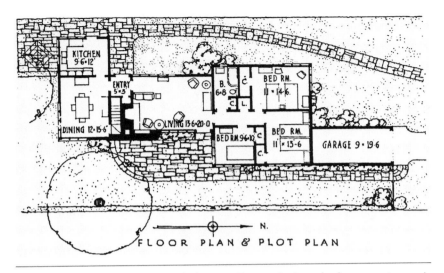

FLOOR PLAN & PLOT PLAN

In this F. H. Glidden Jr. and Eben D. Finney design, the house entrance is not obvious. One following the sidewalk on the left passes the garage, and two sets of bedroom windows, before rounding the corner to an entrance to the living room. Taking the sidewalk on the right means walking even farther, nearly to the back of the house, to the main "entry." (*Prize Homes*, 45.)

requires walking past the attached garage and two children's bedrooms to enter; one still must go past half the house's footprint, not even counting the garage.[29]

Rooflines tip the observer: a flat or shed roof is a modern one. Twenty-six *Prize Homes* houses had flat roofs, and another seven had low-sloped shed roofs. Four houses combined flat and pitched roofs, placing sundecks

R. W. Tempest's "cottage" positions a flat-roofed garage in front. (*Prize Homes*, 57.)

on the flat portion. Many houses—thirteen of them—had conventional roofs but implemented a flat roof for the attached garage, often a snout one.

A flat roof in a small house carries a significant price. While the flat roof might allow for a second-floor deck, a flat or low-pitched roof prevents the addition of an attic, which could be valuable storage space in a small house. Copy only once pointed out a flat roof, with Connie Weibezahl's design, although Puckett's "shed roofs give interest."[30]

But those houses were the most likely to earn descriptions of contemporary or modern, or even beyond: among the flat-roof designs, Zook's house and Duprey's were "original,"[31] Alling's and Lackner's houses were "unusual,"[32] while one of Myhrum's houses was "highly original."[33] The originality drew current owner Ursula O'Hayer to the house when she and her family bought it in the early 1970s; before that, as a teenager, Audrey Hellinger liked it when visitors entered and exclaimed, "what a cool house!"[34]

Aside from the obvious traditional or modern elements of a house that would have been easily visible to the reader, *Prize Homes* copy and headlines often, though not always, described a house's style. Adjectives like

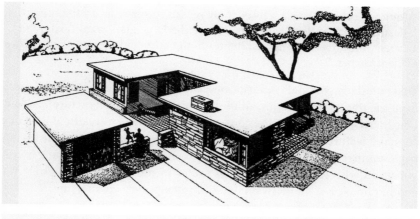

Connie Weibezahl's house and unattached garage (top) have flat roofs, noted in the copy; Olen Puckett's staggered shed roof (bottom) "gives interest." (*Prize Homes*, 81, 38.)

"traditional," "conservative," and "colonial" contrasted with "modern" and "contemporary." Sometimes, however, it is not obvious why a house earned one label or another. The appellations did not stem from arcane definitions of style but rather clearly drew from popular usage; the copywriter(s) were not architects but engaged in selling. But even architects might hedge their bets in describing their own designs. When reporting on the construction of the first house in Highland Park, the local paper appeared to have consulted with the architect, to affirm that the house "is of the modern, seven room ranch type, classified by its designer, Howard Uebelhack, as modern colonial."[35] Thomas Hubka shows the challenge of identifying and compartmentalizing vernacular architecture, and the *Prize Homes* copywriters reflect that confusion.[36] The terms' imprecision can be found in the many occasions when copy combined terms, as *Prize Homes* wanted readers to consider every house in the volume. Hugh Garden's problem one house illustrates the way text explained the architectural elements.

> *Warmth and friendliness characterize this home of modern colonial design.* With its steep roof, high gables, central chimney, and picket fence around the front garden, this design has the warmth and friendliness of the traditional colonial home. Closer study reveals its many up-to-the-minute features and modern comforts. Notice the large glass areas facing the street, the large, well-lighted living-dining area, and the practical, efficient kitchen.[37]

That "modern colonial" description separated the interior conveniences from the traditional exterior, although it also included the picture window. One house will "appeal to the conservative homeowner because it includes so many features found only in the new homes of today."[38] On the facing page, another house, while "[o]utwardly conservative, this charming house is packed with features more often found in more radical design."[39] Yet another house is a "modern version of contemporary architecture."[40]

No *Prize Homes* house carries the adjective "ranch," but many certainly could have. The ranch house would become quite popular in the coming years, straddling the divide between a modern and traditional home. Its modernism is found in the house footprint, which, instead of squarish, tends to be rectangular or even L- or U-shaped around a patio or courtyard. Roofs are relatively low-pitched and might have expansive eaves, windows are large (think of sliding glass doors at the back of the house), and interiors are open, often with a combined living and dining room. On the other hand, the style harkens to an earlier age, as it was colonial vernacular in the American West and Southwest. Five houses are labeled "rambling"—all one-story homes—which was frequently used to describe ranch houses, spread out on only one floor.[41] Other descriptors fill in the blanks. Uebelhack's "modern colonial" could be called a ranch; it is instead offered as "a good example of the currently popular one-story house." Bradley's house is a "rugged country home," while Puckett's "suggest[s] the simple adobe houses of the American Southwest."[42] The best example of this is a house by Charles Hogan, whose ranch has not one but two weathervanes, shutters, and a wagon-wheel gate to the backyard. But it also has a front projecting garage and a combination living-dining room, and although the kitchen is not open to the rest of the house, it is at the front of the house, right by the front door.[43] Glidden and Finney's "rambling frame house" also sports a weathervane.[44]

Just as the midcentury ranch house was a modern version of a colonial design, *Prize Homes* designs mixed architectural elements, and accompanying text noted this. While the designer of a modern house would not add shutters to a glass brick window, or a Dutch colonial roofline to a ranch, architects of more conventional designs might add modern features. As mentioned earlier, a few conventional house designs added a snout garage, sometimes with a flat roof. Davis's two-bedroom house is for "conservative tastes" but has some high strip windows and glass brick in the bathroom.[45] A house by Sanford Full is "conservative in design"; its dining room has a full window wall rather than traditional windows.[46] Copy occasionally pointed out contemporary architectural features in otherwise conventional houses: Garden's "traditional colonial" was also a "modern colonial" with a large picture window.[47] Davis's house, referred to above, "contains so many features found only in the new homes of today."[48]

This "modern colonial" by Hugh Garden has the highest pitched roof of the collection. (*Prize Homes*, 23.)

Arnold's house is "outwardly conservative" but packed with radical features.[49] Sloan's is a "combination of both new and old design."[50] "Without a radical department in exterior design from the conventional house," Wayman's design "includes numerous present-day conveniences."[51] *Prize Homes* labels a three-bedroom, one-story house by R. W. Tempest a "cottage" with "charm," romantic words not usually associated with modern architecture. Tempest's elevation shows flowering window boxes and a box hedge around the house; it has also a conventionally gabled roof. But the snout garage is flat roofed, the main entrance is on the side, and one living room wall is all glass, leading to a courtyard.[52]

A couple of the houses are almost brutalist in their modernity, both by Myhrum. One of his "unusual" houses is flat roofed and brick, and it has few windows. Kitchen and living room windows are high strips.[53] A second Myhrum design shows no street-facing windows on the first floor. On a large expanse of plain façade on the street-facing second floor, windows

NORTH (STREET) ELEVATION

Contrast the back of Arthur Myhrum's house, with plentiful windows, to the street-side front. In the built iteration, front windows were added to the street side. (*Prize Homes*, 74.)

illuminated the bathrooms in the middle of the design, but the corner rooms, bedrooms, had no street-facing windows. The back of the house has plenty of windows, and the main elevation is shown from that more appealing rear side. Despite Myhrum's instruction that the back, windowed façade face the south, it was not favored with that placement when built in Deer Park: the back of the house with the windows faces north, and the relatively windowless street side faces the south.[54] Even then, the back-facing banks of windows, when built, were rejected in favor of conventionally sized windows.[55] The stark street front was modified, and in construction, builders added windows to the corner bedrooms, softening the exterior and letting in more light and air.

Next door, however, Shimon Langer thinks his south-facing windows on the street side of the house are one of his favorite features of his house, even though that design, by Hanson and Martorano, specified just the opposite siting.[56]

If readers needed to be reminded that a traditional house served their modern needs, sometimes the *Prize Homes* copy assured them that a modern house did not stray too far from the desirable or comfortable. The "almost windowless front wall" of Thies's design, buyers should know, disguised light available from the back and side windows.[57] Woolford and Peterson's modern house plan would be "appropriate to any neighborhood," so residents could be sure their house choice would not be too extreme.[58] (Windows were also added to this design in construction.) Blachmik's

Robert William Blachmik's stark house would be "softened" by appropriate landscaping. (*Prize Homes*, 61.)

modern plan has a façade with a random ashlar pattern, which, together with landscaping, tends to "soften the severity of the design," while Pierce's "contemporary design" would be "softened by color contrasts."[59]

In Barry's individual article on one of Tempest's flat-roofed houses, competition advisor Boyd Hill pointed out "a low-pitched roof might be substituted for the flat one . . . without detracting from the house's appearance."[60] Buyers could amend the plan if they were deterred by too much adherence to contemporary features.

Some criticism of the Prize Homes winning designs came contemporaneously. Not from the *Tribune*, of course; reporter Edward Barry and people quoted in *Tribune* articles had nothing but praise for the winning and additional designs. *Architectural Forum*'s 1946 article on the competition, however, began by pointing out what the *Chicago Tribune* itself could not: the point of the contest was not only to promote houses and house building, but also "to give its Sunday Edition a timely topic to talk about." If the *Forum*'s purity of motive permitted unblinking criticism, the journal suggests, the *Tribune*'s attention to crass commerce corrupted its own discernment. Quoting Boyd Hill, the *Forum* indicated more than half of the entries were of contemporary design; this was only natural, concluded the *Forum*, when there was so much emphasis on practicality. Specific design trends found among the winners included "provision of space for relaxation and open air living . . . position of garage at the front of the house . . . inclusion of more than one bathroom and . . . location of laundry facilities on the ground floor." The *Forum* included sketches, floor plans, and its own commentary on ten of the houses: six for problem one and four for problem two. Their choices reflect their affection for modern design, as only one of the ten they featured can be called traditional, whereas the *Tribune* jury split winners evenly: half modern(ish) and half traditional(ish).[61]

Two modern designs, by J. Floyd Yewell and a co-design by C. S. Woolford and R. D. Peterson, merited no complaints at all in the *Forum*; those houses were practical, convenient, and spacious. But the other eight earned some—or even a great deal of—criticism. Privacy was a point of contention: some laudably preserved privacy from the street and from neighbors, but others sacrificed it by putting the living room in view of the street. The Heidt Associates' plan made a "questionable" decision to put all the bedrooms facing north—and in doing so put the living room facing the street, indicating some inconsistency with their criticism (after all, some part of the house must face the street). Several designs failed to take full advantage of the lot. Lucille McKirahan, the one woman among the twenty-four winners, saw the inclusion of her design among the ten featured, but the *Forum* found her house "generally undistinguished," although they acknowledged her good room arrangement. Eric Wenstrand's modern design generated sarcastic commentary, here in its entirety:

> Again, privacy and garden beauty are ignored. Here the designer has caused the few windows of his living room to face directly upon the street; and, in addition, he proposes to make a summer porch even nearer the street by providing overhead doors on three sides of the garage. The remainder of the lot apparently has nothing to do with the house, the bedrooms being arranged in tight formation with very small windows, and connected by a completely dark corridor. Size of chimney suggests open hearth cooking practised [*sic*] in the 18th century.

Designers' favorites did not seem to be the same as the public's. If, as Hubka asserts, "the most important 'prototype' examples of common houses are actually those that have been built and confirmed in greatest number," the *Architectural Forum* missed the mark.[62] Of the ten featured by the *Forum*, half were never known to be built (including the much-admired design by J. Floyd Yewell), two were built once, and one was built twice. Loathed by the *Forum*, Wenstrand's house, a favorite among *Tribune* readers and the Art Institute visitors, was built at least five times, and four still stand.

On the surface, house owners faced oppositional choices. Did they want traditional houses, like Cape Cods or colonials, with multi-paned, double-hung dormer windows; gables and shutters; and high-pitched roofs? Or did they prefer to live in modern houses, with walls of glass, flat roofs, and clerestory or corner windows? The *Prize Homes* collection presented options for both of those home buyers. About a third of the houses fit a conventional notion of modern exteriors: flat roofs and large expanses of glass. Three or four of those designs might earn the label "international style"—very asymmetrical, flat roofed, boxy, and lacking any external ornamentation.[63] At the other end of the spectrum, about eight or nine houses clearly borrow from traditional styles. But most of the Prize Homes were largely what Smiley calls "modified moderns," less stark than they could be, with blended features, designed to appeal to a broad market rather than a rarified one.[64] Few were so unusual that they would repel buyers wanting a house that would not disrupt the neighborhood, the in-laws, or the bank. *Tribune* inquiries about the twenty-four winners, and visitors to the Art Institute of Chicago exhibit of 172 who voted for their favorites, showed similar preferences. The *Tribune's* own analysis of mail inquires indicated readers "favore[ed] a traditional rather than a contemporary style," and the five favorites were "versions of traditional styles." Art Institute visitors selected seven favorites, overlapping with three of the *Tribune* favorites; the other four were also at the traditional end of the spectrum.[65]

America's preference for a more traditional aesthetic could be found in home furnishings and décor. A *Chicago Tribune* ad for the Spiegel store, in March 1946, featured the Wenstrand house and described it as a "practical contemporary design." The store's recommended furnishing for the house? An "Early American" bedroom suite and living room pieces that include an "18th Century Georgian Lounge Chair" and an "18th Century Kneehole Desk."[66]

The *Tribune* solicited professional decorators to recommend furnishing, even providing sketches, for two winning designs. For Garbe's very

Spiegel department store recommended colonial furnishings and décor for what the store itself called a "practical, contemporary" house. (*Chicago Tribune*, March 10, 1946, 17.)

traditional house, with a "somewhat formal character," the decorator used conventional furnishings and chintz floral for upholstery. Finney and Glidden's rambling ranch—one of the few with a fully separate dining room—presented a challenge. "When decorators were planning this interior they decided to face a problem which occurs frequently," admitted Agnes Hunter, of the design firm selected. "Many people who admire and want a modern house prefer to furnish it in a traditional manner." Hence they decided to use English-style furnishings and printed fabrics, and they placed a china plate collection over a Williamsburg-style mantle.[67] Other decorators must have felt similar pressure. A sketch for Myhrum's modern design does have a modern dining table, but right next to it is an open hutch with colonial detailing, meant for displaying dishes and bric-a-brac. Recommendations for Sackville-West's house put a wingback chair in the living room and a frilly, flowered skirt around a bedroom dressing table.[68] Suggested décor was carried through to the building project. Sears, Roebuck and Company furnished the Cedarstrand house in the Deer Park subdivision. Sears's own sketches of the kitchen décor describe the "colorful peasant wallpaper" in the kitchen; the pictures show sheer, lacy curtains and a scalloped valance. The range, however, is state of the art, and the kitchen table has hairpin legs; the chairs surrounding it mimic Marcel Breuer's iconic Cesca design: cantilevered chairs of tubular steel. Cedarstrand's rather conventional design has a modern window wall of large-paned glass overlooking the backyard; Sears draped it in floor-to-ceiling floral fabric, nicely accompanying the rest of the home's neo-colonial furniture and fabrics.[69]

In contrast to the cautious choices of the jury and whoever selected the additional sixty-eight designs included in the *Prize Homes* book, the twenty non-winning houses featured by *Tribune* reporter Edward Barry leaned toward a less compromised modern aesthetic. Barry admired Ralph Rapson and John Van der Meulen's modern house, a design that made it to the Art Institute show but not the *Prize Homes* book. He liked a submission from Eileen and I. M. Pei that did not appear in the book. Of the twenty non-winning designs he wrote about, only four can be described as falling into the traditional camp: houses by Edward Dwyer, Charles Hogan, Miriam Hurford, and Hugh Garden, all included in the *Prize Homes* book.

Barry's choices are not only modern—they are more starkly modern than even the most contemporary designs jurors selected. Of the sixteen modern houses, seven merited inclusion in the book, but nine others did not. Those nine are very modern, and the copy often acknowledges this. About the Rapson and Van der Meulen house, Barry wrote, "This remarkable design . . . will appeal strongly to persons who are sympathetic toward contemporary architecture."[70] In presenting Kazumi Adachi's design—also omitted from the book—Barry opined about the state of architecture.

> This admittedly extreme design has great value as an illustration of certain advanced ideas which architects have been turning over in their minds. These ideas have not, at least in this part of the country, been incorporated into very many homes. But if the history of design repeats itself, and the radical ideas of one era continue to become the commonplaces of the next, such devices as the use of skylight and clearstory [*sic*] windows as principal means of illumination and ventilation may be familiar to everybody a few decades hence.[71]

Adachi's butterfly-roofed house had no conventional windows, relying exclusively on clerestories and skylights; Barry was right to label it an extreme design. Decades later, clerestory windows and skylights are not principal means of illumination and ventilation.

7

Competing Visions
Other Architectural Competitions

The Prize Homes competition occurred alongside other, similar competitions, as shown previously. As well, publication of the *Prize Homes* book catalog came along when people planning on, or even just dreaming of, building a house had many house plan books to choose from. Comparisons to other competitions and catalogs indicate *Prize Homes* houses were both similar to and different from what was available from other sources. Competitions sponsored by architectural publications were likely to be ideas competitions, with no plans to build any of the winning designs. Unconstrained by middlebrow tastes, conservative Federal Housing Authority (FHA) appraisers, or cautious builders, they offered the public the most modern designs, largely eschewing traditional house design. Beyond juried competitions, small house designs curated by architectural publications reflected editors' perspectives, and their choices generally mirrored those of the juries. More commercial enterprises, however, such as house plan catalogs, did not stem from competitions but culled the most "buildable" designs from competitions or other sources. Catalogs offered house plans to a middle-class and largely conservative house buying market that mostly embraced a more traditional house style. The ninety-two houses chosen for the *Prize Homes* book straddled both worlds, presenting buyers with choices at both ends of the spectrum.[1]

Architectural periodicals promoted the most modern designs, including few if any traditional house designs among their winners, if in a competition, or among editorial collections. A review of collections and competitions reveals their preferences. *Architectural Forum, Architectural Record, Pencil Points/Progressive Architecture*, and *Arts & Architecture* monthly magazines each had different sensibilities and somewhat different audiences. Taken together, they reflected largely consistent architectural choices: a strong attachment to modern and a rejection of traditional style.

One of the largest competitions, with over 2,000 submissions, was the House for Modern Living competition co-sponsored by *Architectural Forum* and the General Electric Company.[2] It solicited submissions in 1934 and announced winners in 1935, a decade earlier than the Prize Homes competition. The partnership between G.E. and *Architectural Forum* exemplifies much of what has already been documented about house competitions. General Electric's agenda, of course, was to highlight its modern electric appliances and utilities. Submitted floor plans had to include furniture, cabinetry, and electrical appliances; designers went far beyond the standard kitchen appliances and water heaters, indicating where electric lamps, clocks, irons, hair dryers, and radios could be placed within the home. *Architectural Forum* looked to promote design, create content for its pages, and give underused architects something to do during the Depression. Rather than specify how many rooms the houses must have, the architectural problem described a particular family, the Blisses, and asked for designs appropriate for them at two life stages, a decade apart. Initially, the Blisses are a young couple in their early thirties. Mr. Bliss is a professional engineer; he is a meticulous man who likes things in their proper places. Mrs. Bliss, a stay-at-home mother, also has a college degree. They have a four-year-old son. Mrs. Bliss does all the housework, because they cannot afford a domestic laborer but also because she enjoys it. "Electricity is her servant."[3] But ten years later, the family would need a different house, based on family size and rising affluence. Now they can afford a live-in maid and a second car, neither of which fits into their first home. Shortly after they moved into the first house, they had another child; their son is now fourteen and their daughter is nine. Opposite-sex children cannot share rooms, requiring another house adaptation. And where in the United States would the Blisses live? The competition asked submissions to be suited to either northern or southern climates, creating four categories of potential prizes.[4]

The House for Tomorrow jury of a dozen was quite large; their names were withheld until after the competition deadline had passed. Seven architects served on the jury, another represented the real estate business, one juror represented the construction industry, and one electrical engineer juror was to help with that technical aspect of building. Two women jurors, experts on housekeeping and child rearing, "contributed to the women's angle." The *Forum* helpfully categorized the "sympathies" of the twelve: three were unknown (the two women and the builder), three were strongly modern, one was modern, two were conservative, one more generally conservative, and one more "conservative but open to suggestions."[5]

The moderns won. Whether the Blisses' starter home or the one they "moved up" to, whether in a southern or northern climate, the house interiors are midcentury conventional: few separate dining rooms, bedrooms separated by placement on the second floor or along a buffering hallway, children with their own bedrooms, and the owners' room with a private bath, at least when the Blisses upgrade. Exteriors are modern: of the 107 designs shown, only about fifteen can really be called traditional, using elements found in colonial or Cape Cod designs.

Some of the few traditional houses even have snout garages, and some of those garages have flat roofs. Beyond the winners and mentions determined by the jury, *Architectural Forum* included an additional forty-eight houses it thought worthy of discussion. These "selected designs" are even more modern than the jury selections (Arne Kartwold submitted a fanciful round house with glass exterior walls; the detached garage is perhaps on a turntable[6]). Among them, only four can be called traditional. Copy describing the traditional houses often points out that aspect, nevertheless assuring readers that the house really is modern. One design is "one of the few submissions in which the architect has succeeded in designing the exterior in one of the traditional styles of design without great sacrifice of efficiency of plan," while another house is "another successful reconciliation of modern requirements of plan with an exterior resembling traditional form."[7]

The House for Tomorrow competition, despite its stated intent, did not generate "small houses." Mr. Bliss was already established in a professional

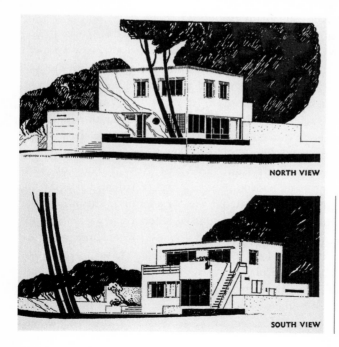

NORTH VIEW

SOUTH VIEW

Stephen Alling won first prize for the smaller Bliss home for a northern climate. The exterior is modern: protruding garage, flat roof, glass brick, and boxy frame. (*Architectural Forum*, April 1935, 293.)

career when the couple bought their first house; they have a car and a garage to put it in, and despite having only one child, they were not expected to occupy a two-bedroom house; they were usually given a third room for guests or a study (or the new baby). Their houses were chock-full of G.E. appliances, as per the competition requirements. A decade later, their houses are even bigger, making room for the second child, the maid, and the additional car, and the houses still have a fourth (or even fifth) extra bedroom for guests or a study. As for exterior design, the *Forum* expected the Blisses to embrace modern style. When describing the few traditionally styled houses, the editors often assured readers that the conventional exterior wrapped around a completely modern house. Conversely, the *Forum* never felt the need to assure that despite a modern exterior, a home was warm and comfortable. When announcing the winners, the *Forum* heralded an architectural break from the past.

> 1935-Another great war has come and gone. In its wake have come the consequent spiritual readjustment and depression. A new modern movement is under way. Wright in Taliesin is now an authentic prophet. Gropius, Le Corbusier, Mendelsohn, Mies van der Rohe, to name but a few, are the disciples each preaching a different interpretation of the same gospel. The following pages show the trend of small house design today in America.[8]

Jurors rewarded the new, modern movement. Old houses reflected a sensibility that had not been "spiritually readjusted."

Six years later, in April 1941, *Architectural Forum* used its pages to feature eighty-one small houses. These choices did not arise from a competition; rather, the editors selected them as examples of good "new" houses. All were built homes, recently constructed. It was to be the first of a semi-annual search for the best small houses in America. Their timing was right: the Depression had abated, and the war had not yet begun for Americans. Without the parameters of a competition's rules, the house sizes varied, as did their locations, the *Forum* dividing them among five regions: West Coast, Southwest, South, Midwest, and East Coast. Three had only one bedroom, while another had no bedrooms at all, asking residents to use a communal sleeping porch (copy indicated it was for a family). This house may have been a weekend or vacation home; a few others clearly were. Despite *Architectural Forum*'s declaration, not all the houses were small; a significant number had a bedroom for a live-in maid, or even two.

Although a few houses display some oddities (one house had no hallways at all, the bathroom sandwiched between the one bedroom and the kitchen, accessible to both rooms), the floor plans rely on familiar conventions: bedrooms mostly located on the second floor, if there was one, or through a hallway; separate dining rooms were rarer than dining ells/ alcoves or living-dining spaces (when a dining room was separate, the copy emphasized that); attached garages; and designated laundry facilities. The smaller the house, the more likely there would be no separate dining room or no entry hallway.

Many houses relied on vernacular styles, especially on the East Coast, where Cape Cod and colonial styles dominated. Those houses had dormer windows, multi-paned glass, shutters, and classical pediments above doors and windows. West Coast houses displayed the most modern features, while southwestern houses tended to be one-story ranches. Some houses combined stylistic elements. *Architectural Forum* approved of the mix.

> In examining this group both old and new tendencies in design are apparent. The fundamental cleavage between period and modern design remains—but the gap is growing perceptibly smaller. It is not news that "modernistic" has been giving way to something closer to the popular conception of the home—but it can now be seen that the period house has also been changing. It no longer relies so heavily on the tricks of eclecticism. Replacing the sagging roof lines, imitation half-timber and "correct" detail is a return to the traditional concern with contemporary problems of building. Between the plans of many period and modern houses in this issue there is little choice, and almost the same can be said for the more thoughtfully designed exteriors.[9]

Modern houses looked modern, with flat or sometimes shed roofs, corner windows, window walls, glass block, and high strip windows.

But the many Cape Cods relied on an open floor plan and dining ells; if they did not have window walls, they had picture windows, and if sliding glass doors were not included, French doors might lead to a backyard terrace. Traditional styles might nevertheless have corner windows. The garage was rarely a snout, but often attached, front-facing, and accessible directly into the house. Harris Armstrong designed a large house with room for two live-in maids but eliminated a separate dining room. The *Forum* noticed this omission: "The trend toward combined living and dining rooms has come a long way when it is considered preferable, in a house of this size, to replace the dining room with a study."[10]

Contrasting the 1935 *Architectural Forum*/G.E. competition with the eighty-one houses selected in 1941 underscores the difference between juror preferences in an ideas competition and what was built, as the latter had to have a buyer who approved the house plan. Choosing from over 2,000 designs gave the House of Tomorrow jurors plenty of latitude, in 1934, to favor what they considered the best designs. They overwhelmingly

Two admired houses in the *Architectural Forum* collection of eighty-one new houses. A "contemporary colonial" has a U-shaped kitchen, a dining ell, a front entrance open to the living space, shuttered windows, an attached garage to the side, and plenty of closets. On the next page, a modern house combines living and dining, the two-car garage protrudes from the front façade, the entrance is deep into the house footprint, and the design uses corner windows, strip windows, and glass brick. ("81 New Houses," *Architectural Forum*, April 1941, 137–138.)

THREE BEDROOMS, TWO BATHS, MAID'S ROOM AND BATH, RECREATION ROOM

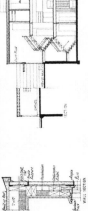

TWO BEDROOMS, ONE BATH, STUDY-GUEST ROOM, LAVATORY, ATTACHED GARAGE

OXFORD, OHIO. POTTER, TYLER & MARTIN, ARCHITECTS, A.I.A.

The influence of early dwelling types of Ohio and upper New York is visible in the small second-floor windows which fit into a narrow horizontal band on the front elevation. The effect is confined to the front, however, as the other exterior view is a display of contemporary Colonial in all of its complexity. The plan is excellent: compact, economically arranged, with adequate rooms and good closets. Cost: $8,964. Cubage: 31,865.

CONSTRUCTION OUTLINE

STRUCTURE: Exterior walls—cypress siding, waterproof paper, yellow pine sheathing; inside—lath, plaster with sand plaster. Floor construction—yellow pine sub-floor, oak finish and yellow pine finish.
ROOF: Covered with red cedar shingles.
INSULATION: Rock-Balsam wool, West Corrosion Co. Weatherstripping—Chamberlin Metal Weatherstrip Co.
WINDOWS: Double-hung and storm sash, Glass—single strength, quality B, Libbey-Owens-Ford Glass Co.
HARDWARE: Lockwood Hardware Mfg. Co.
FLOOR COVERINGS: Kitchen and bathrooms—linoleum, Armstrong Cork Co.
ELECTRICAL INSTALLATION: Wiring system—3-wire. Switches—Bryant Electric Co.
KITCHEN EQUIPMENT: Range, refrigerator, dishwasher and garbage disposal unit—Hot Point, Edison-General Electric Appliances, Inc. Cabinets—steel, Sears-Roebuck.
BATHROOM EQUIPMENT: By American Radiator-Standard Sanitary Corp. Cabinets—Miami Cabinet Div., Philip Carey Co.
PLUMBING: Water piping—copper tubing. Water softener—Permutit Co.
HEATING: Forced warm air system, Rudy Furnace Co. Grilles—Tuttle & Bailey, Inc. Thermostat—Minneapolis-Honeywell Regulator Co. Water heater—Edison-General Electric Appliances, Inc. Fan—Victor Electric Products, Inc.

rewarded modern-style houses, presumably discarding what must have been hundreds of traditional houses. Six years later, however, when the publication chose the best from already built houses, it presented a mix of modern and traditional.

Pencil Points/Progressive Architecture magazine sponsored and co-sponsored a few ideas competitions throughout the Depression. In 1930, it held a competition for an eight-room residence; four years later, it partnered with the Flat Glass Industry for another house competition. Walter J. Thies won first prize for a concrete house in a *Pencil Points* competition in 1936; as was shown earlier, his winning design for the Prize Homes competition appears to have borrowed heavily from that 1936 submission.

Joining the Pittsburgh Plate Glass Company and Pittsburgh Corning Corporation, *Pencil Points* called for submissions in December 1944 for a small house competition. The Pittsburgh competition, as it is known, announced winners in May 1945. In stipulating the rules to the Pittsburgh competition, *Pencil Points* acknowledged "this is an educational competition, and none of the houses are to be actually built," a caveat that might have influenced the designs. The competition had only one theoretical family to accommodate: G. I. Joe, returned from the war, Mrs. Joe, and their ten-year-old boy and six-year-old girl, comparable to the Prize Homes problem two. Also, in line with the Prize Homes problem two, *Pencil Points* limited the square footage to 1,400 (excluding garage and basement). Joe, in his early thirties, had just returned to his prewar job with a promotion in the wings; he's an average man, constrained by a budget. His house should not only be affordable to buy but also require low-cost maintenance. Mrs. Joe, who has no servants, needs an easily maintained home so she can "have more time to devote to her children from whom she had to be separated during the war." Joe wanted modern amenities, a house full of light, and up-to-date building materials, but he and Mrs. Joe did not wish their house to be conspicuously different.[11] This latter condition was a warning; the house should not be so modern as to stand out in the neighborhood.[12] Some Pittsburgh entries came from those who also entered the Prize Homes competition: I. M. Pei, Ralph Rapson, Leon Hyzen, Oliver Lundquist, Elmer Babb, and C. H. Chau.

While *Prize Homes* includes thirty-one houses in the problem two category, *Pencil Points* awarded four winners, with an additional seven special mentions; another eighteen additional designs earned mentions. Twenty-nine Pittsburgh designs can be compared to thirty-one *Prize Homes* choices. All four Pittsburgh winners, five of the seven special mentions, and twelve of the eighteen mentions contain only one floor. As two-story houses easily solve the problem of bedroom and bathroom privacy—by locating most if not all those rooms exclusively on the second floor—Pittsburgh designers had to address the problem of privacy in a single-story house. As in *Prize Homes* houses, placing private rooms in a separate wing could do the trick; absent a separate wing, clustering bedrooms around a separate corridor achieved the same privacy. Pittsburgh architects largely adhered to this privacy norm. Fletcher and Fletcher's first-place winner creates two parallel units, one with living, dining, and play space, and the other with bedrooms; the two units are connected by service rooms of kitchen, utility, and baths. But other designs wrestle with the problem unsuccessfully. Six houses allow bedroom access directly from public rooms; two of those are even the owners' bedrooms. The houses accommodate separate bedrooms for children, adhering to the norm that same-sex children should not share rooms; designers who specify rooms, in designs where one child's bedroom is closer to the parents than the other, place daughters closer than their brothers, by a seven-to-three margin. Five of the houses appear to use a movable partition to separate the children's bedrooms, rather than a fixed wall. Copy accompanying one such house, by Stuart Perkins, commends the "flexible two-in-one treatment," but while that arrangement might suit a ten-year-old boy and six-year-old girl, a few years later, those older children—and their parents—might well wish for a more substantial barrier.

Few houses have owners' bathrooms, in keeping with the insistence that the house be modest and affordable. Pittsburgh house designs maintained

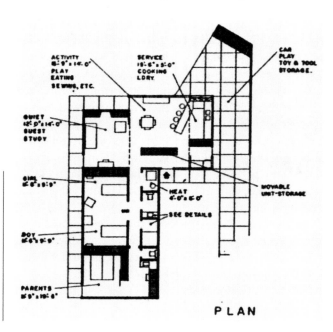

Stuart Perkins was one of five winners or notables in the *Pencil Points* Pittsburgh competition to use a flexible partition between the children's bedrooms. (*Progressive Architecture*, May 1945, 33.)

PLAN

a great deal of open space in the public areas, as well. A third of the houses use a dining ell, while the rest combine living and dining into one space. Carports are not unusual, but then, many of the houses were intended for mild climates, in California, the South, or the Southwest.[13]

Later that year, in October, *Pencil Points/Progressive Architecture* sponsored a second, similar competition, in this case a "realistic house for a family in Georgia." Winners of this "purely educational effort" were announced in April 1946.[14] As in the earlier competition, the hypothetical family was a married couple but this time with younger children: five-year-old boy and two-year-old girl. It would need to be affordable, have plenty of storage in the form of an attic or basement, and be suitable to the Georgia climate (the call for submissions helpfully included average temperatures, rainfall, and sunshine for the region). Unlike the 1,400 square footage of the Prize Homes or Pittsburgh competitions, the Georgia houses needed to be even smaller, no more than 1,350 square feet. If an open or screened porch were added (a feature that would get significant use in the Georgia climate), half of that square footage would contribute to the total. Though held at virtually the same time as the Prize Homes competition, with the announcement publicized in October 1945 and the winners announced in April the following year, there is little known overlap between Georgia submitters and Prize Homes entrants. Prize Homes winner J. Floyd Yewell earned a mention, as did I. M. Pei.

The Georgia competition problem indicated that houses must be suitable for an "established residential section of a still growing city." This criterion pointed directly toward the need for a house to sit comfortably alongside its neighbors.

> The clients for whom you are to design the house are average people who have been looking forward for a long time to having their own home. They have been studying the pages of current magazines and are sympathetically aware of the contemporary trend in design, especially in regard to its greater promise of comfort, convenience, and freedom from a good deal of household drudgery. They definitely do not wish conformity with any traditional "style." At the same time they are desirous that the house they build shall take its place gracefully among its older neighbors. They have an idea that a good architect can give them something that is thoroughly modern and thoroughly appropriate to the region, not at all stodgy and imitative, yet so well proportioned and pleasant of aspect that it will excite general admiration rather than amazement.[15]

For both the Pittsburgh and Georgia competitions, the message rang clear: give us a modern house, advised the jurors, but not too modern, not terribly unusual, and nothing that would stick out in the neighborhoods where these families would live.

Like the Pittsburgh competition, jurors for the Georgia competition chose four winners, from among 568 entries, granting a special mention for a Georgia-based architect and twenty-four additional mentions. Jurors expressed disappointment in the submissions.

> Practically all entries leaned toward complicated plans and extensions which would be wasteful of capital costs as well as undesirable from the point of view of family life, or at least not productive of results commensurate with the investment. . . . [S]ome jurors regretted the scarcity of good two-story plans. . . . There was disappointment over the relatively small number of entries that made use of sloping roofs, since in Georgia the sloping roof is not only conventional and acceptable, but also of great utility for purposes of insulation.[16]

Only three of the twenty-nine houses had two stories, leaving twenty-six designers to consider how to maintain bedroom and bathroom privacy in a small home. Hugh Stubbins's first-place winner, a U-shaped house around a front terrace, created a bedroom wing quite separate from the house's public areas, but it accommodates the "occ guest" through a partition in the living room. A window wall separates the dining room from the street view; a low wall screens the house from passersby. David Kuechle's design warranted a mention, but even the copy notes a particular problem: the owners' bedroom opens directly onto the living room. He found space for two bathrooms, one a Jack-and-Jill between the children's bedrooms and other

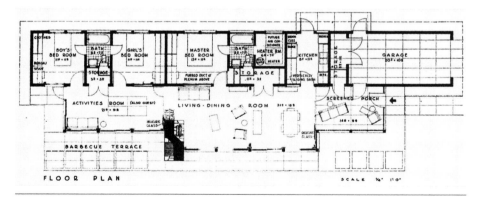

Without a bedroom corridor, David Kuechle's plan puts children's bedrooms open to an activity ("also guest") room, while the owner's bedroom opens onto the living-dining area. He brings in a second bathroom, but both are accessible only through the bedrooms. (*Progressive Architecture*, April 1946, 82.)

accessible through the owners' bedroom. This arrangement, however, is highly unusual; conventional privacy considerations disfavor a plan where guests must go into bedrooms to use the lavatory.

Despite competition advice that architects should "keep in mind not only the present needs of the family but its future needs as the children grow up," twelve Georgia designers separated the children's bedrooms through a flexible partition when those children might grow to want more privacy.[17] One design also makes a wall between the owners' bedroom and living space movable although adult couples may not have wanted to use their bedroom for entertaining. Georgia houses take more care than Pittsburgh houses to separate dining from living. Seven houses have separate dining rooms, while another twelve have dining ells. Only ten, then, completely integrate dining and living.

Most Georgia designs have window walls and snout garages. About half have flat or low-sloped roofs, and six of the conventionally roofed homes also have a flat-roofed garage. Strip and corner windows are common. William Wilner won the special prize for a Georgia architect, and his house is more conventional: two-story, gable roof, attached garage flush with the front door, conventional windows, and separate dining room. Each design includes brief commentary from the jury, on the house's "good points" but also what they perceived as the design's shortcomings, and the commentary on Wilner's arrangement is telling: "This solution rated high during the discussion of the jury because it seems economical and realistic in terms of popular acceptance."[18] It was the only allusion to public taste.

Georgia jurors confronted the problem of snout garages compromising the main entrance of the home.

> There was general agreement that garages should not be at the back of the house or to the rear of the lot because of the wastage of land area for driveways. There was an inclination to regard the garage, or other provisions for parking the car as the most frequently used entrance to the house; in effect, its main entrance. For that reason, there was much doubt whether the open car shelter close to the street is really an acceptable solution, since the car shelter would normally attract a good deal of clutter, exposure to which is undesirable. This consideration was taken into account in rating entries which required one to pass through the car shelter or along its open side in order to enter the house. There was some criticism of garages (and particularly open carports) that stood detached in front of the house, fully exposed to the street. The jury felt that garages look bad enough in their unusual rear location and that if it became general practice to place similar detached structures in the front, the appearance of the streets would be greatly damaged.[19]

There is a "damned if you do, damned if you don't" sensibility here. Small lots cannot have rear garages if they want to have reasonably sized houses and/or yards, but the front-facing, snout garage creates a new set of aesthetic problems.

Monthly periodical *Arts & Architecture* showcased the most up to date in architecture, but it did not stop there. Among the ads and articles found in any architectural publication—on building materials, fixtures, drafting tools, features on specific buildings and houses, architect profiles—*Arts & Architecture* included articles focusing on jewelry, sculpture, film, literature, visual arts, and even social issues. The publication sponsored two small house design competitions close to the Prize Homes competition. In April 1943, "Designs for Post-War Living" asked for a house for a modern worker, his wife, one child, and "perhaps a mother-in-law," a concession to multi-generational living that the Prize Homes competition did not allow. This American worker will "not only accept but demand simple, direct, and honest efficiency in the material aspects of the means by which he lives."[20] Competition rules provided no guidance as to minimum or maximum square footage, number of rooms, lot size, or climate.[21] Architects clearly wanted more direction, for a month later, the editor defended the original call, asking readers: "Please don't accuse us of being vague or unrealistic."[22] Eero Saarinen and Oliver Lundquist (the latter's non-winning submission is included in the *Prize Homes* book) earned first prize with a co-designed three-bedroom house built from preassembled parts. A shared second prize for I. M. Pei and E. H. Duhart (the former also submitted to Prize Homes), and a third-place award to Raphael Soriano rewarded equally modern designs.[23] The five honorable mentions show the same design elements: flat or shed roofs, window walls, open plan, and small bedrooms with more space for common areas. Most are one story. Several among the eight are shown in community with other houses; *Arts & Architecture* thought postwar American workers wanted to share garages and playgrounds with their neighbors rather than insist on private amenities.[24] The magazine featured two more submissions that did not win but that the publication thought interesting enough to bring to their readers. Ralph Rapson and David Runnells created a fabric house; the publication conceded "this shelter is an insulated tent" but admired its flexibility. Using the barrel and the silo as inspiration, Theodore Luderowski designed a house comprised of cylindrical units; more units could be added after original construction.[25]

A year later, in 1944, *Arts & Architecture* promoted a "Small Post-War Home Design" competition, cosponsored with the U.S. Plywood Association. The program offered more direction than that of the previous year, asking for a prefabricated plywood house for "the average American family—a man, his wife and perhaps one or two children," with a suggested price of $5,000 to $6,000. Like the year before, first, second, and third prizes were awarded, with five honorable mentions, and the magazine also featured three more "distinctive and modern" houses. First-place winner Charles Wiley created a three-bedroom, one-bathroom house with attached garage. Dining and cooking areas are clustered, while living space is divided between quiet activities (visitors, music, and books) and noisier activities, "the place where the family can make a mess and leave it!" Its dissimilarity with *Prize Homes* houses is the lack of a bedroom corridor; the bedrooms are accessed directly from the common areas, and even the bathroom is in the middle core rather than tucked away.[26]

Russell Amdal designed the second-place winner, a two-bedroom, one-bath residence. His house preserves bedroom privacy, by creating access through a hallway, but also compromises it: the owners' bedroom is accessed through a hallway door, but the wall between that bedroom and the living space is only a partition, not a permanent wall. The third-place winning design, by Eduardo Catalano, locates the two bedrooms and one bathroom on one side of the house; the public areas combine living and dining but separate the kitchen and create a "hobby" room off the kitchen.[27] All three houses have one floor, flat roofs, and window walls.

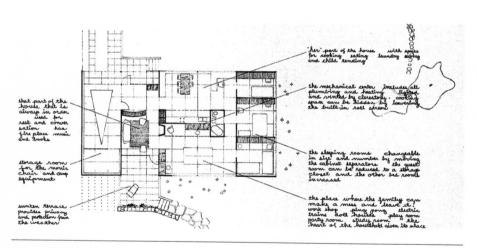

Charles Wiley's first-place winner in the *Arts & Architecture* competition for "Small Post-War Home Design." Wiley separated the living room from a family room. Rather than combing living and dining space, he combines laundry, kitchen, and dining (it is "her" part of the house). In the center is the mechanical and plumbing core, and the bathroom is located there. Bedrooms open directly into common rooms. (*Arts & Architecture*, February 1945, 32.)

Arts & Architecture sponsored the Case Study Houses, announcing the project in January 1945.[28] While not a competition—participating architects were chosen by the editor, and four of the first eight architects selected were either associate editors or on the editorial advisory board—the program nevertheless provides a good opportunity for comparison. The Case Study program has been widely reviewed by architectural historians and is credited with being the best of midcentury modern style. Like *Prize Homes* houses, Case Study houses were meant to be built, *Arts & Architecture* going so far as to purchase a few acres in Los Angeles to complete the project.

> The house must be capable of duplication and in no sense be an individual "performance." All eight houses will be opened to the public for a period of from six to eight weeks and thereafter an attempt will be made to secure and report upon tenancy studies to see how successfully the job has been done. Each house will be completely furnished under a working arrangement between the architect, the designer and the furniture manufacturer, either to the architect's specifications or under his supervision. This, then, is an attempt to find out on the most practical basis known to us, the facts (and we hope the figures) which will be available to the general public when it is once more possible to build houses.[29]

Lot sizes and square footage were left unspecified, and it appears that the architects could themselves determine the family problem to be accommodated; those families included married couples with one, two, or three children, as well as a married couple without children and another house for a lone occupant. Most of the architects were based in California (the publication had until only a few years earlier been *California Arts & Architecture*), and because the land purchased was in Los Angeles, the house needed to conform only to the California climate.

Between February 1945 and March 1946, *Arts & Architecture* featured thirteen designs each month, and they are analyzed here. Square footage is not always available, but when it is, the houses are larger than even the largest cap on a *Prize Homes* house. One exception—and *Arts and Architecture* makes note of the small size—is a J. R. Davidson house of only 1,250 square feet, designed for a couple with one child. The other houses are roomy, with guest rooms, plenty of bathrooms, open living, and play areas. Some have pools or water play areas on the grounds. Garages are more likely to be open shelters than enclosed, certainly due to the friendly California weather. Other than the two designs by Richard Neutra, which placed a separate dining room in the house, all have dining ells or living-dining spaces. Many include work or hobby spaces; the occupants are artistically minded and will want to pursue photography or other arts. None have basements, so space for hobbies or laundry or children's play is exclusively aboveground. Only Case Study No. 1, by Davidson, has two floors, and even that design makes the partial second floor home to a guest room and bath, with access to an upper-level terrace. (Although this discussion does not incorporate the houses as built, architects could change houses considerably. Between drawing board and execution, Davidson's design lost the second floor.[30]) Like *Prize Homes* houses, bedrooms and bathrooms (other than a guest lavatory) are mostly separated from the public spaces of the house, using hallways.

Case Study houses go well beyond even the most modern *Prize Homes* house features. Since the houses are meant to be situated together, complementing each other in the "neighborhood," there is little worry about whether a house will "fit in" with its companions. Some designers note which views will take in the sea and which will overlook the mountains; this is a far cry from the narrow, rectangular lots found in the typical postwar suburb, where the typical view is that of one's next-door neighbor and her laundry. Other than one shed-roof design by Neutra, all houses have flat roofs, and all have window walls. The houses incorporate outdoor living in all the designs, using glass walls to break the divide between indoors and out. Integration with the landscape resulted in Charles Eames's house design jutting from a small hillside, most of the house supported by columns.[31]

Ralph Rapson's innovative design deserves special attention. Case Study No. 4, called the Greenbelt house, divides a squarish house into three distinct segments. The top third is an owners' suite, two more bedrooms, and a bathroom. Except for the bathroom, the bedroom walls are partitions, open to the middle third, a common space. This arrangement is unusual in that it does not have the hallway barrier between public and private space, let alone conventional walls and doors. The common space displays a grand piano and a card table, indicating the area is for recreational family activities. The bottom third of the house is the "food-living" area: kitchen, dining, and living, and the latter two spaces are open to each other but can be divided by a partition. The middle third is the "greenbelt," a glass-roofed garden. Sidewalks traversing the greenbelt connect the top and bottom thirds; there are no walls between the bedroom-side recreation area and the living-side dining and living rooms. With no lavatory in the food-living area, residents and guests use those sidewalks to get to the bedroom side. Rapson is generous in using human figures in his drawings, and they are charming ones. Loopy and loose and not strictly proportional (children and adults are the same size), the people depict how inhabitants will live in this modern house. In one sketch, a woman bends over a flower garden outside, while nearby, a man sunbathes on his stomach, reading a book. In another, a man is seen coming or going in his helicopter (the car sits to the side of the house, unused); he waves to a woman hanging or taking down laundry. Another view depicts a woman again administering to her laundry. (Rapson's faith in the future of commuter travel far outstripped his expectation of the household dryer.[32]) The uncredited cover of the September *Arts & Architecture* shows an illustration of the greenbelt; a woman tends the garden while a child tricycles around the perimeter. Within the pages, a lingerie-clad figure is poised before an open drawer in the owners' bedroom. From the kitchen, a woman watches a diapered baby on the sidewalk of the greenbelt.[33]

Contrast the Greenbelt house with the one Rapson and his partner, John Van der Meulen, submitted to the Prize Homes competition for problem one. It did not win, nor merit inclusion in the *Prize Homes* book, but *Tribune* reporter Edward Barry featured it as "remarkable" and appealing "strongly to persons who are sympathetic toward contemporary architecture." Again, the illustrations show residents using the house: In one elevation, a man rakes his yard with his car nearby, the same jalopy in the Greenbelt house illustrations. A woman looks out from the second-floor balcony. In a second depiction, the same woman (the dress is the same) stands at the service counter dividing kitchen from dining room. The house is certainly a modern one; it is a split-level house, and it has extensive window walls, a low-pitched roof, and a front-facing snout garage. The dining room is an ell. Bedrooms and the single bathroom are on the upper floor; the balcony opens out from the owners' bedroom. Barry's article added that Rapson was participating in "an important west coast house program."[34] Rapson and Van der Meulen's house, however, does not in any way come close to the remarkably innovative Greenbelt house. When it came to *Arts & Architecture*, Rapson needed only please the editor; for the Prize Homes competition, a house would need to appeal to a broader constituency.

If Rapson's house is the most unusual, other Case Study plans also stand out. The footprint of Spaulding's 2,000-square-foot house is V-shaped.[35] Wurster's house falls along Rapson's model, with three bedrooms and two baths in one third of the house, and the public rooms on the other side of the house, separated by a covered "porch."[36] Abell's 1,800-square-foot design is a "series of interrelated indoor and outdoor spaces," a plan that adheres to the Case Study requirement that a house be duplicable only if built in accommodating climates.[37] In creating a house for a single occupant, Saarinen places the bedroom directly next to the living room, with a glass wall between, yet a study is windowless. Case Study houses were not meant for average, midwestern middle-class home buyers. They were for Californians seeking the most modern and unique. Saarinen's house was built for the editor of *Arts & Architecture*. Eames's house—with a detached workspace—was

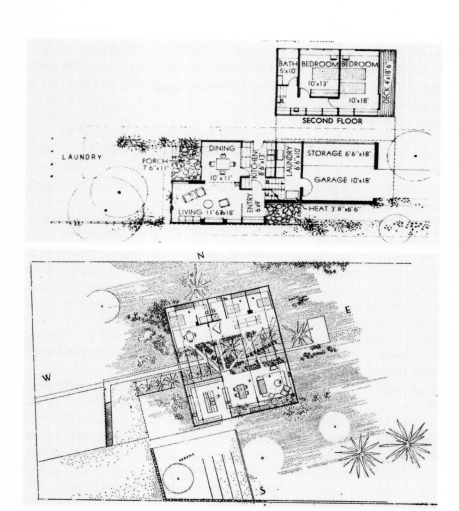

Compare Rapson's *Arts & Architecture* Case Study house (bottom) with the co-submission with John Van der Meulen for the Prize Homes competition (top). The Prize Homes design has a dining ell and locates bedrooms and bath on the second floor. The Greenbelt house combines living and dining; bedrooms and bathrooms open to common space. (*Arts & Architecture*, February 1945, 33; Edward Barry, "A Three Level Home," *Chicago Tribune*, March 17, 1946, C9.)

for "a married couple both occupied professionally" in the arts: for Charles and Ray Eames.[38]

By 1950, the builder subdivision was in full swing, and the architectural profession acknowledged this in one of the era's last small house design competitions. In September 1950, *Architectural Forum*, joined by the National Association of Home Builders (NAHB) and a few other sponsors, announced a competition "To improve the design of builders' houses and to interest more architects in builders' houses." The *Forum* itself called this the "greatest design competition in the history of housebuilding."[39] If the future of house building was going to be primarily the builders' subdivision, with street after street of similar, cost-efficient houses, then architects needed to get on board and "study the home-builder's problem for their mutual benefit and the benefit of the home-buying public." The competition did not describe a particular family but listed a particularly strict set of requirements: the house had to adhere to FHA and VA requirements, rely on materials already commercially available, forgo a basement, and have three bedrooms, and it had to do all of this in 1,000 square feet.[40] No other small house competition had ever required such a tiny footprint. Without a basement, the house's laundry, storage, and recreation spaces could not be shunted into "free" areas, and utilities located on the first floor would have to eat into square footage. Further, the house had to sell for $10,000 or less. Prizes would go to national winners but also to the winners of the seven regional categories. No house had two floors; perhaps this was a condition unmentioned in the ad but specified in the competition program. This was a competition that truly asked for a house design within the financial reach of millions of Americans.

Despite the restrictions, the competition drew 2,727 submissions, a number the *Forum* called "record-breaking." Prize money was substantial, and since architects could submit and win in multiple categories, the potential for financial reward was significant. Winners were announced in the March 1951 issue of *Architectural Forum*.[41] An article accompanying the winners' announcement was especially detailed, as was the jury report, which quoted the five architects and two builders, who served as jurors, at length. Two architect jurors—L. Morgan Yost and Philip Will—practiced in Chicago, the former submitting to the Prize Homes competition.

Editors at the *Forum* had great hopes that the competition would marry the size and financial constraints of the builder to the imagination of the architect.

> But the competition's real significance is best measured . . . by the simple fact that such a competition was sponsored by the nation's home builders (who last year recognized for the first time that the design of their product needed professional attention) and that the competition problem was grasped so enthusiastically by the architects (who until recently felt that the small house for the merchant builder was beneath their dignity). Thus the competition's success, however measured, is an important milestone along the road to widespread architect-builder collaboration and better house design for the average American family.[42]

The cozy relationship between architects and builders went further when, in January 1951, the NAHB announced the winners and displayed their designs at their Chicago convention, which drew 6,000 builders.[43]

Jurors expressed disappointment in the overall pool, saying it was "good—but not excellent."[44] They were sorry to find, once anonymity had been lifted, few big names among the applicants. Four first prizes, nine honorable mentions, and twenty-eight regional prizes were awarded. Some duplication occurred, so twenty-nine designs can be analyzed. Comparisons to Prize Homes problem two are limited; the number of bedrooms is the same, but the Prize Homes competition permitted even the two-bedroom house to have 1,100 square feet plus a basement. Nevertheless, the jury's choices indicate how, given the postwar housing shortage and the rise of builders' subdivisions, architects sought to bring their designs in line with market forces.

Bruce Walker won first place with a design that both adheres to and breaks some conventions. Bedrooms and the one bathroom sat on one side of the house, buffered by hallways. One elevation shows a woman hanging laundry but does not show the placement of her washing machine. The bedroom wing sits opposite a side carport, with the main entrance recessed

alternate elevation 1

alternate elevation 2

alternate elevation 3

Three different rooflines are presented in Bruce Walker's winning design for the 1951 *Architectural Forum* small house competition. (*Architectural Forum*, March 1951, 112, 113.)

in between; one enters a hall and walks past the kitchen to get to the living space. Walker does have an ell in the living room, using it for "conversation" rather than dining; he designates dining near the kitchen in the large living room. Perhaps the most interesting design aspect is that Walker's elevations include three different rooflines: a low-pitched roof, a flat one, and a butterfly.

The main elevation shows the pitched roof, and a photo of a scale model also uses that roof.[45] Ralph Rapson's second-place winner forgoes hallways altogether; the bedrooms and the bathroom open directly into a multipurpose room separate from the living-dining room. Kitchen, bathroom, and utility room form a core, with the living space surrounding them; the kitchen has windows but the other two rooms in the core do not. An unattached carport protrudes in front. The low-pitched roof also has alternating shed roofs, and the carport roof is flat. Clerestory windows bring light into the core.[46]

Third prize went to Wallace Steele, for a house the jury's builders thought had "very considerable selling appeal." Bedrooms, bathroom, and utilities were clustered off a short hallway. One entered the house into a small vestibule. The kitchen, though small, had room for a washer and dryer. Dining was separated from living, though the dining area was marked for not only dining but also work and play. An unattached garage, set back, connected to the house with an overhang; the garage was flat roofed but the house roof had a low pitch. High strip windows, awning windows, and corner windows join the glass walls at the rear of the house.[47] George Matsumoto's fourth-place design minimizes hallways. Bedrooms open to a multipurpose room, while the bathroom is directly across from the U-shaped kitchen. Dining is in an ell, which is unusually positioned; it is around the corner from the kitchen rather than positioned as a room to pass through between living and kitchen. A carport protrudes. If first-place winner Walker showed his main elevation with a pitched roof and more modern rooflines as alternatives, Matsumoto did just the opposite, with a main elevation of a completely flat roof and an alternative with a pitch.[48]

Honorable mentions and regional prizewinners follow similar patterns. There are no separate dining rooms; at best, there is a dining ell, and even that is rare. If most designers place bedrooms and bathrooms along a buffering corridor, a sizable minority put those rooms directly across from a social room, not a living room but a recreation or multipurpose room that is clearly intended for children's play and family activities. Kitchens are quite small, but only a few really open the room to the living space, keeping the kitchen somewhat out of sight, although entrances to that room probably eliminated doors. Limits on square footage made for a predictable trade-off:

designers who wanted to provide living space other than the living room, in the form of a playroom or rec room, had to shrink bedrooms to grab the space; houses with good-sized bedrooms could never include the bonus living space. Every house made generous use of outside areas, often more than one, for dining and recreation. Only two houses managed to squeeze in an extra bathroom. Small bedrooms, which must accommodate beds, dressers, desks, and closets, cannot afford to have low windows that would be blocked by furniture. Liberal use of high strip windows permits furniture up against the walls without obstructing light and air.

All the houses include space for cars but usually in the form of a carport rather than a garage. Many had side entrances. One notable feature: if about half the houses had main entries that went straight into living rooms, another half brought those entering the house into a hallway where the first accessible room was the kitchen. Kitchens did not sit at the back of the house, as in the most traditional room configuration, but at the front. This preserves privacy, as the living spaces' window walls can take that rear spot and face the backyard, but it brings guests in proximity to the smells and clutter of the kitchen.

In a final concession to modern style and the preferences of conservative builders and their conservative clients, designers frequently presented houses with alternative roofs. So many included this that perhaps the competition program asked for it. Main elevations with flat roofs included an alternative, smaller elevation with a low-pitched roof, and the converse was true, as elevations with a pitched roof also displayed a flat one. But a third alternative appears, one unseen in *Prize Homes* houses: the butterfly roof, which inverts the conventionally pitched roof. This option gives the house a more modern style, although it would have construction and materials implications. Among the twenty-eight winners, mentions, and regional award winners, only four included a single roof in their drawings. The rest included one or even two alternatives: eight designers included all three options. Moreover, like a flat roof, a butterfly roof would at best compromise attic storage but most likely eliminate it altogether; residents of a house with no basement, and rarely even an enclosed garage, would want to make use of every storage opportunity they could. Lacking a basement or attic, Alysa Slay and Alan Edelman, current residents of the Coder Taylor two-bedroom house, removed soffits to build kitchen cabinets up to the ceiling and installed a tankless water heater just to increase their storage by inches.[49]

Moderating the extremely modern sensibilities found in architectural publications, popular periodicals also sponsored architectural competitions and featured the winners in their publications, reaching millions of middle-class readers. *House Beautiful* conducted annual small house competitions throughout the Depression and into the 1940s. Rather than holding ideas competitions, the magazine considered only houses that had already been constructed. Chapman's overview of the competition winners and their house features documents the growth of modern style over the years; she argues that over a decade-plus of house competitions, *House Beautiful* accepted more and more modern features in their selections of winners. Despite the contest's title, however, the winners and mentions were not small: the houses were designed for specific clients and built for specific sites, most had maids' quarters and large lots, and the smallest ones tended to be weekend or vacation homes.[50] Entries could contain between five and twelve rooms (a stipulation that did not include bathrooms, pantries, or porches).

A small house competition sponsored in 1938 by the *Ladies' Home Journal* drew 700 submissions. Published floor plans indicate a parents' room and a room each for a boy and a girl; perhaps the program rules mandated that family constellation. The *Ladies' Home Journal*, a far cry from the highbrow discourse of architectural publications, sought a small, affordable house for an average family. A jury, comprised of four architects and a designer, seems to have been pleased with the submissions. Jury chairman Miles Colean commented in *Architectural Forum* on the overall patterns the jury discerned from the submission pool. Only "a small percentage" were one story, in contrast to the overwhelming number of single-story houses chosen in architectural publication competitions and collections. Every one of the nineteen money-earning prizes went to a two-story house, which better addresses the house privacy conundrum. Most designs developed the backyard as an important living space, in contrast to "developers, who still generally cling to the notion that the homeowner prefers the diversion of the street to the privacy and repose of his own garden," an admission that artistic sensibility and commercial interests could conflict. (In this case, the architects were largely correct: Americans were coming to prefer their backyards.) Most entries combined the living and dining spaces, and basements were rare. Despite those two modern trends, jurors expressed surprise at the lack of modern style. "Although the trend in design was perhaps less distinctly modern than in some recent competitions, that trend is emphatic none the less. The jury suspected that references in the program to FHA acceptability may have added to the caution displayed in facing the issue of design and expressed the hope that the influence of government in the housing field would not act to prejudice the development of new forms and new treatments of form."[51] Colean's complaint that the submissions were too conservative echoed Paul Cret, who, as a juror commenting on the 1930

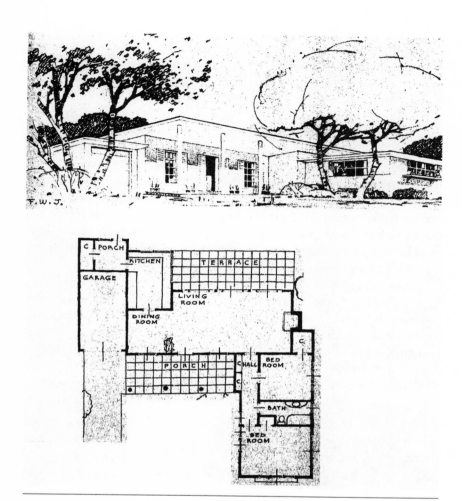

Typical of Paul Williams's blended designs, the "Louisiana" keeps traditional shutters, even around the doorway, but adds "streamlined columns and the wide overhanging flat pitched roof." (Paul R. Williams, *The Small Home of Tomorrow*, Murray & Gee, Hollywood, 1945, reprinted Hennessey + Ingalls, Santa Monica, 2006.)

free, to its customers. Rather than specify family constellations, the rules merely indicated the number of bedrooms: two, three, or four. But within each bedroom category, they also distinguished between contemporary and traditional design. That the competition separated traditional from modern suggests that it considered them to be for two separate audiences. The eighteen winning designs in the 1947 booklet are the first-, second-, and third-place winners for both contemporary and traditional houses in each of the bedroom categories. In a hint that the families dwelling in these houses might be above the middle class, two of the houses noted bedrooms for maids; perhaps this makes sense given Bloomingdale's reputation as an upscale business.

Whether traditional or contemporary, Bloomingdale's houses largely adhered to established patterns. All houses separated bedrooms from living space through placement on a second floor or a bedroom wing, and all two-story houses had at least a lavatory on the first floor, ensuring that visitors need not breach family privacy by ascending the stairs. Two-bedroom houses had one shared bathroom (the exception was the lone two-story house in category one, which had a lavatory on the first floor). All the four-bedroom houses contained owners' suites. Whether a house was of contemporary or traditional style had no bearing on where residents would dine: most houses used dining ells or dining areas. Only three houses had clearly separated dining rooms, two of those modern styled.

In the contemporary category, houses contained the predictable elements. They had flat roofs, were mostly one story, and had corner windows and window walls. Garages protruded. Entrances were sometimes deep into the house, alongside a garage, or at the side. One of the more interesting examples of mixed style is a house by Erling Iverson, who won third prize for a two-bedroom traditional house. Its gable roof is traditional, as are its shuttered, conventional windows. It has a snout garage and a hidden

Bloomingdale's architectural competition awarded third prize in the traditional house category to this two-bedroom by Erling Iverson. The ranch house has shutters and a moderately pitched roof but a protruding garage, with the entrance deep into the house floor plan. The back of the house eliminates traditional right angles, placing the living room diagonal to the rest of the house. (Bloomingdale's, *Prize Winning Designs in Bloomingdale's Architectural Competition*, 1947, 15.)

entrance; one must walk past the protruding garage on one side of a sidewalk and the two bedrooms on the other side to reach the main entrance. The section of the house with the living area has walls that are diagonal to the rest of the house.[61] Take off the shutters and flatten the roof, and it would fit nicely in the contemporary category.

Whatever modern meant, competitions sponsored by architectural publications and juried by architects preferred it and had preferred it for some time. In the 1934 *Pencil Points* Flat Glass–sponsored competition, jurors warned submitters that the hypothetical client would not be receptive to anything too extreme, but they gave awards to modern-style houses (with, of course, large windows); especially notable is the Dukelski and Shilowitz flat-roofed, corner-windowed second-place design, reminiscent of Frank Lloyd Wright design.[62] At least a third of the mentions are flat roofed. Jurors in the Portland Cement–sponsored competition of 1936 complained that some architects thought all one needed for a modern house was to add corner windows; apparently the jurors found this detail insufficient to make a house truly modern.[63] Their winners and mentions were overwhelmingly modern, with flat roofs and corner windows, and some were starkly modern.[64] The *Pencil Points* "Suntile" competition in 1938, for a residence for a doctor who could practice out of "his" [*sic*] home, repeated its preference for modern style.[65]

Prize Homes–winning architect Edward Burch preferred colonial houses and became an expert in that style but, according to his son, submitted a modern-style house because he thought that was what consumers wanted.[66] Burch's assessment was misplaced; enough buyers clearly liked traditional styles that his beloved colonial was a marketable option. But the editors of architectural publications largely ignored conventional styles in favor of not merely modern but starkly modern design, to an extent that even some of their readers found objectionable. In one month alone, three letters to the *Architectural Forum* in February 1946 complained about the publication's dedication to modern style. Walter Dunlap's letter succinctly lays out the problem.

> My policy is to find out the kind of house the customer wants and to build that kind. Your recent survey showed that about 95 per cent of the customers do *not* want modernistic houses [emphasis in original]. Yet your magazine is devoted 100 per cent to just that. It takes but a few minutes to look through your magazine for there is nothing there I want to see. I am fed up with it. Why don't you feature the kind of houses customers want to buy?[67]

Another reader concurred, claiming that in fourteen years of practice, he had never received a request for a country house in a "modern" style.[68]

In contrast with the selections discussed above, whether juried or chosen by editors of architectural publications, people compiling small house plans for catalogs did not need approval from architectural elites. They answered, instead, to banks, government agencies, builders, and, especially, consumers. These conservative voices lowered the tolerance for any extreme house features that would make a house stand out among its neighbors, risk resale, discourage a lending agency, or bring disapproval from an average house buyer.[69]

The Federal Housing Act of 1934 significantly influenced housing policies when it established the Federal Housing Administration (FHA). By regulating and insuring home mortgages, the legislation encouraged speculative building projects, since developers could be confident buyers would be able to get mortgages. The FHA opened opportunities for middle-income and even lower-income buyers with the regulation of mortgages and interest rates; established mortgages with low down payments; showed builders how to use large-scale planning to create housing developments; created a market for architects and builders; and helped standardize house design.[70] In 1938, the agency could insure a mortgage for up to 90 percent of the value of a house, amortized for twenty-five years, at 4 percent interest, and this insurance widened the pool of potential home buyers.[71] The FHA did not itself build houses; rather, it created conditions and incentives for private developers. Entrepreneurs could build outside of FHA guidelines and regulations, but doing so would significantly restrict their pool of potential buyers.

Working with the program also brought some constraints. FHA loan guarantees, for example, would be granted only to houses complying with standard building codes and practices.[72] As for house design, the FHA, in considering a home's purchase value and future resale value, preferred conservative, trusted architectural styles. The agency instructed its assessors to reduce the scores of houses with modern features like asymmetry and flat roofs.[73] Qualifying for an FHA-approved mortgage required a house appraisal by an FHA employee, so the agency had power to enforce its preferences.[74] Nelson and Wright's *Tomorrow's House: How to Plan Your Post-War Home Now*, the 1945 publication by *Architectural Forum* editors that emphatically dismissed any architectural style other than contemporary, conceded FHA rules might keep bankers from approving financing. Most of the "outstanding early modern houses," they admitted, "were built by wealthy men [*sic*] who could pay for their houses without applying for a mortgage." The authors urged people interested in modern design to either persuade their mortgage brokers or shop around for sympathetic ones.[75]

If the FHA helped moderate-income home buyers to enter the housing market, the Veterans Administration went even further. The Servicemen's

Readjustment Act of 1944 passed in June of that year, and a 1945 amendment, came to be known as the G. I. Bill of Rights. Congress wanted veterans to return to their lives they lived before the war: going to college, purchasing farms, starting businesses, and buying houses, but they had been unable to save up capital with which to do those things. The omnibus legislation contained subsidies and payments for college tuition and vocational training, unemployment compensation for those with a slower reentry into wage work, and business and agricultural loans. To spur house buying—which helped veterans and the economy—the federal government would guarantee low-interest mortgage loans, secured with no down payment, a benefit available up to ten years past discharge. In 1950, the Balsams bought their Uebelhack house in Highland Park with that benefit; Burton Balsam had been in the Navy.[76] Like any vet, he could have qualified for a loan guarantee up to $4,000, amortized at up to twenty-five years.[77] Even though substantial barriers prevented African Americans and women from accessing the benefit, the number of eligible veterans ran into the millions.

The combination of FHA mandates, G. I. Bill policies, and conservative banks that issued mortgages under the federal government's direction influenced house design. Houses had to be small and affordable; Friedman notes that "architects in the field were forced to redirect their practices away from ornate, decorative, and stylish dream houses; post war housing required functional, practical and economical solutions which were appropriate to family homes."[78] Editors of *Architectural Forum* in 1941 promoted a style that bridged the traditional and the modern: "the modern house sufficiently camouflaged to keep lending agencies from getting nervous."[79] The G. I. Bill of Rights set out specific guidelines: qualifying mortgages would be given to houses costing between $6,000 and $8,000, ranging between 800 and 1,000 square feet. In skipping a mortgage and paying for a house outright, a wealthy client could bypass restrictions on cost, size, and style. Certainly, the average postwar home buyer could not. Purveyors of house catalogs catering to the latter audience made their selections accordingly.

A 1950 RKO/Pathe short film, bearing the seal of the United States of America War Office, depicts the life of a White veteran union worker and his family in Detroit. In a flashback scene, he and his wife check their bankbook to determine whether they can afford a house (they can). He flips through a house plan catalog, the 1946 *APS Home Plans* book.[80]

Americans had long relied on catalogs for housing options. As a distinctive home designed by an architect was out of financial reach for all but the very affluent, even well-to-do homeowners relied on the house catalog, and certainly the middle class did. Builders rarely developed a house, or houses, on spec prior to FHA loan guarantees in the 1930s. A buyer who wanted a

Selecting designs from house plan catalogs was how many, if not most, Americans purchased new-built homes in the early half of the twentieth century. A 1950 short film, sponsored by the United States War Office, depicts a couple perusing the APS catalog shown on page 55. (Title unknown; RKO/Pathe.)

new home chose a neighborhood and lot, selected a house plan, and found a builder to execute the design. Today, the Sears, Roebuck house plan books are well known, but in the early half of the twentieth century, Montgomery Ward had a thriving house catalog business, too, as did Aladdin homes; all three sold their designs with or without the corresponding house-building kits. Reiff's history of the catalog industry shows that the business thrived for decades, waning only with the rise of the tract or builder's home, when developers could build houses on spec with relatively little risk.

American Builder used the title of its 1939 catalog, *Buyer-Approved Homes of Known Cost*, to assure buyers that they would not be duped into paying extra. The company could promise the houses were practical and affordable because the catalog included only built homes, including photographs and floor plans.[81] A good number of the built houses are in the Chicago suburbs; at least one was built by Irvin Blietz, Prize Homes juror. Decrying the "strange and radical" designs that are "sensational and upsetting," the editor observed that if one reviewed all the Depression-era house foreclosures, one noticed "the house of conventional design was sold quickly and at a fair price while the abortive architecture was a drug [*sic*] on the market; no one wanted them at any price."[82] Emphasis is on a traditional façade. Among the eighty-seven single-family houses, colonials and Cape Cods dominate, with an occasional French or English house, and sometimes the colonials have an adjective modifying them, such as New Orleans

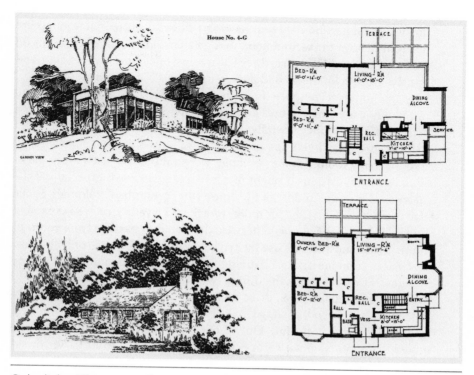

Only slight differences in floor plan (placement of stairway and closets) separate models 4-A and 4-G in Glaser's *Designs for 60 Small Homes*. Despite the similarity, the houses earn the labels "English Cotswold" and "Modern." (Samuel Glaser, *Designs for 60 Small Homes* [New York: Coward-McCann, 1939].)

Small Homes Prepared by a National Association of Architects implored people desiring a new home to hire an architect, even if purchasing the plans in the book.[89] Despite promoting the profession, none of the house designs is credited to any named architect, though the illustrations and floor plans clearly reflect that they were drawn by different people. The book shows one house per page: a large sketch elevation (or, in two cases, a photograph of a built home), the floor plan of the first and second floors (every house has two stories), descriptive copy, and usually one additional sketch, most often an exterior or interior detail like a doorway or fireplace. Interested readers could write to the bureau, either to purchase plans or make inquiries. Purchased plans could be returned, for a small fee, if buyers changed their minds after examining them.

The bureau kept to its small house commitment. Fourteen houses have only two bedrooms, while all the rest have three. Eight houses have a small additional room on the second floor, labeled seven times a sewing room, and once a study.[90] Only seven houses have separate bathrooms for the owners' suite, and only four have first-floor lavatories.[91] Bedrooms are nearly always on the second floor, though a few houses have bedrooms on the first. Only one house has three bathrooms: one in the owners' suite and one shared bath on the second floor, plus a first-floor lavatory.[92]

Many houses have space usage that defied the usual economies found in small houses. Small houses had long eschewed the entry hall, but these architects did not: they liberally used halls, vestibules, and foyers to buffer the entry from the living spaces. In only five houses did one enter directly into the living room.[93] Some vestibules were quite small, just a token partition, but many designs brought one into a large hallway, especially if the stairway was in the middle of the house (the "center hall" colonial). Space that could have been used for more storage, or a lavatory, or even expanded living or dining space, was otherwise dedicated to passage from room to room. While most houses use the typical dining ell or alcove, only three go so far as to combine living and dining space into a single room.[94] Thirty-one designs entirely separate the dining rooms from the living space (mostly using a buffering hallway). Plans do not usually make room for cars; only fifteen houses attach the garage to the house (presumably, one could have a garage elsewhere on the lot). Only three of those fifteen protrude from the house.[95] The others place garages either flush with the front façade or set back from it; three houses put the garages below ground.[96]

As for style, the bureau helpfully used headlines and/or descriptive copy to enlighten the reader. Only a dozen houses are unlabeled, though they are easy to categorize. Whatever the modifier—Cape Cod, New England, saltbox, Southern—colonials dominate; forty-one of the houses have that label, and five more are clearly in that style. Other styles include about a dozen English, three Georgians, two French, and one each of Spanish and Swiss. One house is described as having "no definite style formula."[97] One unlabeled house displays two possible exteriors, but both are traditional: one colonial and one English.[98] Another house shows the exterior in brick or stucco, with some alteration of the roofline and window styles, but both are traditional.[99] Multi-paned windows, dormers, shingle-shakes, pediments over the front door, and shutters repeat through the designs.

The four modern designs stand out among the traditional. One is for the "homebuilder seriously interested in the modern style." It has a protruding garage and is one of two houses that combine living and dining, albeit in an unusual way. The designer has a section of the living room labeled for "social dining," but a separate room off the kitchen is for "family dining." While the roof is hipped, the garage roof is flat, used as a deck or a future bedroom. Casement windows lack ornamentation, though none are corner windows. The exterior is horizontal siding.[100] A second house is a with houses too distinctive and out of step with those of their neighbors. Group warned his readers of the risks of buying modern in 1946.

> If you lean toward the Modern, remember that simplicity of line and mass requires skill in this design, unusually fine workmanship, as well as the best grades of material, if the result is to be effective and remain in favor over a long period of time. Also remember that as far as can be seen today you must anticipate a very limited resale market for Moderns. No records are available to prove whether the Modern house is to be an accepted style of tomorrow, or possibly turn out to be a passing fad.[109]

The economic risk is twofold. First, the modern house would be more expensive to build. It is not obvious why a simpler house would cost more; perhaps builders might be challenged by a wall of plate glass or a flat roof. The latter scare, however, is the stronger one. Will the value of your home hold steady or increase? Will you find a buyer when ready to resell? Since the 1920s, the movement to increase home ownership centered on the economic benefits of building equity in your house, an equity of little use unless and until you sell. Group cautioned readers about the realities of home buying. It would not only be the "biggest financial obligation ever undertaken in their lifetime," but it also would be so for the next few decades. He warned: "Newspapers, magazines and intriguing advertisements have in some instances made the purchase of a home appear to be no more trouble or a no greater financial transaction than buying an electric refrigerator or an automobile."[110] Buyer, beware.

All but eleven of the forty-eight houses in Group's book carry a label of a specific architectural style. His preference for traditional-style houses is clear; copy accompanying each design uses the word "colonial" to describe seventeen houses, often with modifying adjectives: Dutch, Cape Cod, Southern, Early, or New England. Other traditional houses might be "Regency" or "cottages." The Vernon drew "inspiration from our founding fathers," the Endicott reached "back to the old salt-box tradition," and the Upton brings the family back to "old-time country life." Only nine houses can really be called modern, with one of those, the Lincoln, "as modern as television, without striving too hard for effect," suggesting the house is modern but not so modern as to be off-putting to the average home buyer.[111]

The Trent is a "modern suburban cottage" that looks pretty traditional, as is the Piedmont.[112] The Ulster, Irvington, and Nassau houses have flat roofs, but the page devoted to the Ulster displays an "Alternate Rendering showing Pitched Roof," which renders the design immediately more conventional. Inside, the houses are barely distinguishable from each other in style. Rather, the real differences are among house sizes. Eleven houses

"The Lincoln" from the *House-of-the-Month Book of Small Houses* is one of the few "modern" styles, yet it is still fairly traditional in exterior and interior. (Harold E. Group, *House-of-the-Month Book of Small Houses* [Garden City, NY: Garden City Publishing Co., 1946], 41.)

have clearly separated dining rooms, and seven floor plans, mostly in the very small, two-bedroom houses, contain no dining designation at all, but the rest have dining spaces that are not significantly separated from the living space. At best, those houses have a dining ell, where turning a corner brings one into a dining area, or an extra-wide open doorway separates living room from dining room. The Sutton, a "modern adaptation of Regency architecture," has a "dining space" designated in the living room, while the Judson, a "modern adaptation of Colonial style," has a separate dining room.[113] In the traditional Saginaw, "[a] cottage that is thoroughly American as the Fourth of July" (the elevation shows someone raising the American flag), residents would eat in the dining alcove that is part of the kitchen.[114] Rather than refer to the centuries-old vernacular design of the "keeping room," which historically combined eating and cooking, the Saginaw arrangement is touted as of assistance to the housewife, who will find that her children can be near but not underfoot.[115]

Group's selections reflect an assumption that potential buyers of modest homes, who needed to be careful with their dollars, wanted to be conservative when choosing a house. He was not alone. A 1946 booklet from *American Builder* magazine (which included a "modern adaptation of a French farm house" by Prize Homes juror Philip Maher), added some "modern" houses to its collection.[116] One design, by Henry Otis Chapman and Randolph Evans, is accompanied by the headline "5-Room Sensible Modern

Design." Copy describes the house as "exterior as modern as tomorrow, but sensibly so—no freak architecture, just straightforward styling." (Although the house is not starkly modern, the front door enters directly into the kitchen, which is very unusual.)[117] A house built in Seattle is "done in a contemporary manner, yet with a distinctly Colonial feeling in the entire composition."[118] Maurice Thornton's "modern American home" remains risk free, as its "stability of design assures years of value."[119] The most modern house in the booklet is designed as an office and residence for the architect's, Ernest Peterson's, personal use. The shed-roofed, corner-windowed residence has a carport rather than a garage. The house is modern but "not too revolutionary."[120] A colonial house "is the kind of home [architects] believe home buyers want because of its familiar charm and homey appeal."[121]

Also in 1946, John Dean and Simon Breines brought forward *The Book of Houses*. The foreword is dated January 1946; the volume incorporated information about immediate postwar G. I. benefits for mortgage assistance. Dean and Breines contributed a rare, moderating voice to the home-buying boom: renting is not always less cost-effective than buying, the housing shortage was driving prices up so far up that buyers might not get their money back at resale time, and young buyers do not yet know their families' size and thus needs. Their down-to-earth attitude led them to eschew artists' sketches of dream homes in favor of realistic photos of houses next to other houses, on streets, with electric wires overhead and bare landscaping.[122] Veterans pushed into buying houses might be acting against their own self-interests: vets were less likely to have stable families (experts "estimate that at least one-quarter of the war marriages will crack up"), job prospects and salaries are uncertain, and future desire to move will be hampered by home ownership.[123] In chapters titled "What It Costs to Buy," "Legal Pitfalls," "Safety at Home," and "Purchasing a Neighborhood," the authors list a host of cautions: construction quality of new houses is completely uncertain, houses always end up being more expensive than the sticker price indicates, houses create endless opportunities for fatal falls and fires (they fret about stairs, especially basement stairs; bathrooms and bathtubs can only be made safer with grab bars, a feature they highlight), and neighborhoods develop unpredictably and can quickly turn undesirable.[124]

Some of their caution, however, relates to house style. They are not anti-modern; they feature many houses with modern features, and in one example, they directly contrast the warm sunlight shining into a modern house over the darkness of a traditional Cape Cod. Reality, however, intrudes.

> Most of the structures shown have traditional styles because most of the homes you will find for sale are traditional—Cape Cod, Georgian, Ranch house, what-not—and the chances are you prefer these kinds anyway. The

authors believe that in a house designed in the modern functional style you get more for your money. But there is no point in including primarily "modern houses" when the average home buyer won't be likely to find more than a few in his locality. Besides, most of the beautiful modern designs (replete with modern furniture) are slanted at the $20,000–$30,000 pocketbook—not yours and ours.[125]

They couldn't be clearer: the average house buyer does not want modern, cannot find modern, and cannot afford modern. For those who might want to build, "remember that 'pioneering doesn't pay' and especially in a low-cost home it is unwise to try innovations or anything that has not been tested or proved."[126] The bespoke house may not comport with the neighborhood, and if it is too unusual, it will be difficult to sell.[127]

While not a catalog of houses for purchase, the book does have two chapters on model houses, and they include photos and floor plans. Since the authors are not trying to sell the designs, they have some latitude to criticize them. The first of those chapters, "The Basic House," shows a dozen one-story houses, including the Museum of Modern Art–approved war housing project designed by Hugh Stubbins. To those unacquainted with modern style, "the house may look a little like a shack," but the authors approved of its simplicity. Combining the living and dining spaces creates an expansive area. A tiny kitchen is made more convenient with an adjacent utility room. Windows are awning styled but conventionally sized and placed.[128] But the other houses in this section have more conventional appearances, with exterior features like shutters and multi-paned windows. Some combine elements: an otherwise Cape Cod–style house by architect Carl Paulsen, built for his own residence, has high strip windows in the living room, as seen on the front façade.[129] Another house built by an architect for his own use has vertical siding and a flat-roofed garage perpendicularly attached to the side; it is "not too unconventional."[130] But *The Book of Houses* offers no flat roofs or glass walls.

The following chapter, "Two-Story Houses," presents eleven houses. Dean and Breines suggest the "widespread demand for a traditional American two-story house with all bedrooms on the second floor reflects the public's slow-changing resistance to styles and plans which might satisfy their housing needs more simply." Two-story prejudice stems, they say, from outdated ideas about efficiency in construction and home heating costs, and privacy concerns that could be abated by better design; a two-story home should have at least one bedroom and bathroom on the first floor for the benefit of children, the elderly, and the infirm.[131] (They address neither lot size nor lot-eating garages that might make a two-story house a practical choice.) Of the eleven houses, only one (a design from their own firm) can be labeled modern: a shed roof on the second floor, a flat roof over part of the first floor, a two-car garage, and an angled wall separating the dining room from the outdoor terrace. Comporting with their instructions, it has a first-floor bedroom and full bathroom, in addition to the two bedrooms upstairs.[132] But the other houses? Colonial, Georgian, or French, with shutters and dormers, and three of the eleven with separate dining rooms.

The Scale Model Home Planning Company's *Book of Small Home Designs* was discussed earlier. Its first edition, issued in 1948, and its third edition in 1951 included Prize Homes houses by Sackville-West, Wenstrand, and Taylor. (A second edition is unavailable, but because all the first-edition houses are in the third edition, it is reasonable to assume the second edition also included the three Prize Homes houses.) The 1948 publication offered buyers "a home that has individual design and livability—and not just a house that looks like all the rest of the houses on the block."[133] Despite the promise of individuality, the houses are conventional and truly modest (there are no owners' bathrooms, for example). Fourteen of the twenty-six designs show window shutters; two houses display both corner windows and shuttered windows. Houses are one story (one is a split-level), but copy accompanying five houses promotes second-story expansion. Two of those expandable houses have dormer windows. Roof pitches vary, but the low pitch is rare, and the flat roof is nonexistent. Taylor Coder's long and low design stands out.

Competitions sponsored by architectural publications, and collections determined by those publications' editors, selected designs far more modern than those seeking to sell house plans to the buying public.[134] The two competitions most similar and contemporaneous to the Prize Homes competition, the *Pencil Points* Georgia and Pittsburgh competitions, reflect the difference. Despite their caveats that putative owners wanted houses that would fit in with existing architectural aesthetics and be modern but not too distinctive, both the Pittsburgh and Georgia competition juries overwhelmingly rewarded bold, contemporary designs. Pittsburgh winners, special mentions, and mentions displayed flat or very low-sloping roofs, glass walls, corner windows, clerestory windows, and unseparated dining areas in asymmetrical floor plans. Georgia jurors rewarded mostly the same styles, albeit with fewer flat roofs.[135] The *Tribune* competition, at least for problems one and two, asked for a house roughly similar to the Georgia and Pittsburgh houses. They drew from the same pool of architects. But while *Pencil Points* rewarded modern-style houses, the *Tribune* jury awarded prizes to traditional, modern, and blended designs. And even those that can be categorized as contemporary might be better called only moderately modern. Two of the twenty-four winners had completely flat roofs, and other modern designs made do with low slopes. Picture windows prevailed in living and dining rooms, but walls of windows were rare. Many of the winners are two-story homes with regular sized windows and conventional roofs. Houses by Cedarstrand, Uebelhack, and Garbe have shutters, anathema in contemporary design. Some winners combined living and dining space into one room, but more winners separated dining with an alcove, an ell, a nook, or a separate room. Unlike the Case Studies houses and the Georgia competition, Prize Homes jurors split the winners evenly between one-story and two-story houses, with twelve each.

The Prize Homes catalog does not look like its contemporaries, neither the ground-breaking designs architectural publications promoted, nor the conservative choices house plan purveyors offered. Unlike the catalogs displaying page after page of "Southern" or "New England" colonials, English cottages, or Tudors, Prize Homes houses are not so easily categorized. There is not a single Tudor style; nor is there anything remotely French or English. Nothing harks back to Southern colonial architecture, and the label "Cape Cod" is never implemented, quite rightly. Federal pediments are absent, as are gambrel roofs. One house is labeled, in headline and copy, Georgian.[136] Hugh Garden's "modern colonial" has two street-facing dormer windows, while Edward Dwyer's house had a single street-facing dormer over the setback, attached garage, but those are the only two with dormers.[137] None of the problem one houses have shutters, only two of the problem two houses do, and four problem three houses display them.[138] William Boedefeld submitted a house with the "universal appeal of the colonial design," but the facing page shows Harold Zook's "unusual" modern.[139] Minimizing traditional design, however, did not lead those who selected the Prize Homes houses to wholly embrace modern design. At the very least, the texts assured potential buyers that the modern houses provided warmth and hominess. Arthur Myhrum's modern house has a "sedately modern" layout; Zook's "unusual" house had "comfort."[140]

No treatment of post–World War II architecture is complete without reference to the 1948 film Mr. Blandings Builds His Dream House, and it should be remembered what that dream looked like. The character of Jim Blandings epitomized the postwar home buyer; indeed, his family might easily have been a "problem" for an architectural competition. Blandings is not a young man with a new bride and a new infant; he and his wife are in their mid-thirties or older. College-educated, married for fifteen years, earning $15,000 a year (over $180,000 in 2020 dollars), he uses new selling techniques to promote postwar products. One Blandings daughter is a pre- or early teen, the other a couple of years younger, and they attend a progressive school. The family has occupied their New York City apartment for many years, perhaps the entirety of their marriage, and it is big enough to provide live-in quarters for the maid. But it is far from ideal; the living room is too cramped for entertaining, their two daughters share a bedroom, there is only one bathroom for the family, and the bedroom and hall closets are overfilled.

Upon reviewing architectural plans for a new house, Mrs. Blandings finds them a bit too conventional. Mr. Blandings concurs: "If we were going to build a house, well, you know, we'd want it a little bit different." But the alterations they seek are quite conventional: more bathrooms, bigger bedrooms, a sewing room for her, a bigger study for him. Mr. Blandings's education, urbanity, and modern profession notwithstanding, he and his wife do not want an open-plan, one-level, flat-roofed house with window walls for their dream home. When searching for a better way of living, Mr. and Mrs. Blandings go back in history, choosing a two-story colonial with a salt-box roof in Connecticut. Their children leave behind the Manhattan progressive school for a rural, probably public school that must be reached by bus (one day a storm washes out a bridge, keeping the children from returning home after school). With dormers and sixteen-paned, double-hung, windows, every window and even the front door is shuttered. Unusual even for its time, the dining room is separate, neither an alcove nor ell. The family has a live-in maid (who has her own room and bathroom), so the kitchen is not a place for the household to eat. If not the dining room, the Blandings family uses a breakfast room/dining alcove for more casual meals. No garage is visible, but it is certainly not attached. (The conceit of the story explains why the family must build this house anew—they have already bought the land—when Connecticut must have had thousands of such houses already available for purchase.) They clearly bought new furniture upon their move, matching the outside of their Connecticut house with colonial décor inside, down to the pewter candlesticks, Windsor chairs, ruffled and floral fabrics on upholstered furniture and drapery, and old-fashioned fireplace tools. Scenes of their Manhattan apartment display contemporary furniture—the furniture suite in their cramped dining room set looks modern—but the roomier dining room in the Connecticut house contains a colonial-styled dining room set.[141]

The Blandings family should have wanted a modern home; McCoy claims the market for modern houses was "often professional people with moderate incomes—progressives, they were called."[142] Editors of architectural publications and jurors of architectural competitions wanted to build houses for those progressives, only throwing in a few traditional houses, if any at all, among their choices. Those promoting modern style envisioned a White market, but they might well have looked to the Blandings family's

Black maid or middle-class Black house buyers when seeking potential consumers. African American house buyers understandably felt no nostalgia for colonial homes, furniture, or décor; Margaret Ruth Little's research indicates that Black home buyers sought and welcomed contemporary architectural styles that broke with American vernacular tradition.[143]

Prize Homes winning designs, and the subsequent collection found in the *Prize Homes* book, offered consumers a liminal house. If the houses did not have immediately identifiable historical roots, in the case of the colonials and Cape Cods, neither were they glass and steel boxes. They were modern houses that did not look too modern. Reporter Edward Barry admitted that the mail to the *Tribune* indicated readers favored traditional over contemporary designs.[144] Williams, Group, Dean and Breines, Robinson, and even the readers of the *Architectural Forum* thought that buyers desired conventional houses. Editors of house plan books gave the public what they wanted, and *Prize Homes* did, too, but they brought readers a gentler, softer modern house, and an up-to-date traditional one.

Mr. and Mrs. Blandings' purchase of new furniture might be a clue to some house-buyers' sensibilities. People can furnish their homes as they please. One can fill one's Cape Cod two-story with Eames chairs, Saarinen tulip tables, and other sleek, midcentury pieces. Likewise, no one is prevented from furnishing the modern house, with its glass walls and flat roof and wide-open interior, with wing chairs covered in flowered chintz or Windsor chairs. But in creating domestic space, even those without a trained decorator or architectural eye may well have been sensitive to what "fits" a house's style. Could a barrier to buying a modern-styled house have been the lack of the appropriate furniture to put in it? Buying a house, as consumers had been warned, was (and is) a major purchase. Moving is expensive. Adding the additional costs of "appropriate" furniture might have been too much. Family heirlooms and hand-me-downs, pieces already owned, what was available in second-hand shops, or even what was available to buy new but on layaway, at affordable prices from Sears or Montgomery Ward: these might have dissuaded the average home buyer from selecting a modern house where their furniture might have felt out of place. Not everyone, like the Blandings family, can replace all their existing furniture. Add to this a common notion at the time, deserved or not, that modern furniture was uncomfortable, with more hard angles and less cushy upholstery than the overstuffed chairs people might be used to.[145]

Without being privy to the conversations Prize Homes jurors had among themselves when choosing the twenty-four winners, we can imagine that their different sensibilities pulled them in opposite directions. As argued earlier, architects unconstrained by market forces fancied starkly modern and innovative houses, dismissive of the conventional (but popular) Cape Cod or colonial. Builders and developers, in contrast, considered the buying public to be conservative, fiscally constrained, and wary of anything too innovative. The Prize Homes jury found middle ground. Reporter Edward Barry described the process.

> On the aesthetic side, too, practical considerations were kept constantly in view. A design for an exterior might be so striking that the temptation to accept it immediately would be strong. But the questions were asked: "Could it be built economically? How would it be to live with?" "What will the owner think of it 10 years hence?" Would he lose a large part of his investment if in some emergency he had to sell it quickly?"
>
> The freakish and the merely startling were ruled out immediately. There were debates and lengthy discussions of designs that were considered border line. In the end the trained and experienced architects and builders who made up the jury concurred in the 24 designs which are now being submitted to the public.
>
> Because of the character of the judging, The Tribune believes that a house based on one of these winning designs will be something that a man [sic] can come home to happily, live in comfortably, show to his friends proudly, and if necessarily dispose of easily.[146]

Barry's *Tribune* review of *Prize Homes* stressed the broad selection available in the publication: "Small and medium sized homes, simple and fairly lavish homes, traditional, contemporary, and even 'radical' homes." Whatever one's design preference, the catalog offered practicality, as "the designers are more interested in seeing to it that the kitchen windows command a view of the children's play area than they are in experimenting with novel materials."[147] The dominant aesthetic seemed to be modern, but not too modern.

8

Breaking Ground

The Building Project

As stated at the competition's outset, the *Tribune* sought to build some of the winning designs, and this enterprise began quickly on the heels of the winners' announcement. Since the competition explicitly sought to provide needed shelter and jobs for workers, from the beginning, the paper wanted families to think seriously about commissioning houses immediately on publication of the winning designs.[1] This promotion of the built houses distinguished the competition from others, even from the paper's own 1926 iteration. Putting builders on the jury signaled, from the outset, the building project's seriousness. This would be no mere ideas competition. Several factors compromised the ambition, however, and the building project was at best a mixed experience for potential home buyers. In the end, it did not present a realistic solution to the Chicago housing shortage.

As predicted, the United States suffered from a postwar housing crisis. Despite President Truman's commitment to prioritizing veterans' housing, policy-makers clashed on how to confront the problem. Government agencies wanted more control and oversight over new construction; banks and contractors wanted less. In one Chicago-related example of the conflict, Truman's national housing administrator, Wilson Wyatt, sought authority over other governmental agencies and private industry. Wyatt admired prefabricated solutions to housing, thinking the speed of prefabrication could address the urgency of the housing problem. Builders, and especially banks, were skeptical; prefab houses had no proven track record, and lenders were skittish about whether the houses would hold up.[2] (A *Tribune* article in 1947 told of the prefabrication industry's attempt to avoid the stigma by promoting the label "factory made."[3]) Wyatt planned to commandeer a Chrysler/Dodge auto manufacturing facility in Chicago and turn it over to the Lustron corporation, a pioneer in prefabricated houses. Truman (later no stranger to seizing manufacturing plants) refused to grant Wyatt the sweeping authority he wanted, and the plant continued making cars. Only a few weeks later, Wyatt resigned, also frustrated with Truman's lifting of price caps on building materials and a Congress that viewed government regulations as "socialistic" practices to be resisted.[4]

Chicago ended up with 100,000 homeless veterans, according to 1945 data; add spouses and children, and the number increases significantly.[5] The *Tribune* covered the crisis as it played out locally, highlighting veterans and their families' personal stories. In the fall of 1946, several articles confirmed the emergency. Desperate for housing, George Rasse and his wife were willing to pay six months' advance rent to secure a bungalow. Once they moved in, a representative of the real owner showed up; the family had been defrauded, the legitimate owner wanted to sell rather than rent, and the family had to move. Their "rent" had disappeared.[6] Another human-interest feature also confirmed the importance of newspapers—in particular the *Chicago Tribune*—in the process of securing housing. Nineteen-year-old Darwin Gilmore, a Navy veteran, waited overnight on a Saturday with his wife and seven-month-old baby in the lobby of the Tribune Tower, hoping to get first crack at the real estate listing in the Sunday paper. They had no family nearby with whom they could live and—the very next day—were due to lose their temporary lodgings in a Homewood hotel. The Gilmores' sad story drew the *Tribune*'s particular attention, but other house hunters had the same idea, also camping out in the Tribune Tower lobby.[7]

Even more dire was the story, told over several weeks, of a battle between veterans and the Chicago Housing Authority (CHA). Approved for housing but fed up with waiting for assigned apartments, a group of White veterans stormed the office at the Airport Veterans' Housing project where units were finished (or nearly so) but still unoccupied. They overpowered the site manager, seized keys, and moved their families into sixty units. The CHA sought assistance in removing the squatters; neither the mayor nor the police department was willing to step in. Personal testimonies of the veterans show why hesitancy and delicacy were required.

Paul Principato, 31, who served 2 ½ years in the European Theater—They'll have to get troops to move us out. These buildings are for veterans, and there are veterans in all of them. I've been living with my mother and my wife and the kids have been living with her sister. There's an example for you of why the courts are full of divorces.

Mrs. Adele Seibert, whose husband, Victor was wounded as a gunner on a navy torpedo plane—Even if they throw us out it was nice while it lasted. I guess we'll have to go and live at the city hall. We haven't anywhere else to go.

Willis Abeln, 33, overseas with the navy for 21 months—My wife, June, and Judy, 4, have been living in a basement all the time I was overseas, and I've been there since I got out.

Roman Pezdek, 27, a navy veteran with 18 months overseas—If they throw us out where can we go? My wife has been sleeping with her mother, and I've been sleeping in the basement. Four years in service and when you come out there's no place to live.

Mrs. Margaret Gianis, 26, whose husband William, 31, was an infantryman in Europe for two years—We and the baby, Anne, 4, were evicted from a one room place where we had been living since last August. When we read about this we just came over and moved in. The only thing the housing people ever referred us to was a four room flat with stove heat over a garage. But children weren't permitted.

Mrs. Robert Boggs, 21, whose husband was a 2d lieutenant in the air training command for three years—We'll stay here till we're kicked out. Then I don't know where we'll go. We've had an application in for a place here since the first of the year. I hope they let us stay.

Robert Kakuska, 20, a navy veteran with 18 months overseas—My wife is pregnant, but I can't bring her up from Alabama until I got a place to live.

Jack Crawford, 22, navy signalman with 23 months overseas—We've been living in Elmhurst but my folks got notice to move. We read about this and moved in when we found it open. This will be my first Christmas home in four years. I've never spent Christmas with Jill. She's just 3.[8]

The CHA, despite lack of assistance from other political stakeholders, fought back. Sympathetic as their stories were, the squatters had jumped ahead of veterans who had also been waiting and had been on the list for far longer than the occupying families, some for as long as a year. Those veterans had equally compelling stories. The Frales, with four children five and under, had been living with the wife's mother, eight people sleeping in two bedrooms. The Heys and their two sons were living in hotel room; it lacked private toilet and cooking facilities.[9] To counter the complaint that the units were "sitting empty," the CHA quickly put the finishing touches on the units (they still lacked stoves and some heating), renting them to approved tenants.[10]

The CHA implied the squatters had another agenda. "Ugly rumors have been heard that the squatters moved in because they heard Negroes might be allowed to occupy part of the project," said an official. "CHA treats all veterans alike, regardless of race, creed, or color. Negroes have been invited to move in and we welcome a squatter spokesman's statement in a radio talk Friday that the squatters support the CHA policy."[11] Six offenders (thought to be the leaders of the action) were charged with criminal trespassing, and by the end of November, the remaining squatters had agreed to vacate the premises.[12] Despite the assurances of Wilson Wyatt, Truman's administrator of federal housing policy, that housing for veterans was "certainly not intended just for white people," policy did not overcome culture.[13] An apartment unit was reassigned when its original designees, Black veteran Theodore Turner and his wife and infant, declined the opportunity to live there, "after he realized the feeling against Negroes in the neighborhood."[14] In December 1946, when two Black families moved in, White people rioted, injuring police officers and the press, overturning cars, and throwing rocks. The Turners were not the only Black families to decline the housing opportunity, though they must have been as desperate for housing as any other veterans' families.[15] The fate of the six charged with trespassing is unknown. The *Chicago Defender*, Chicago's daily newspaper catering to the interests and perspectives of the city's Black population, covered that riot and other acts of violence and intimidation, concerned that the housing situation was worsening, not improving, for Black veterans.[16]

In May 1946, a new federal law planned an ambitious national building program, setting a target of 2,700,000 houses for veterans. The federal government would subsidize the production of building materials and increase loan protection to banks, which then could release more mortgage loans. To be eligible for the federal benefits, new house prices were capped at $10,000 and house sizes limited to no more than 1,500 square feet. Builders of low- and medium-priced units got first access to scarce materials.[17] Any newly built house for sale, any newly built apartment for rent, and any building being converted into a habitable dwelling had to be made available first to veterans, for thirty or sixty days after completion. The national housing agency issued official signs and posters proclaiming new housing "Held for Veterans."[18] Builders jumped, planning construction of single-family houses, rental apartments, and cooperative apartments. Modest projects hoped to provide forty-two, sixty, seventy-four, and seventy-eight units.[19] Other builders planned on a grander scale: 530, 1,500, and 1,650.[20] Anton Reminih, giving an end-of-the-year review in the *Tribune*, wrote:

> Historians of the future, seeking the pattern of life following the end of the greatest war in world history, will do well to look up on the files of the Metropolitan section of the Chicago Tribune. They won't find Washington datelined stories of sweeping governmental decrees promulgated to fight inflation, expedite reconversion, or create housing for returned war veterans. The files will reveal, however, a humanized version of these stories, and the pulse of the people, the home, and the community in 1946, the year of the great readjustment. And from the Metropolitan stories the

chronologist will be able to evaluate the meaning of the decrees to Mrs. and Mrs. Average American in terms of dollars and cents and human emotions.

At the top of Reminih's list: housing, lack thereof, and gratitude when even too-small and inadequate housing could be procured.[21]

Given the urgency, the *Tribune*'s contribution to the housing problem was certainly welcome and much needed. Its initial publicity noted that a successful Chicagoland Prize Homes competition would lead to some number of built houses. The competition rules booklet sent to those who had registered an intent to submit a design confirmed that aspiration: the jury would select "those solutions which provide the best designs of dwellings which are marketable to the public and attractive as investments to builders and lending agencies, and which can be executed into finished homes by the average small home building contractor and at total costs which would not be considered excessive, uneconomic or wasteful in relation to the floor area."[22] Boyd Hill's letter to registrants, dated October 30, 1945, outlined a major building project.

> The present plan is to build 56 in the Chicago metropolitan area and 88 in outlying cities within a radius of 300 miles of Chicago. It is felt that every entrant should know that in case he [sic] is a winner in the competition, his winning design will not be merely a dream house on paper but, conditions permitting, will actually be built.[23]

That ambitious plan for 144 houses, however, was never reflected in the newspaper coverage. *Tribune* articles referred to the "more than a score" of houses to be built.[24] The latter number is more accurate; research has turned up not much more than two dozen houses.

The organization created to realize the building project remains an enigma. Edward Barry's June 2, 1946, article on the first groundbreaking ceremony added detail to the *Tribune*'s ambitions of making the houses a reality. In announcing the ceremony, Barry shared that it "officially inaugurates the Chicago Tribune Building program," an entity previously unmentioned in the *Tribune*.[25] By the next day, however, in what is only the second of five *Tribune* references to the program, Barry cautioned that the program had "now reached a stage where no new applications from builders or veterans can be handled."[26] Brief references appeared three more times, twice in Barry articles: December 29, 1946, and June 22, 1947; and once more in an article by Ward Walker, on October 12. In June 1946, *Arts and Architecture* referred to the program in a notice about the June groundbreaking, and in January 1947, Bryant Gas Heating referred to it in an advertisement in a Gas Appliance Merchandising publication. Running twice in the same issue, the ad touted that the Bryant gas heater was used in the "Prize Homes Building Program."[27] The *Tribune* did not finance the houses but made drawings available to builders, partnering with the Chicago Metropolitan Home Builders Association. It seems likely that the association matched builders with potential owners. Who ran the program, how it was administered, what comprised the application process, how long it lasted: these questions cannot be answered.

While the *Tribune*'s first call for submissions indicated its intention to see winning designs through to the building phase, in 1945, the *Tribune* never mentioned the houses would go specifically to veterans. It is not clear when that decision was made—or by whom. By the spring of 1946, however, when the paper promoted house building, from groundbreaking ceremonies to model home showcases to just-moved-in families, they highlighted that Prize Homes houses would go to veterans, featuring six particular veterans. This practice dovetailed with the *Tribune*'s overall coverage of the housing crisis, in putting a personal and familial face on the problem (and revealing the *Tribune* to be a problem solver). Given the *zeitgeist*, the paper *had* to make the houses for vets; if the cultural pressure to support veterans was insufficient, federal policies after May 1946 demanded it.

To promote the house-building enterprise, the *Tribune* enlisted its radio station, WGN, to broadcast groundbreaking ceremonies and open houses. When completed, each house would be open to the public for thirty days before the new owner took up residence. Newspaper coverage of the first ceremony included Barry's caution that the program could no longer accept any more applicants from builders or veterans; the *Tribune* had never mentioned, let alone publicized, an application process for veterans, so it is not clear how builders or veterans would have known when, where, or how to apply.

James McDaniel, a twenty-five-year-old Navy veteran, was awarded the first house, at 100 W. Washington, in the western suburb of Lombard. Barry's article on the June 2 groundbreaking ceremony noted that although the veteran had been released from active duty months earlier, he had not yet secured a home for himself, his wife, and his infant son. In what might not be a coincidence, it was designed by veteran W. R. Burns. Barry mentioned specific plans for the construction of eight more houses, listing the neighborhoods or suburbs where the houses would be erected and the builders assigned the construction.[28] One day after the groundbreaking ceremony, the *Tribune* featured it again, with a list of local luminaries in attendance (DuPage County and Lombard city officials, builders, bankers, and competition advisor Boyd Hill); the article also pictured McDaniel, shovel in hand, posing before a WGN microphone.[29]

Veteran James McDaniel at the groundbreaking ceremony for his home-to-be in Lombard, a Chicago suburb. ("Vet Starts Dream Home," *Chicago Tribune*, June 3, 1946, 40.)

Only a week later came the second ceremonial groundbreaking, for a Wenstrand house in Blue Island for dentist Taylor Bell, his wife, and their two sons. Along with Blue Island officials, that occasion drew some members of the jury, but builders rather than architects: Arthur Fossier, John O'Connor, and Irvin Blietz, in addition to Hill. The *Tribune* reprinted the elevation sketch and floor plan.[30] Ceremonies—all broadcast on WGN—followed on June 16 for a Chicago house[31]; sometime in the same week, a house in Wheaton[32]; June 24 in Highland Park[33]; and sometime in that same week in Palatine, the latter three locations in Chicago suburbs.[34] Four photos with substantial captions updated readers on the 100 W. Washington house in Lombard, the first to start construction.[35] In November, Edward Barry featured the house again in the Sunday Grafic Magazine, with a cover photo and inside story, reporting construction delays but also noting some changes from the original plan. Because of the lot, the house was reversed from the original, and additional windows were added so the corner bedrooms could be cross-ventilated. Barry reported the house would need another two months for completion.[36]

The first house built within the Chicago city limits went up on Sunnyside Avenue for Hugh J. Falvey, an Army veteran; his wife, Anne, had been an Army nurse. Groundbreaking for that house, by Chicago architect Charles Schroeder, took place on June 16, 1946. Falvey told people listening to the WGN broadcast that "his present task was more enjoyable than digging foxholes." The accompanying photo shows the smiling couple, with Anne Falvey holding an umbrella over her husband as he shovels into the ground.[37] Houses in Lombard, Blue Island, Chicago, Wheaton, Highland Park, and Palatine, plus a second Lombard house right across the street from the first one, are the seven houses—outside of the ten built in the Deer Park development in West Rogers Park—that the *Tribune* promoted. An eighth house went up in Kankakee but drew only cursory attention from the paper.

The Deer Park subdivision drew the most publicity from the *Tribune*. Built on vacant land in West Rogers Park, the simultaneous building of ten houses for veterans was really the competition's acme. Precedent existed for such a building program: in 1927, developers Phelps & Hayward bought a Highland Park farm, turning it into Briargate Estates. Ten houses from winning designs in the 1926 competition were sited there, although without any fanfare from the *Tribune*.[38] In the later iteration, the Deerfield Company solicited builder Joseph T. Carp, Inc., and consulted with Boyd Hill, who selected the designs for two-, three-, and four-bedroom houses, each specifically arranged on three streets—Pratt, Francisco, and Farwell—at the edge of what would become a multi-acre development. Criteria for choosing which houses and where they might be placed are left unknown. Myhrum's design, one of the ten, emphasized that the street side of the house should face north, so the expansive windows in the rear receive southern exposure; despite the opportunity to do that, Hill did just the opposite. Hill chose various styles, from Garbe's very traditional to Myhrum's very modern. Sizes vary, too: Sackville-West's garage-less, two-bedroom house is perhaps the smallest among the winners, at 900 square feet, while Garbe's design supplies four bedrooms, two full bathrooms and a lavatory, a study, a good-sized first-floor laundry room, and, as built, a two-car garage. Groundbreaking for the first house, at 6820 Francisco, occurred on November 27, 1946. Original Chicago building permits exist for only three of the houses, all on Pratt. At the place on the permits where it asks for the name of the architect, instead of naming Myhrum, Hanson and Martorano, and Wenstrand, the permits name B. Hill or Boyd Hill; the architect's address on one is "Chicago Tribune," and on the other two, it is "Tribune Tower."[39]

The *Tribune* noted the Deer Park choices were "not of the inexpensive type," conceding for the first time that the winning houses might not be affordable to the average homeowner.[40] The original city permit indicated the Wenstrand house, built on a corner lot, would cost $14,000, while the other two houses for which permits exist, built in the immediately adjacent two lots to the west, would each cost $18,000.[41] They ended up even more expensive than those original estimates. Despite concerns about costs, the paper could boast further that the Prize Homes contest moved housing ideas into reality, at least for some. Barry praised the Deer Park project in the summer of 1947, lauding the variety of styles, the quality of each design, and the grouping of them into a single neighborhood rather than building them piecemeal. He reported the *Tribune* had engaged a landscaping planner to develop the area, and he reminded readers that upon completion of construction, which was near, the houses would be open to viewers for thirty days.[42]

The *Tribune's* plan for open houses was a novel practice in 1946. Around the turn of the century, some builders had opened to the public newly finished row houses in urban areas, and immediately after the war, did the same with single-family houses in new developments. But prewar and immediate postwar houses open for inspection were not furnished or decorated. Nor were appliances regularly supplied; house buyers were expected to bring their own refrigerators, stoves, washers, and dryers. Rather, the idea was to show potential buyers the floor plan; they could purchase an identical house down the street or a block over. As discussed in chapter 1, some prewar model houses were erected, but they were temporary; after their display, they were moved or torn down. Jacobs marks the late 1940s as when the furnished display home began as a promotional tool for builders; the practice grew considerably in the 1950s. By that timeline, the *Tribune* was an innovator.[43] Parades of Homes eventually proved to be a successful way of pulling in buyers looking for a first house or, as time went on, an upgrade. But the Chicago open houses promoted house-buying in general, since the houses visited were, in theory, mostly spoken for. The empty lots west of the Deer Park Prize Homes houses did not stay empty for long; Greer Braun, whose family was an original owner of the Thies house until 1957, recalled the new construction and, as she was growing up, forty children on her block.[44] Tribune photos taken just before the open houses reveal the partially built houses just adjacent.[45]

Furnishing and decorating the houses required partners to share in the cost. This pairing likely was welcome, as businesses were eager for the publicity. Even in spring of 1946, when the war's end was not yet a year in the past, *Tribune* articles and advertisements advanced the idea that postwar spenders could find what they needed in local stores. Spiegel Furniture—with four Chicagoland locations—featured Chicagoland prizewinning designs in ads on March 10 and 17, matching illustrations of furnished rooms with *Tribune* sketches of the Wenstrand and Sloan houses, respectively. Copy in the March 17 ad encouraged "Mister and Mrs" to dream of the home they would soon have.[46] When the Kankakee house was ready for public inspection the following year, developer Romy Hammes listed his sponsors, who included suppliers of building materials, appliances, and furniture, but also a provider of "flowers and objects d'art." The kitchen must have been stocked, too, since the Borden Co., and General Mills were among those contributing "food stuffs."[47] Deer Park houses, too, had food in the refrigerators.[48] A 1949 feature on Wenstrand's house there included color photos of the display, showing a child's bedroom with toys and books, and a kitchen outfitted with dishes and potted plants.[49]

Boyd Hill designed interiors for the Blue Island house, and the *Tribune* featured his sketched recommendations, juxtaposed with photos of the house under construction.[50] Having invited two professional landscapers to design plans for the Sloan and Uebelhack houses, the *Tribune* promoted their efforts with an Edward Barry article featuring the designs on July 7, 1946, with large illustrations on the front page of the Sunday Grafic section and continuing inside the section. What was good for the outside of the house was good for the inside: the *Tribune* also invited interior decorators to supply designs to furnish and decorate the same two.[51] Myhrum's and Sackville-West's houses received coverage on August 11; as did Burns's and Uebelhack's on September 5. The series of three articles featured color drawings and commentary directly from each designer, who, unsurprisingly, praised the exterior and interior recommendations. Decorators uniformly emphasized spaciousness and light, and use of color, and suggested how inhabitants might use their homes: homework at a dining-room table, for example, or hosting bridge parties.[52]

Once the built Prize Homes opened for public inspection, a few advertisers boasted of their connection to the project. Absent a complete record of ephemera, we do not know what house viewers collected on site from the companies that provided the utilities, appliances, and furniture in the houses; they could have given away pamphlets, flyers, and even promotional items. Upon opening the ten Deer Park houses to public view in fall of 1947, some *Tribune* ads connected to the display houses. In October 1947, three businesses seized the opportunity: Iron Fireman, an oil burner manufacturer, urged readers to check out its appliances at the Deer Park open houses.[53] Lynn & Healy, makers of case goods, offered "prize homes" for readers' record collections.[54] Montgomery Ward, chosen by Deer Park developers to furnish the Myhrum house, thrice repeated an ad featuring a sketch of that house and its suggestions for furniture.[55] John A. Colby & Sons, promoting the return of its exclusive "Precedent" furniture line, reminded readers of those pieces' inclusion in a prize home and did this as late as 1948.[56] The Zimmermans, original owners of the Cedarstrand house in Deer Park,

Publicity poster from Sears, possibly displayed in its stores, promoting its furnishings and decorations in one of the Prize Homes houses. (Poster owned by Valerie and Bill Kanter; photo by author.)

preserved and passed to subsequent owners a poster from Sears, Roebuck, which furnished and decorated the home with its "Harmony House" line.[57]

Sears publicized its efforts on its own. The company used its own store windows to display "adaptations of the Prize Homes furnishing," and the poster alerted readers to the house's location, even supplying a street map and the days and times one could visit the house.[58] Over time and across the country, appliance and furniture makers, paint and wallpaper suppliers, and even utilities joined the practice of presenting furnished and decorated houses.[59]

Free open houses of completed, furnished homes drew visitors, and the *Tribune*, along with WGN radio, made the most of the events. Front-page coverage of the first displayed home, in Palatine in July 1947, included a recap of the Prize Homes contest and noted the assistance of several manufacturers who supplied materials in construction, including Kohler, Frigidaire, and others, who "helped break supply bottlenecks."[60] Reporting on the 3,000 people who visited on opening day, along with a photograph of a long line of those waiting to enter the house, the paper used the opportunity to play up house features, such as sliding closet doors and window screens removable from the inside.

As it would with subsequent coverage of open house events, the *Tribune* focused on the variety of attendees ("old and young, families with children, young couples, and elderly couples") and quoted several of them. Mrs. Carl Butmann liked the easy-to-clean kitchen counters, and Mrs. Charles Opper found the closets "wonderful."[61] Among the visitors in the early days were the house's soon-to-be owners, Leroy and Cecilia Langhamer. They, too, loved the house, having selected the design from the early *Tribune* announcements of winners. Mr. Langhamer acknowledged being placed at the head of the list of veterans eligible for the houses because of his friendship with the builder, a surprisingly honest portrayal of how a few houses might have been allocated among thousands of eligible veterans. In another acknowledgment of the house's $18,000 price tag, Mrs. Langhamer ("pretty

The first house to be opened to the public was in the Chicago suburb of Palatine. Visitors waited in line on opening day, July 13, 1947. ("Thousands See Tribune Prize Home," *Chicago Tribune*, July 14, 1947, 44.)

and blond") acknowledged it is "lot of money" but expressed satisfaction at getting "the very best."[62] On subsequent days, lines to see the house were so long that prospective visitors had to be turned away.[63]

By the time the second house opened for public inspection a month later, the *Tribune* knew to include in its front-page coverage a map for readers' convenience, information about which train to take, driving directions, and a promise that signs would guide drivers nearing the home. The Highland Park Uebelhack house was fully furnished, decorated, and landscaped. Designed for problem three, it is one of the largest houses, with four bedrooms and two full baths, plus a guest lavatory; as one of the largest, it came with a hefty price tag of $30,000.[64] John A. Colby & Sons supplied the furnishings, the same company furnishing the identical house in suburban Wheaton, which opened to the public the following month.[65] The poor Highland Park realtor, anticipating opening the house at 1:00 p.m. on September 7, looked at the long line already in place and instead opened the house at 10:00 a.m., showing the house until 8:30 that evening. Again, visitors liked it, admiring the windows, the multiple bathrooms, and spacious rooms. Mrs. Harold Metzer offered one criticism: the wallpaper and drapes were a little too bright, but she was "crazy about the furniture."[66] The two Lombard houses, across the street from each other, opened October 5; Mrs. Marion Stutzman, "prominent Chicago interior decorator," chose furnishings and colors for 100 Washington, while 111 Washington remained unfurnished.[67]

Chicago Tribune press coverage of the house tours stressed that women would be primary users of the houses and thus how much the houses would appeal to them. Journalist Gladys Priddy's September 14 article's headline said it all: "Found: The Home of Our Dreams, Women Agree." She reported that many women's clubs visited the Wheaton house as groups: Oak Park's Nineteenth Century Club, the Wheaton Garden Club, the Glen Ellyn Garden Club, the Daughters of the American Revolution, and the Millard Avenue Women's Club. All admired the house unconditionally, noting the beauty of the design but, as was true of much of women's commentary on all the open houses, they especially appreciated design efficiencies that eased housework. A section headlined "No Work in That Kitchen" quoted Mrs. George Kendall: "And think of keeping house with all of these closets."[68] The only visitor quoted from the first day of the open house in Blue Island was Mrs. E. Baumruck, who was struck by the house's beauty but also its convenience.[69]

Reporter Agnes Lynch told of clubwomen visiting the furnished house in Lombard, where members of the Lombard Woman's Club, the Elmhurst Women's Club, and the Villa Park Women's Club admired the layout and décor. Mrs. Harley Lichtenberger found the house "designed with standards of efficient housekeeping in mind."[70] Girls from the Franklin Park high school, Leyden Community High, visited the Deer Park houses with their home economics teacher, Miss Edith Whitehouse, who praised the designs' contribution to home management.[71] Including such laudatory remarks in the press coverage confirmed that the house interiors did, indeed, provide the efficiencies and comforts of a modern house. As has been previously discussed, a modern house bowed to the reality of a servantless household. Women cared especially about ease of housework and layouts that reduced steps when they were the ones doing the stepping. Another highly impressed visitor to that Blue Island Wenstrand house was Esther Hendricks, who fell in love with it. She saved the flyer given to visitors, and when the house came on the market in 1962, she and her husband, on vacation in Florida when they heard it was available, snapped it up and lived there for thirty years.[72] In 1992, the Blacks toured it before it went on the market and, without knowing it was a prizewinner, bought it.[73]

The ten houses in the Deer Park development proved to be a remarkable opportunity to highlight the competition and Chicago commercial interests. It is perhaps the first time in the United States that multiple furnished houses, clustered within walking distance of each other, were available for public inspection.[74]

The *Tribune* thought it important enough to devote three consecutive days of front-page coverage, taking credit for a "community project in which Chicago again stepped out to lead the way to finer living." After a preview day, attended by 5,000 invited guests, all ten houses opened for public inspection on Sunday, October 12, 1947, a little more than two years after the competition's initial announcement. Partnering with well-known local and national furniture and department stores, the developers were able to show the houses fully furnished and decorated. House prices did not include the furniture, décor, drapes, or rugs; house buyers would have to pay for those extras.[75] The Zimmermans, original owners of one of those houses, perhaps bought only a few pieces; the Finks bought none.[76] Secondhand accounts suggest that, perhaps to preserve the cleanliness and crisp newness, perhaps to keep small items from being pilfered, in at least the Cedarstrand house, the second-floor bedrooms were roped off; one could look but not enter.[77]

Deer Park house prices ranged from $22,500 to $37,500; even accounting for the builder's profit, those prices went well beyond the costs indicated in the original permits for three of the houses, which were $14,000 and $18,000.[78] In yet another admission about housing costs, reporter Ward Walker acknowledged, at $400,000 for its total cost, the Deer Park project exceeded projections: "Originally all the Tribune prize winning homes were designed to be constructed within the $10,000 to $17,000 class, but

A full-page display of the ten prize homes built in the Deer Park subdivision in West Rogers Park. ("Open 10 Tribune Prize Homes," *Chicago Tribune*, October 11, 1947, 34.)

increased labor and material costs forced the higher prices."[79] Perhaps reflecting the understanding that the Deer Park houses were not meant for Black home buyers, the *Chicago Defender*, the daily newspaper for Black Chicagoans, made no mention of the month-long open house (nor any of the other house building projects, nor the competition at all).

Despite house prices and selling practices out of reach for all but a few potential buyers, the opening ceremony was a significant celebration: night-time floodlights, new cars displayed in every driveway, 10:00 a.m. to 10:00 p.m. visiting hours, and appearances by Chicago Mayor Martin Kennelly and builder Joseph Carp. WGN radio broadcast the awarding of a commemorative plaque to Colonel Robert McCormick, publisher and editor of the *Tribune*, from the Chicago Retail Furniture Association, in recognition of the *Tribune*'s "part in stimulating public interest in fine homes and furnishings with the two month Chicagoland Home and Home Furnishings festival, which opened September 15."[80] Hostesses, with identifying badges, were on hand to answer questions about the houses and decorations.[81] Sears's own publicity indicated that "specially trained consultants" would be on hand to answer questions.[82] As the WGN television station—owned by the Tribune Company—was only a few months away from its April 1948 debut, an onsite television exhibition promoted that event, setting up a film camera in one of the garages and filming passersby.[83] This drew "shrieks of dismay" from people unused to seeing themselves on television monitors.[84]

At each house, visitors received a paper flyer, printed on both sides. Original owners of the Garbe house, the Fink family, saved copies, passing them along to the next owners, the Domskys. On glossy paper, the black-and-white flyer shows three photographs of the house, and the first and second floor plan (the flyer is evidence of differences between the original design and the actual building). It describes the house layout and particularly the décor, down to the "amusing pink elephant pattern with a metallic silver background" that papered the powder room.[85] Although not original owners, the Scheckermans, too, possessed the flyer for their Wenstrand house. Beyond that, they preserved another important piece of ephemera. The *Tribune* or the developers distributed an envelope for visitors to collect the flyers from each of the ten houses. One side of the envelope recaps the competition, promoting it as "the most extensive building and home equipment project ever sponsored by a newspaper." Credit is also given to the Deerfield Company, owners and developers of the land, Joseph Carp, Inc., the builder, and Freeman Nurseries, the landscaper. The ten stores that furnished and decorated the houses also received credit: the New Boston Store; the Fair; Goldblatt Bros., Inc.; Petersen Furniture Co.; Rusnak Bros.; Sears, Roebuck & Co.; John M. Smyth Company; the Stylecrest Group; Montgomery Ward & Co.; and Wiebold Stores, Inc. On the other side of the envelope, along with hours and days the houses were open to visitors (1:00 to 9:00 p.m. Monday through Friday, 10:00 a.m. to 10:00 p.m. on Saturdays and Sundays), an aerial map of the ten houses includes both the house numbers and the designated competition winning numbers.[86]

Same-day coverage of the open house reiterated the information from the previous day, reproducing some of the photos and providing readers information about buses and parking availability, plus a map for drivers. Reporter Ward Walker deemed this the "climax" of the open houses; it was, arguably, the climax of the contest itself.[87] Although the houses would stay open until November 9, more than 50,000 people attended on the opening day (the *Tribune* used adding machines to get an accurate count). Mayor Kennelly praised the *Tribune*, as the "housing situation today is a very critical problem in all large cities. . . . For Chicago, it is a real emergency." Colonel McCormick was happy to take credit in a public address, for in the Deer Park project, "the Tribune presents the most extensive building and home equipment project ever sponsored by a newspaper"; a self-serving claim that is nevertheless arguably true. The weather cooperated: a large, front-page photo of the Sunday crowd shows a sunny day and many men with their shirtsleeves rolled up.[88]

The next day, Monday, many women returned for a second visit with friends in tow,[89] another 5,000 returned on Tuesday,[90] and another 6,000 on Wednesday.[91] Crowds grew so large that the American Red Cross contributed a volunteer at the first aid unit.[92] The *Tribune* kept up its publicity, offering on October 21 that any visitor would receive a souvenir program with photos and descriptions of each of the ten houses; no such program has been found, but as noted above, individual flyers were distributed at each house.[93] By the time the houses closed to the public, the *Tribune*

Over 50,000 visitors attended the first day of the month-long display of the ten Deer Park houses. ("51,819 Inspect 10 Tribune Homes on Opening Day," *Chicago Tribune*, October 13, 1947, 56.)

As noted, developers consulted with Boyd Hill in selecting the ten Deer Park houses. If Chicago architects were overrepresented among the winners—at least half of the twenty-four winners practiced in Chicago or its suburbs—that was even more the case with houses built: of the thirteen designs that are known to have been built, nine were from Chicagoland designers. The built homes supply some hint as to home buyers' preferences, at least as seen through the eyes of builders and developers: they quite clearly wanted houses that leaned more toward the traditional than the starkly modern. The thirteen designs seen to completion reflect the overall pattern of Prize Homes winners and inclusions in the book, with a range of conservative to modern, but nothing extreme. Woolford and Peterson's house, built once in Lombard, is labeled by Barry as "contemporary" and has a low-pitched roof, with a flat roof over the garage, and unusually placed windows. Arthur Myhrum earned a "highly original" label from Barry; his house has a flat roof, a hidden entrance, and only one second-floor window facing the street. Built once, the developer modified the original design, adding more front windows to give bedrooms additional air and light but eliminating the expansive windows in the back in favor of more traditionally sized windows. Coder Taylor's design, built in Highland Park without any *Tribune* publicity, has high strip windows, a low-pitched roof, a dining-living room, and an open courtyard between garage and house. Burns's house, a low one-story house, might be best cataloged as a ranch. The roof is low pitched, and its dining and living space are combined. Plans for Charles Schroeder's house show corner windows on the first and second floors, with very large ones on the front façade. As built, the house has quite conventional windows.

A second Uebelhack house in Highland Park, just blocks from the one that garnered so much attention from the *Tribune*, reflects the way builders adapted designs. Built in 1950, the Balsams, with one infant daughter and two more to come, arranged to have the four-bedroom, two-and-a-half-bath house built with only three bedrooms and one-and-a-half bathrooms, using the G. I. Bill to help get a mortgage.[106] While two other houses from the same design kept the architect's shuttered, centered windows, the Balsam house has a corner window in the street-facing bedroom.

By 1950, the competition had already begun to be forgotten, as the three children had no idea their home was a prizewinner or in any way architecturally distinctive, and they never knew that another version of their house existed only a few blocks away. Their parents, though, chose the lot and picked the house, perhaps from the *Prize Homes* book.

A few house designs can be called very successful, in that they were built multiple times. Reporter Edward Barry called the Wenstrand house "a

While the first two iterations of Howard Uebelhack's house retained his window design, one in Highland Park moved the front bedroom windows to the corner, giving the house a more modern look. (*Prize Homes*, 77; contemporary photo by author.)

modern version of contemporary architecture."[107] Not nearly as modern as other houses, it has a regularly pitched roof and a separate dining alcove; it displays large picture windows on two sides of the living room, but not the walls of windows more characteristic of modern houses. The *Tribune* publicized two of the iterations, the one in Deer Park and the one in Blue Island. At least three more were built, in Deerfield and Highland Park, Illinois, and Whiting, Indiana. Although *Architectural Forum*, reporting on the competition in the spring of 1946, singled out Wenstrand's design for scathing criticism, house builders—and buyers—clearly thought differently.

A second design also seems to have been built at least three times, twice in the Chicago area. Arthur "Jack" Sackville-West's design was an Art

Institute top seven design, and it won a *Tribune* "readers' vote." Ground-breaking in Palatine and Deer Park received *Tribune* coverage. In Kankakee, a small city about fifty miles from Chicago, local builder Romy Hammes made the Sackville-West house the centerpiece of his new Marycrest subdivision; the *Tribune* mentioned the August 8, 1947, groundbreaking, citing Hammes's intention to have the house finished by October 15.[108] He seems to have been successful in hitting that target; the *Tribune* reported on October 18 that the Kankakee house would open to the public the following day. For the next month, Kankakee citizens could walk through the fully furnished house with its modern appliances, such as a dishwasher and garbage disposal.[109]

Howard Uebelhack's house seems to have been erected at least four times. Houses in Highland Park and Wheaton received much attention from the *Tribune*, but another iteration erected only a few blocks away from the Highland Park house, plus two other prizewinners built in the same neighborhood the following year, went unmentioned by the paper.[110] In 1950, the *Arlington Heights Herald* real estate listings advertised "Tribune prize winner #18" (Uebelhack's design) for sale, and the ad promised that the house was "95% finished," in the suburb of Bensenville.[111] Lack of an address makes that house difficult to trace.

If the newspaper had the power to get houses built, furnished and decorated, publicized, and then sold, the question remains why the *Tribune*'s housing project fell short of its stated ambitions. By June 1946, the *Tribune* specified the number of vets who would receive Prize Homes houses through the program: only twenty, a tiny fraction of those in need.[112] The newspaper recorded the erection of seventeen houses in the Chicago area, and one more in Kankakee, a number far short of Boyd Hill's stated expectation of 144. If one confined one's *Tribune* reading solely to the stories about the Chicagoland Prize Homes, the picture is rosy. But elsewhere in the paper, obstacles to providing veterans' housing appear again and again.

Both federal policies and Chicago municipal building policies served to restrict building, not facilitate it, many people thought. A 1,500 square footage limitation on approved new housing was intended to ensure affordable housing, but the Chicago Metropolitan Home Builders Association, by the end of 1946, worried the city faced a glut of too-small houses. Raising the square footage requirement would, in their estimation, permit construction of more two-story, three-bedroom houses, residences better suited to families. They also wanted construction projects begun before legislation passed in May 1946 to be grandfathered into new rules.[113] Some found the government regulations a deterrent to building at all. A report from the National Association of Real Estate Boards cited one response from a builders' representative: "We represent five builders who are ready, willing, and able to produce 500 houses in the next 12 months. Government red tape is responsible for their failure to produce. Home building is at a standstill in this area." Another builder knew who to blame: "Government controls, restrictions, and changing policies have completely discouraged us from building more homes for sale or rent."[114] Chicago building codes that dated back to 1939 came in for even more criticism. Their stringency deterred certain kinds of house framing, required too much spacing between houses and other buildings, and discouraged prefabricated housing. After strong lobbying efforts, the city council planned for some emergency measures to ease building requirements, seeking an advisory board that included Chicagoland Prize Homes jurors Philip Maher and A. N. Rebori.[115] Emergency revisions eased some barriers, but not all of them. Rehauling the codes would be a long-term project. Chicagoland Prize Homes juror John O. Merrill, advisor to a subcommittee of the Chicago city council, at the end of 1946 embarked on what he said would be a year-long review and revision of city codes.[116]

At the most essential level, the ambition to build outpaced the availability of materials. Despite a call immediately after the war's end to favor residential over commercial construction, the pace of retail store and business building rose faster than residential building; labor power and raw materials for the former meant less available for the latter.[117] Wage stabilization policies were blamed for preventing brickyards from being able to hire enough labor to keep up with demand, creating a major shortage of bricks.[118] The *Tribune* reported on a half-finished, fifty-house project in Homewood, stymied by the brick shortage and the lack of available flooring, sewer tile, and electrical conduits.[119] The American Legion accused the government of hoarding building supplies of all kinds: toilets, nails, and paint. One Chicagoland Prize Homes juror, builder Irvin Blietz, weighed in. "A builder must search a long time to find materials, place an order, and then wait—and wait," adding that there could be no movement on large building projects until supply chains opened up.[120] Shortages created a thriving black market.[121] Desperate for a home, some buyers moved in before their houses were finished.[122]

Such delays may have influenced the houses' quality. Rich Schneider, owner of one of the Lombard houses, described his home as extremely well made.[123] In contrast, the Halpers had a very different experience. Their Uebelhack house in Highland Park developed ceiling cracks, the floors were uneven, and the basement flooded regularly, spewing up sewage from the basement toilet, an annual problem they lived with for forty years.[124] Steve Smedley, in junior high, visited three houses with his father when they were house hunting. They rejected one house because there was standing water, and that tipped the family to buying the Wheaton Uebelhack house, which, ultimately, also flooded regularly.[125] Both houses were torn down in the mid-2000s.

Shortages, delays, and black-market prices, in turn, drove up the cost of the houses, and the "affordable" part of the program to provide housing for vets fell away. The average cost to build a house fell in 1946, from a peak of $8,350 to a low of $7,500 in May, but this number did not include everything; the cost of land and utilities added another $2,000 to $4,000, and even that did not include any profit for the builder.[126] A war department survey from December 1945 showed that only 12 percent of discharged "men" could afford a house that cost more than $6,000; even the dropping prices were still too high.[127] In theory, people buying more expensive housing freed up less expensive accommodations when they moved up; those wanting to build expensive houses would have to convince the general public of the communal benefits of pricier houses. Note, too, the internal conflict between veterans' needs: they needed houses small enough to be affordable but with enough square footage to accommodate their families. Developers—and buyers—must have been frustrated in trying to achieve such contradictory goals.

A push toward building residences for purchase faced backlash. Despite the G. I. Bill's offering of down payment–free mortgages, despite the availability of good employment, purchasing a house was out of reach for many. Yet government policies and builders' preferences leaned toward creating units for sale rather than rent. Many people thought the solution was to build more rental housing. Apartment buildings needed fewer building materials, used less land, and required less costly commitment to street paving, sewage and water, and utilities.[128] A report from the Chicago Housing Center suggested that 97 percent of vets wanted to rent.[129] Renting was a common enough practice; over two-thirds of families residing in Chicago rented in the 1920s, continuing to rent well through the Depression.[130]

After Wyatt's resignation as Truman's housing "czar," federal policy changed again. By mid-December 1946, the *Tribune* ran a banner headline on its front page: "Priorities on Homes Ended." Federal policies canceled the $10,000 house price ceiling eligibility for vets, ended priorities and subsidies on materials, and allowed anyone, veteran or not, to build a new home, though vets still would get preference on any non-custom housing for purchase or rent. Truman's administration promised to simplify the permit system, indicating that if the priority had been houses for sale in 1946, 1947 would prioritize rental housing. Square footage would still be limited, however, and probably would be well short of the 1,800 minimum that builders wanted.[131] By December 1946, however, construction on Prize Homes houses had already begun, and the program was tied to its commitment.

Against the backdrop of the shortages, cost overruns, and a small market for expensive houses, the *Tribune* had to concede that the expectations for the Prize Homes building project would have to be adjusted. The newspaper admitted that "increased labor and material costs" brought house prices to $22,500 to $37,500, nearly double what had been anticipated.[132] In reporting on the Kankakee house, the *Tribune* revealed damaging information. "Hammes [the Kankakee developer] was one of 98 contractors in Chicagoland outside Cook County who contracted to build a Tribune prize home—a program that the federal housing agency refused to expedite. Ninety-seven of the contractors, unwilling to buck the scarcity of materials and the uncertainty of the market for a custom-built house, let the program drop." Hammes persuaded the Kankakee American Federation of Labor (AFL) chapter and business leaders to build the house regardless, but as the showpiece of his Marycrest subdivision, it was the only custom home among a neighborhood of far more modest, repeated designs. Perhaps Hammes, who was already a successful entrepreneur, considered the Sackville-West house he built there as a "loss-leader" to bring potential home buyers to the neighborhood.[133] It is not clear who contracted with the ninety-eight builders; was it the Chicago Tribune Prize Homes Building program mentioned only a few times, and then only cursorily, in the *Tribune*? Its obvious lack of success might be why it fell from view.

As noted, the Prize Homes contest rewarded sufficiently conventionally styled houses that would appeal to average house buyers, but it missed the mark in both size and price. More than half of the submissions addressed problem number one: a family consisting of parents and one child. The birth rate had dropped in the 1930s, during the Depression, and only children were not uncommon. Two-bedroom houses could accommodate multiple children, but only if they were the same sex; it had been many decades since Americans had found it acceptable for brothers and sisters to share rooms. Three-bedroom houses, then, would quickly become a housing standard. Also, Prize Homes houses, even the *Tribune* admitted, were just too expensive. Despite the contest's goal of creating affordable housing for the regular family, Prize Homes houses were singular enough to be accessible only to the more affluent buyer.

The *Tribune* identified six specific veterans who were to purchase houses. Their stories illuminate both the dire need for housing and the difficulty in providing it. James McDaniel, the first veteran to break ground, at one of two Lombard houses, hoped in June 1946 to move his family into his house by the fall. Post-groundbreaking, the *Tribune* twice reported on construction status and indicated things were not progressing. Four photographs with substantial captions appeared in the paper at the end of July, showing a building half constructed. The *Tribune* reminded readers the house was for

McDaniel, and that other "homes based on the contest's winning designs are being built for veterans in other locations in and around Chicago."[134] But the hoped-for fall move-in never happened. In November 1946, Edward Barry wrote an unusually forthright description of the challenge of building the house. After the framework, walls, and stonework were finished in August, construction came to a halt.

> No soil pipe was available, and for about seven weeks virtually nothing was done on the house. In the latter part of October the soil pipe arrived, but it was not installed because a shortage of box cars had made it impossible to obtain the cement necessary to construct the slab which is to be laid over the pipe. As this is written the cement still has not arrived. When it does, the house will be about two months from completion.[135]

That house and the Prize Homes house across the street were not ready to show for nearly another year, opening to the public on October 5, 1947. When the *Tribune* publicized the Lombard open houses that October, they omitted naming James McDaniel as the homeowner of 100 W. Washington and, indeed, did not mention veterans at all.[136] Agnes Lynch's article (with six accompanying photographs) interviewing visitors to the open house also neglected any reference to an owner.[137] But in December 1947, a local publication, *Oak Park Oak Leaves*, advertised both Lombard houses for sale. At least three times between December 4, 1947, and January 8, 1948, readers saw this real estate listing: "TRIBUNE Prize Homes No. 5 and No. 16. Five rooms, gas heat, attached garage, $19,750. Six rooms, 2 baths, 2 fireplaces, gas heat, 115 ft. corner lot $29,950. Both in Lombard. Immediate possession. Phone Lombard 417." By April 1948, one had sold, and *Oak Park Oak Leaves* had this ad: "Real Estate for Sale . . . Tribune Prize Home No. 5 gas heat Att. Gar., util room and base. $19,000."[138] The price of the smaller Woolford and Peterson house dropped. The McDaniels family did not, in the end, buy the house; the most likely first owners Marjorie and C. Galen Sedgwick (ages fifty-three and fifty-four) lived there with their adult son in 1950.[139]

Other veterans faced the same constraints. Reporting on the groundbreaking ceremony to come in Wheaton, the *Tribune* on June 16, 1946, featured the former Navy officer Madison P. Neilson, now, in civilian life, a thirty-five-year-old attorney for United Airlines. He and his family were desperate for housing.

> For six months, the Neilsons followed want ads and jumped at tips, but always in vain. They returned wearily to a room in a south side hotel, where the raising of a 4 year old boy is no joy. But one afternoon recently the John Cummings Lindop real estate company told him he was eligible for a Tribune home which the Lindop firm had arranged to construct on a subdivided country club at Wheaton.[140]

The *Tribune* ran a photo on June 30, with Mr. and Mrs. Neilson and the four-year-old, Billy, all three cheerful at the groundbreaking ceremony.[141] A year later, however, an August 10 article promised the house would be completed by September 1, and then open to the public for a month-long showing. The article quoted John Lindop, head of the real estate company, saying the house "has not been sold."[142]

The Neilsons' Wheaton house design came from Howard Uebelhack, and that same design was used for the Highland Park house designated for retired veteran Matt Kane. The Kanes presented an appealing story. Lieutenant Colonel Kane retired from the Army after recovering from an arm injury sustained during the war. The Kanes (Mrs. Kane's first name is never mentioned) and their two children had been unable to secure housing; Lieutenant Colonel Kane, working in the Loop, resided with his mother in the Chicago area, while the rest of the family lived with Mrs. Kane's mother in Des Moines, Iowa.[143] A year later, the coverage of the open house made no mention of the Kanes; the house's first owners were likely the Grossmans, a couple with a one-year-old child, who lived there in 1950.[144] Perhaps the Kanes, like the McDaniels, either could not afford the cost of the house or could not wait so long to occupy it. Likewise, Hugh and Anne Falvey, both of whom served in the war, were slated for the two-bedroom Sunnyside Avenue house; they attended the groundbreaking ceremony and had their pictures in the *Tribune* coverage of that event. Chicago phone directories indicate a Hugh Falvey did live in Chicago in 1947 and 1949 but never at the Sunnyside address.[145] In 1950, Charles Kelly, his wife, Ann, and their one-year-old daughter resided there.[146]

Taylor Bell and his family were to occupy the Wenstrand house in Blue Island; they were featured in the *Tribune*, having attended the groundbreaking ceremony. Before the war, Bell had a dental practice in the area, and clearly the family wished to stay in the area. Bell's son, five years old at the time of the groundbreaking and shown in *Tribune* photos playing in the dirt with a toy shovel, confirmed that his family never lived in the house designated for them. His mother saved copies of the *Tribune* pictures and articles, but the Bells stayed in the bungalow they owned before the war until 1948, when they moved to new house a few blocks from the Wenstrand house. The Bell family story is that Bell fairly quickly lost interest in the Prize Homes house when he realized that neither the house nor the lot would be big enough to accommodate an in-home dental practice. He soon pivoted to the idea of a custom home, found a large lot just a couple of blocks away, and hired an architect to design a family home with a separate entrance to a dental office: two examining rooms, lab space, a reception area, and a half-bathroom for patients.[147]

Only one of the six designated families appears to have bought and resided in a Prize Homes house. The two-bedroom house in Palatine—a Sackville-West house—had a groundbreaking ceremony, but at the time, the *Tribune* did not name a specific veteran occupant. Only when the house was completed, and the open house ready for public viewing, were the new owners named: Leroy and Cecilia Langhamer. Mrs. Langhamer, according to the *Tribune*, appeared to have been the prime mover in choosing the house.

> Leroy was an army sergeant serving with the corps of engineers in the Philippines. Cecilia was in Chicago waiting for him to return and working on designs for the home they planned to build. In the second set of prize winning designs, published Feb. 10, 1946, she saw the floor plan and artist's representation of Arthur J. Sackville-West's five rooms. "I knew at once it was exactly what I wanted," said Mrs. Langhamer, who is pretty and blond. "I saved the page to show to my husband. He came home March 22, 1946, and was just as enthusiastic about it as I." "It happened that the general sales manager of Arthur T. McIntosh & Co., the builders, is a friend of ours," said Langhamer. "We were the first to call about the house, and were put at the head of the list."

The Langhamers acknowledged the high price of the house—$18,000—but were happy to pay it.[148] A 1948 telephone directory confirms the Langhamers did reside at that address. The Langhamer family story differs from the other five in certain ways. They had no children at the time of the house purchase, and Mr. Langhamer served as a corporate vice-president; perhaps higher income and childlessness reduced pressure to secure housing. But more important, they seem to have come to the process of buying the home late enough that the house price would not have come as a surprise. They knew what they were getting and knew the cost.

In its extensive coverage of the Deer Park houses, the *Tribune* abandoned the practice of matching a named veteran to a specific house. By the time the houses were completed, and Chicagoans had had the opportunity to walk through the decorated houses, seven had been sold; the *Tribune* did not specify to whom.[149] In October 1947, a *Tribune* classified ad indicated the Deerfield Company was still offering three of the houses: Garbe's four-bedroom, and Sloan's and Wenstrand's three-bedroom houses. Prices were, respectively, $37,500, $35,000, and $33,500. The ad made no mention that the purchaser had to be a veteran, only that they were "for the discriminating buyer only." Buyers could take immediate possession.[150] Among the male first owners of the Deer Park houses, neither Harry Scheckerman nor Milt Fink was a veteran.[151] Others were not likely to have been vets, either. Nathan Krupnick, who lived in the Sackville-West house, was not only born in Russia but also was about fifty years old in 1940, beyond the 1941 draft age of forty-four. Probably outside of the draft age window, as well as being born in Austria, was Alex Schoenfeld, who was fifty-four years old in 1950.[152] It is a good bet that Abraham Zimmerman (alias Joe White), who bought the Cedarstrand house, was not a veteran, either. Convicted of income tax evasion in 1939, his name is listed as "Joe Zimmerman" on the 1950 census form, and despite the name change, he was investigated, arrested, and rearrested multiple times for running illegal gambling schemes.[153]

Other than Bell's interest in having room for a dental practice out of his home, two other reasons might explain why veterans did not, in the end, buy the homes they had hoped for. As noted earlier, the house prices ended up much higher than expected. The G. I. Bill offered a generous mortgage—with no down payment—but borrowers still needed a salary ample enough to make a monthly mortgage payment, pay property taxes, and cover home maintenance costs. And, were the cost of buying not prohibitive, the building delays may have been. House construction begun in early summer of 1946 but not completed more than a year later may have left would-be buyers to seek other arrangements. The *Tribune* related the dire circumstances of the McDaniels, living in a hotel with their young child while searching for housing. The Kanes, at groundbreaking, were living apart. Even had they been able to afford a house that turned out to cost $30,000, twice the expected price and already well beyond what most veterans could afford, they may well have preferred arrangements that would bring them together in weeks or months rather than in over a year.

Despite the *Tribune*'s declaration that the competition would bring attractive and efficient houses to average Chicagoans, only half of that turned out to be true. The house designs are beautiful and modern, but average Chicagoans could not have afforded them. If only 12 percent of vets could afford a house priced above $6,000, even the *initial* expected price of the most modest house, by Sackville-West, at $9,000, would have been 50 percent more than what 88 percent of vets could afford. Sackville-West's house ended up costing twice that: $18,000. Had the builders waited until building supplies were plentiful—the *Tribune* reported in mid-1947 that construction costs were expected to drop, and the "scarcity premium" would be gone by 1950—the houses still would have been beyond the reach of average home buyers.[154]

What ultimately solved the housing crisis—in Chicago and nationally—was a two-pronged solution. First, developers began to build apartments and row houses for rent. Throughout 1946, the *Tribune* reported on grand plans for new single-family residences, but in January 1947, the new year began with a story on how newer federal policies were loosening money for developers to build rental housing.[155] Seven projects for rental housing in Chicago and its northern suburbs were announced in April; construction of six apartment buildings in suburban Evanston and Chicago was announced in July.[156] The *Tribune* reported in June 1947 that Chicago would be home to the most expensive FHA project to date: a $27.5 million endeavor to build more than 3,000 rental units, in the form of row houses and duplexes, in a brand-new, unnamed suburb. That project included an additional project to build 8,500 single-family homes. "We are building for families with children," said the developer. "We want this new suburban city, with an expected eventual population of about 25,000 to be a place where people of moderate incomes can enjoy living." The new suburb, on Chicago's South Side, was initially unnamed, with developers expecting residents to suggest names.[157] However, their placeholder name stuck: Park Forest.

Park Forest also exemplifies the second solution to affordable housing: building single-family houses using economies of scale.[158] Randall's history of Park Forest locates the town in the context of the economic and supply restrictions. Levittown and its like had not yet begun, and without that business model, builders of individual houses—or even a small cluster as in Deer Park—could not turn a profit by building houses sprinkled here and there. When planning the first single-family houses, Park Forest developers settled on an 828-square-foot house, with two bedrooms, a small kitchen, and likely no dining room. A carport would later be added to the design, and plans were to eventually include some three-bedroom houses. Developers worked hard to shave off any unnecessary costs, moving the house closer to the street, for example, to shorten the materials and labor needed for sewer and water connections. Suppliers delivered building materials directly to the lot, cutting down delivery time. In 1952, this kept a house price down to $12,000.[159] The iconic Levittown Cape Cod design, although it possessed an attic space that could add two more bedrooms as families and incomes grew, adhered to an even smaller footprint, at 750 square feet, and at $7,500, a much lower price.[160] Tract homes eliminated basements, building right on top of a cement slab; roofs were not usually flat but tended to be low-sloped; high-pitched roofs cost more, in labor hours and materials. Builders saved money by keeping the house completely square or rectangular. Designing the bathroom and kitchen to share a wall efficiently put the plumbing together.[161] Park Forest houses were no anomaly: in 1950, the average square footage of a newly constructed house was 983, and nearly half of new houses had two bedrooms.[162] In the end, it was the builders' tract house development that got Americans into their own homes, not the piecemeal offerings promoted by the *Chicago Tribune*.[163]

Houses in Flux

Prize Homes Houses Evolve

That the *Tribune* promised to build houses and made good on that promise—even if on a smaller scale than initially thought—sets the Chicagoland Prize Homes competition apart from others. Other architectural design competitions generated a few houses, but such houses are difficult to trace. The *Tribune*'s publicity makes it possible to identify many of the built Prize Homes. At least in the Chicago area, about thirty houses were built from thirteen different designs; addresses are known for twenty-three of them. While three of the known houses have been torn down, those remaining have been remodeled and expanded, bringing them in line with late-twentieth-century house expectations. The evolution of Prize Homes houses reflects residents' changing needs over the decades since the houses were built.

As the previous chapter indicates, some modifications came from the original builders, who already knew what people wanted in houses and what could feasibly be delivered to them. Perhaps they also conceded to shortages in construction materials and labor power. They reversed designs, repositioned or added windows, expanded the square footage by stretching exterior walls, and rearranged interior walls. The first residents, too, did not wait long before making their own changes. Some of those changes were minor: finishing basements, screening in porches, and adding window awnings. Other modifications, as we will see, were more substantial.

Five problem one designs were built, but not all of them as originally planned. Arthur Sackville-West's two-bedroom house was built at least three times. His house is the most modest among those built, perhaps the most modest among the ninety-two. *Prize Homes* described it as 900 square feet, in line with the small houses the tract housing developers were beginning to build. The house has "a combination living room and dinette," a small bedroom about 10 by 10 square feet and a larger bedroom that is 14 by 10. The "dinette and kitchen are small; but when guests are invited for dinner, the dinette table can easily be extended into the living room."[1] In 1946, the APS Home Plans booklet featuring the house extended the dining and living room by two feet, indicating a concern even then that the house was too small.[2] A two-bedroom house was a gamble; it worked for the smallest family but would challenge the household with the addition of another child, especially if of the opposite sex. Sackville-West's house was one of three Prize Homes houses chosen by Home Planners, Inc., to be included in all three editions of its catalog. Dean Robinson's series of syndicated columns featured it, and that article was carried dozens of times throughout the country. Coder Taylor's two-bedroom house was also included in all editions of the catalog and featured in Robinson's columns. It is impossible to know how many of these houses were built.

For a married couple with only one child, designers often thought two bedrooms were insufficient. Ten of the thirty-one problem one designs either included a third bedroom outright or added another room that could be used as a bedroom. Woolford and Peterson's design included a small third bedroom labeled for "study/guest." As built, however, that small bedroom was eliminated in favor of creating a large closet off the larger bedroom; that the house has only two bedrooms is a disadvantage, even for the couple who currently own the house. Although it is just the two of them, the owners wish there were a third bedroom, and they have contemplated turning the existing living room into a primary suite, since a family room addition is the main living space.[3] Builders of two other problem one houses were savvier. The Walter Thies design is nominally a two-bedroom house but, according to the copy in the *Prize Homes* book, "Although this house is designed for a family of three, the size of the storage room and the good-sized study on the first floor suggest that the house could comfortably accommodate a larger group when required."[4] Deer Park builders took that advice; when the *Tribune* announced the project, the Thies house was described as a three-bedroom house.[5] Builders did the same with Charles Schroeder's house, as one of its two bedrooms is quite large and has a large dressing room; it was built as a three-bedroom house.

Demand for two-bedroom houses waned. The Palatine version of Sackville-West's design, subject of a month-long spate of oohs and ahhs from visitors, was torn down in the 2000s and in 2020 remained a vacant lot. (Whether any modifications occurred before the teardown is unknown.) A version built in Kankakee, Illinois, exists but now with an attached garage and what is likely a kitchen addition; it is still probably only a two-bedroom house.[6] The Deer Park iteration still exists but has been expanded in two directions: a second-story addition can be seen from the street, and a rear extension is visible from an aerial view. There is at least an additional bedroom and probably at least one additional bathroom; its current square footage probably doubles the original.[7]

Coder Taylor's two-bedroom house was built in 1948 with an unusual bathroom configuration: side-by-side bathrooms had one room with a toilet and sink, while the other had a tub and sink. The current owners have remodeled, creating two full bathrooms, but it is still a two-bedroom house, with one tiny "storage" room currently used as an office. The footprint is unchanged, and there is still a one-car garage. The galley kitchen—which the Moran family found too small sixty years ago—is still quite modest. Before the current owners remodeled that room, it lacked a full-size refrigerator, instead relying on side-by-side counter-height refrigerators.[8]

Schroeder's problem one house also has undergone significant alteration. Access to the garage comes through a back alley. When the current owners, the Valdezes, moved in around 2002, there was already a two-car garage where there likely was only a one-car garage originally. A bay window has been added to the front façade. Schroeder's design placed a minimal canopy over the front door; now, the house has a conventional porch with enough room for a couple of chairs, and pillars supporting a larger overhang. Centered windows, the bay window, and the porch give the house a very different appearance from the original; it looks like a Chicago vernacular design generally known as "Georgian."

The family's own renovation pushed out the back of the house, possibly doubling the original footprint. That addition turned the small kitchen into a sizable bathroom, attaching a bedroom to create a primary suite. A new, large kitchen opens to a new dining space.[9] What was designed as a

Two of the Moran babies in high chairs, in the galley kitchen of the Coder Taylor house. (Photo courtesy of Ann Moran.)

two-bedroom, one-and-a-half-bathroom house was built with three bedrooms, and now it has four bedrooms and one more full bathroom.

Modest two-bedroom houses are now relics of an earlier age, certainly undesirable for families with children. As a twenty-year-old newlywed in 1958, Ann Moran was thrilled to be able to buy the Coder Taylor house in Highland Park. But four years later, she and her husband had had three children, finding no other space for the baby's crib than the five-by-eight-and-a-half-foot storage room that current owners use as an office. Because the Morans expected to have even more children, they left the house for one that would accommodate their expanding family.[10] As mentioned above, even by the time of the competition, Americans had become accustomed to the social practice of giving children their own bedrooms. The Morans' experience echoed national trends. Only a third of new houses built in the early 1950s had three bedrooms; by the end of 1955, two-thirds of new houses did.[11] It is no surprise that, by the turn of the century, a two-bedroom house would be outdated and would need to be either replaced or expanded. Only Taylor's Highland Park house is substantially unchanged. The current residents, a couple with no children, find it just right for them but fear that whenever the time comes to sell, buyers will be merely interested in the large lot and will tear down the house in favor of new, roomier construction.[12]

Charles Schroeder's original design has corner widows and a minimal canopy over the front door. It was built with centered windows, and at some time, a bay window and larger porch and overhang were added. These changes make the house look like what Chicagoans call a "Georgian." (*Prize Homes*, 12; contemporary photo courtesy of Scott McDougall and Lake Forest College.)

Designs for problem two, the family with a boy and girl, required three bedrooms to comply with the housing standard that opposite-sex children should not share rooms. Eric Wenstrand's submission for that category is a modest house: the three bedrooms, one shared bathroom, a dining alcove, and a garage attached to the house but inaccessible directly from the house. It was built five times in the Chicago area. A version in Deerfield, a northern suburb of Chicago, was torn down and replaced by a newer, probably four-bedroom house. Before the Golans moved there in 1979, a powder room had been carved out of the utility area. The Golans built a garage in back, turning the attached garage into a family room.[13] The one in Blue Island, subject of much *Chicago Tribune* publicity, has also been remodeled. The Hendrixes, the second owners, built a detached two-car garage at the back of the lot, so the third and current owners converted the original attached garage into a primary suite, which gives the house four bedrooms and two bathrooms.[14] The Highland Park version has been altered significantly. As

Four iterations of Eric Wenstrand's house still exist. The one in Whiting, Indiana (bottom right), is unmodified. The Deer Park version (top right) got an early rear addition, but the garage is intact. The Blue Island (bottom left) and Highland Park (top left) garages have been turned into living space: in Highland Park, that space is a home office, and in Blue Island, it is a primary suite with bathroom. Compare to Wenstrand's original sketch on page 57. (Photo of Whiting house by the author; others courtesy of Scott McDougall and Lake Forest College.)

it occupies a large lot, the garage, like in Blue Island, has also been incorporated into the house's living space; there is also an added two-car garage just next to it. One owner turned a bedroom into a dining room and used the dining alcove to expand the kitchen, then built out the back of the house to create an owners' suite and another bedroom. The current owners, the Creinins, removed the upper wall between the kitchen and the living room, opening and brightening the space even further.[15] Adaptations over the years give the house a dedicated dining room, a larger kitchen, four bedrooms, and two bathrooms, plus a two-car garage. The original occupants of the West Rogers Park version have not been located. They did not stay long, but when the Scheckermans moved there in 1949, the two-year-old home had already been modified with a rear addition that added a primary bedroom suite.[16] A version in Whiting, Indiana (just over the Illinois border and essentially a suburb of Chicago), appears from the outside to be unchanged.[17]

Burns's house, with three bedrooms, one shared bathroom, and a second bathroom accessible from the both the hall and the primary bedroom, was built twice. The Lombard iteration, built in reverse from the architect's drawings, is significantly bigger today than it was in 1946. The original one-car garage is now living space, likely an expansion of the kitchen. To the side is a two-car garage, with a second floor above that; it would not be a surprise if the upper story contained a primary suite. Street views indicate the high strip windows in the back of the large combined living and dining space have been replaced, either by sliding or French doors or large windows.

Six of the ten houses built in the Deer Park neighborhood were three-bedroom constructions. One was a duplicate of Burns's Lombard house; *Prize Homes* includes a photograph of the house as built in Deer Park. Comparing that photograph to the house today reveals the same one-car garage, but part of the original outdoor terrace in front has been enclosed, increasing living space. At some point, the modest primary bedroom was enlarged. The toilet and sink of the primary bathroom, which was also accessible via a hall, were closed to the bedroom and accessible only through the hall, creating a half-bath. The renovation created a new primary bathroom; the three-bedroom, two-bathroom home now has an additional half-bath and a much larger primary suite.

Sloan designed a large house: it has a two-car garage that can be accessed through a laundry room, an owners' suite with walk-in closet and full bath, and a shared bathroom on the second floor. The family can eat in the very small breakfast nook in the kitchen, but otherwise the dining and living space are combined; Sloan shows the placement of a couch to divide the area.[18] In the late 1950s, the probable first owners expanded the house, adding a large dining room; the current owners, the Horoviczes, can seat twenty guests. Below that addition, the remodel extended the basement, adding a full bathroom. Accessible from an external door, the basement addition could be used as a separate unit; the Horoviczes' newlywed grandson lived there with his bride while both were finishing school.[19]

Hanson and Martorano's three bedroom offered 1,400 square feet, not including basement or garage. Two full, shared baths occupy the second floor along with the three bedrooms. The second floor also has an alcove, labeled "sewing room," a space that would not be big enough for a bedroom but perhaps could serve as reading nook or play area. The first floor has a lavatory; the kitchen includes a snack bar. One additional three-bedroom house has also undergone changes. Carl Cedarstrand's two-story house has been expanded in three directions. At the front, the jutting garage has

The original Carl Cedarstrand house and the post-renovation version. Current owners bumped out the second floor above the garage to create another bedroom. (*Prize Homes*, 42; contemporary photo courtesy of Scott McDougall and Lake Forest College.)

an addition on top of it, adding a fourth bedroom. In the back of the first floor, a significant addition expands the footprint, creating a larger kitchen and family room. Renovations also went down, expanding and finishing the basement under the rear addition, which adds a guest room, a bathroom, and an additional kitchen.[20] As the house already had a primary suite bathroom, albeit a modest one, the house comports well with late-twentieth-century American house standards: primary suite plus four other bedrooms, three and a half bathrooms, and a large family room. Only the single-car garage is a throwback to an earlier era.

Seven four-bedroom houses were built. Four of the seven were the Uebelhack design; the *Tribune* heavily promoted two of them, among the first six Prize Homes houses built, in Wheaton and Highland Park. With four bedrooms, two shared bathrooms, plus a lavatory, the house allows a family with three children to occupy their own rooms. A good-sized entry gives

The Wheaton iteration of Howard Uebelhack's house was built in reverse. A watercolor painting owned by the Smedley family shows the second-story addition. Contrast with the first Highland Park version. (*Prize Homes*, 7; photo courtesy of Eleanor Smedley.)

access to a lavatory, and in addition to a dining ell, the "kitchen includes a bay window, which should provide a sunny breakfast nook." The Wheaton house had already been significantly expanded when the Smedleys moved there in 1971, with a second-story addition (dating back to the late '50s or early '60s) above the garage and kitchen, which added two more bedrooms and a bathroom, rendering it a six-bedroom, three-and-a-half-bathroom home.[21]

Despite the size of the Highland Park and expanded Wheaton houses, both were torn down in the 2000s, replaced by larger houses. The replacements may not have more bedrooms or even more bathrooms, but they certainly have more garage space, closets, and modern updates. Just a few blocks from the widely promoted Uebelhack house in Highland Park, another iteration was built. Original owners, the Balsams, delayed the construction of the fourth bedroom and second full bathroom. When the family expanded the house, they put an additional bedroom and bathroom in the same place as on Uebelhack's original floor plan but made it a dedicated owners' suite. At the same time, they enclosed the porch to create a family room; as has been shown, over the 1950s and '60s, that space became an attractive place for casual family activities and to put the television set. Sunny Balsam remembers the television, previously in the basement, available in the new family room in time to watch the Beatles on the Ed Sullivan show, dating the renovation to 1963 or 1964.[22] The Chicago suburb of Bensonville also had a Uebelhack house, but the address is unknown.[23]

The three other four-bedroom houses are in Deer Park. Arthur Myhrum's design is quite large. On the first floor, living and dining space meld together; the kitchen is adjacent to a laundry room and a large "storage" room, plus a lavatory. The garage accommodates two cars. On the second floor is an owners' suite that boasts "upstairs sitting space," three additional bedrooms, plus one shared full bath. (The original plan had two side-by-side bathrooms, one with a tub and the other with, perhaps, a shower. The builders just made one larger bathroom.) *Prize Homes* called it a "highly original design"; its flat roof and unusually stark front façade make it the most modern of any of the built homes, although as built, the front façade was softened by the addition of second-floor bedrooms facing the street, where there were initially none. Myhrum's submission, very unusually, does not portray the front of the house but instead gives a rear view, showing a small ornamental pool and patio. Despite the house's size, the original owners expanded the footprint, adding another living space, with fireplace, behind the garage and then adding a screened patio beyond that.[24]

Around the corner is another spacious house, by Garbe. On the second floor, the original plan shows a Jack-and-Jill bath between the daughters' and parents' rooms, but as built, the bathroom is only accessible through the owner's room.[25] Two other bedrooms are marked for son or "daughter or guest," and there is a second bathroom, open to the hallway. On the first floor, a thirty-one-foot-long living room dominates, and there is a dinette (the doorway between the dinette and living room was built as a wider entry than the original plan mandated), a kitchen with a passthrough to the dining room, a laundry room, a study, and a lavatory. Despite the size, a long room the length of the living room was added to the back of the house.

Across the street is the last of the four-bedroom designs, a single story by Burch. Bedrooms are marked: "Mom & Dad" share a Jack-and-Jill bathroom with "Little Janie," while "Billy" and "Mary" have bedrooms separated by a shared bath, also accessible from the hallway. Common areas are large, and the dining room is more separated from the living room than in

Edward Burch's original ranch is significantly bigger in 2022. Current owners have extensively remodeled and expanded, even moving the front door. (*Prize Homes*, 73; contemporary photo courtesy of Scott McDougall and Lake Forest College.)

most houses. A one-car attached garage is accessible through the kitchen. As large as this house was when built, it has been expanded. The current owners have lived there since 1990 and have made multiple alterations. What was the front-facing garage is now a large expansion of the original kitchen. A new wing adds another bedroom and bathroom. The space where the original front door was now leads to a new, two-car garage; the main entrance is now centered in the middle of the house. Behind the new garage, a half-level up adds two more bedrooms and a bathroom.

House modifications are shaped by the cultural norms and preferences of the people who live there. Tracking those changes necessitates reviewing Chicago's patterns of ethnic and racial segregation across the twentieth century. A strong national parish system dating back to the 1800s helped cluster Catholic immigrants in neighborhoods consolidated by religious, ethnic, and linguistic similarity.[26] Among Catholics and Christians of European ancestry, this meant identifiably Irish, German, Swedish, Polish, Czech, Russian, and Greek neighborhoods. Later-twentieth-century immigrants to the city—Latinos mostly from Mexico, Black people migrating from the American South, and Asian immigrants, especially from India and Pakistan—further diversified the city, but those groups still lived in generally segregated neighborhoods. Redlining, restrictive covenants, discrimination, and outright violence kept some groups—most notably Black people—confined to particular areas, largely on the city's South Side.[27] Over time, however, many Chicago neighborhoods' demographic profiles have changed. One area, Pilsen, was named by the immigrants who settled there after a city in their Czech homeland, and in the latter half of the twentieth century, it became predominantly Mexican American. In the twenty-first century, it may be changing again as gentrification brings in younger, whiter professionals. Bridgeport, a neighborhood that contributed five mayors to Chicago (including both Daleys), today is more diverse than its historically Irish identification. Chicago's iconic gay neighborhood recently changed its name from Boystown to Northalsted, reflecting that not only White, gay men live there.

While the publicity surrounding the Prize Homes competition never mentioned race or ethnicity, it did not have to. Assumptions about racial segregation were reflected in the way the housing problem was addressed overall. The calls for more and better housing frequently addressed the need to house residents of specific demographic groups; housing for White people was referred to as housing. An opening address at the 1944 National Conference on Postwar Housing acknowledged that many Black Americans had the savings and income to support home ownership but could not buy in most neighborhoods because of White resistance. The remedy was to encourage developers to build housing specifically for that population.[28] Editors at *Architectural Record* agreed in 1945, insisting "private enterprise must embrace also adequate living accommodations for the foreign-born, Negros, and other races long neglected."[29] For White policy-makers and housing advocates, the lack of adequate housing for Black people and immigrants was not a problem of discrimination but, in the spirit of "separate but equal," merely an opportunity to provide high-quality but specifically demarcated housing options, creating and maintaining separate Black neighborhoods. There seemed to be little interest in opening White neighborhoods to anyone else.

Tracking the demographic changes of the Deer Park development in West Rogers Park and reviewing the architectural changes in the ten Prize Homes houses built there provides an opportunity to see how Chicago migration practices have shaped house preferences. According to Rogers Park/West Ridge Historical Society records, a significant amount of West Rogers Park land—twenty-five acres—had been owned by the Illinois Brick Company and home to brickyard #5, which had both a clay pit and a brick factory. German and Scandinavian workers drawn to the worksite in the early part of the twentieth century lived in the multifamily housing, Chicago's famous two- and three-flats, built in the area.[30] In the post–World War I housing boom, rows and rows of affordable single-family residences were constructed; one neighborhood of bungalows is among the National Register of Historic Places today.[31]

Jewish people immigrating to Chicago in the late 1800s and early 1900s were mostly Russians and Eastern Europeans, many fleeing pogroms. Like new immigrants to most cities, they clustered together; in Chicago, that was along Maxwell Street on the city's Southwest Side. Yiddish was the neighborhood *lingua franca* for Russians, Polish, and German Jewish immigrants. But by the late teens, those families—now one or two generations removed from the mother countries—used new wealth to move to other areas of the city. Many went to nearby Lawndale, which would become Chicago's largest Jewish neighborhood in the 1930s.[32] Others went a bit north to Albany Park.[33]

Many others leaving the Maxwell Street area found a home in the Uptown/Rogers Park neighborhood.[34] Migration in the teens and twenties brought synagogues and shops catering to a Jewish community, particularly on the main commercial street, Devon Avenue. In the 1930s and '40s, what had been a trickle became a flood, when Lawndale Jews virtually emptied their neighborhood. "There was a trend to have a home of your own," pointed out Chicago historian Irving Cutler, also noting "Lawndale had very few single-family homes."[35] Jewish families seeking home ownership had to look elsewhere; the demographics of Lawndale rapidly changed, and within a decade, it went from being predominantly Jewish to predominantly African American.[36] Currently living in a Prize Home, Marilyn Domsky embodies the migratory pattern: she was born in Lawndale, raised in Albany Park, and has lived in West Rogers Park most of her adult life. Her children and stepchildren, at least those living in the United States, live nearby, in West Rogers Park, Skokie, or Northbrook.[37] The Scheckermans left Lawndale when they bought their Prize Home in 1949.[38]

West Rogers Park could offer attractive options to families seeking a home in neighborhood that already had a significant Jewish presence: First, it had a good number of preexisting single-family bungalows, built in the 1920s housing boom. Second, and more rare, it had a lot of vacant land. The brickyard that had once been so crucial to economic life in the neighborhood closed in 1938; children played in the remaining clay pit, but not for long, as the property would soon be developed. The area also had some commercial farmland near the Deer Park development.[39] Joel Scheckerman, growing up on Pratt in the early 1950s, remembers a still somewhat undeveloped area: there was a swamp nearby and a place on Devon Avenue where he rode horses.[40] His neighbor Judy Fink walked to elementary school a few blocks east of her house; there was so little built environment that, from a second-floor window, her mother could watch her daughter, in a bright red hat, as she walked to school.[41] With postwar demand for housing, land within the Chicago city limits grew valuable; the area became one of the last undeveloped areas within the Chicago city limits, according to the Rogers Park/West Ridge Historical Society.[42] The Deerfield Company planned two housing projects for the neighborhood. In late 1946, the company leased six acres for ninety-nine years, right on the east bank of the north channel of the Chicago River, where the developers planned to construct two kinds of housing for veterans and their families: thirty row houses plus seventeen two- and three-story apartment buildings, for a total of 156 units.[43]

In addition to the leased property, the Deerfield Company bought outright twenty-five acres of land that had at least partially comprised the former brickyard. The city built a large, multi-block park immediately west of Sacramento, so the Deerfield Company scooped up an adjacent square of land, bordered by Pratt, Sacramento, Lunt, and California, for the Deer Park development.[44] Beyond those bordering streets lay both undeveloped land and previously built dwellings. Donna Scheckerman Orlove, who lived on Pratt, remembers that the street ended in front of the most western Prize Home; their quite large front yard decreased when the city widened the street while extending it.[45] The developer worked with the

Chicago Plan commission to lay out the streets, which the *Tribune* reported were to be curved (they are straight) and without alleys (there are some alleys). With a nearby bus stop already in place, contracts in place for utilities, and FHA approval of a minimum house price of $10,000, the neighborhood would be attractive and somewhat upscale. (1950 census records indicate the occupations for eight of the ten male "heads" of households: three were business owners, one was an attorney, and three were middle- or upper-level managers.[46]) The *Tribune* noted the project was one of the "first since the depression of the 1930's to improve undeveloped acreages for home building purposes on Chicago's north side."[47] This area of Chicago is as near to suburbs as one can get and still stay in the city, and the fact that the houses were built on undeveloped land, rather than in the wake of demolished substandard housing, would also have been attractive to buyers. While Black, Latino, and Indigenous veterans found it extremely difficult to secure even G. I. Bill–backed loans, Jewish veterans did not, so they could buy newer, modern houses in the area (although the original occupants of the Prize Homes were largely not veterans). The Deer Park neighborhood went up quickly, the development adjacent to older, traditional Chicago two- and three-flats on Lunt Avenue, and more modest houses built after the original ten Prize Homes. By the 1950s, it was the fastest-growing area of Chicago.[48]

Thus, a neighborhood that already had a sizable Jewish population found that community growing, pushing farther north and west. But by the mid-1940s, the Jewish population of West Rogers Park differed from the early immigrants to Maxwell Street. Many were now one, two, even three generations removed from the original immigrants, and their adherence to the ways of their great-grandparents and grandparents had waned. They spoke English, and they mostly sent their children to the excellent public schools in the neighborhood. Their observation of Jewish religious rules and customs varied: as Conservative or Reform Jews, they drove and bought groceries on the Sabbath, and they probably did not keep a kosher home. The Scheckermans wanted to live in a Jewish neighborhood but left the west side three-flat owned by Orthodox parents; the Finks, moving from Skokie, also sought out a Jewish neighborhood. Jewish immigrants to Chicago in the 1930s and '40s included those fleeing Germany, Austria, and Poland; they had Jewish identity but without the same kind of religious observation as those arriving in the late nineteenth and early twentieth century. Census records from 1950 indicate that of the nine Prize Homes households for which data exists, three families had adults born in Austria, Hungary, or Russia, while a fourth had a live-in maid from Germany; the briefest scan of the other houses in the neighborhood shows a similar pattern.[49] The area had plenty of Christians, too; West Rogers Park was also home to many Catholic churches and parochial schools. Still, the neighborhood retained its Jewish identity, and between 1930 and 1960, Jews were the largest single ethnic group in the area, and more than a third of the population.[50]

Over the decades, the neighborhood changed again.[51] The children of those postwar Jewish families grew up, and when establishing their own adult lives, rarely settled in West Rogers Park. They sought specific cities and neighborhoods but in the suburbs. The children of the Balsam and Halper families, both of whom left Chicago for Highland Park, described their parents' 1950s interest in Highland Park as a town where Jewish residents would feel welcomed.[52] With no prohibition against driving on Shabbat or holidays, and when not observing a kosher diet, they did not need the physical infrastructure to maintain Jewish life and identity. Like gentiles in Chicago, they feared urban decay, declining schools, and downward-trending housing values; they headed to Cook County suburbs like Skokie, Evanston, Northbrook, and Glenview, or Lake County cities like Highland Park, with large houses on large lots and the kind of excellent public schools they themselves had attended as children and teenagers in West Rogers Park.[53] This exodus meant that, at least for a while, the Jewish community of West Rogers Park declined, particularly in the 1970s. Those who remained were those who did not want to move to the suburbs, and they were largely Orthodox. When the Kanters were house shopping in 1995, Bill Kanter asked himself whether the neighborhood they ultimately chose would have a significant Orthodox presence in twenty-five years. When they first moved there, their neighbors were Jewish, but only two or three Orthodox families lived on their block. The Kanters made a good call, as their street is now the reverse of that original pattern; there are a couple of elderly neighbors who are Jewish but not Orthodox, and the rest of their block is Orthodox or Haredi.[54] A Catholic family, the Shiels, has had people knock on their door to see if they were interested in selling anytime soon; Rita Horovicz, across the street, reports the same thing. The requests have come from Orthodox families hoping to move into the neighborhood.[55]

Why did Reform and Conservative Jews, but not Orthodox Jews, leave for the suburbs? Orthodox Judaism requires walking, not driving, to synagogues, weekly if not daily, whereas suburban life centers around cars. To leave the neighborhood meant leaving the congregation. While it was and is possible to keep kosher in the suburbs, stores and restaurants catering to kosher customers are rarer than they are in West Rogers Park. When your children already attend private, religious schools, good suburban public thought to be superior to urban ones, and life is considered safer. But a shift to suburbs is not a feasible option for families who want to maintain life in a Jewish community and keep walking proximity to synagogues, and who already send their children to private, religious schools.

The residents of West Rogers Park, then, have had to adapt their homes to their needs. At the most basic level, this means more bedrooms and bathrooms. Four, five, six, seven, or more children must sleep somewhere. Larger families need room for more cars, more bicycles, more books, and more toys. At least three of the current owners have had five children; one of those families may yet have more. In addition to needing room for more occupants, Orthodox households have other special requirements. A trend for most Americans, and the architects who design their houses, has been to view the dining room as an expendable space. As the Prize Homes house designs indicate, the dining room is an expensive piece of real estate. Can a room that most households use only two or three times a year be justified? Increasingly, Americans have said no, choosing instead to eat in the kitchen or in a living-dining space, and using the square footage a dining room would have taken up for larger kitchens, living rooms, or recreation space. But as Ben Zeller, who studies the relationship between food and Judaism, noted, "the table is the center of the Jewish home."[70] Every Friday dinner and Saturday lunch, Valerie Kanter serves the equivalent of a "Christmas dinner."[71] Next door, the Domskys selected their house because they knew the thirty-foot-long living room could accommodate meals for their blended family of seven children. Eventually, they enclosed the porch that ran the length of that room, making it a dedicated room where their children, grandchildren, and great-grandchildren visit weekly for Saturday lunch.[72] Twenty-six people can sit around the tables placed end to end. Add to that the High Holy days, Hannukah, Passover, and other annual celebrations, when there might be four or five sequential meals, and the dining room for an Orthodox Jewish family takes on an importance rarely found in Christian or secular homes.

When the Kanters bought their home, the previous owner had a modest dining table, placed as shown on Cedarstrand's floor plan; the Kanters' dining table expands to twelve feet and stretches along the twenty-six-foot combined living-dining space, taking up nearly half of the room. They even moved the overhead dining chandelier from its position at the far end of the room to center it over their table, where they routinely have a dozen guests and sometimes have more than twenty.[73] Also, following dietary rules is easier with a kitchen that can accommodate two sets of pots and pans, two sets of cooking utensils, and two sets of dishes, glassware, and cutlery.[74] For some, the ideal kosher kitchen has two sinks, two ovens, and two refrigerators. A small kitchen poses a challenge to that aspiration. Preparing a kitchen for Passover meals requires *kashering*, an extensive cleaning and removal of many products. The Kanters' house renovations created a Passover kitchen in the basement, minimizing that extra work.[75]

Americans searching for more living space had long been drawn to suburban towns, with big lots and big houses. For Orthodox and Haredi families, however, leaving West Rogers Park would mean abandoning a significant physical and social infrastructure. The synagogues and schools were in place, and replacing the brick-and-mortar aspects of their community, by building new synagogues and schools, would cost millions of dollars.[76] Community and family ties were long established; how could they be retained if families spread out among many suburban towns? Once abundant vacant land in West Rogers Park, where bigger houses might have been built, was long gone; the *Tribune* reported in 2003 that a new development of forty-two houses sold in a single day, primarily to people who already lived in the area.[77] The remaining option in West Rogers Park is to expand existing housing, and that is what people have done, "right up to the lot lines," according to the *Tribune*.[78] In 2000, amendments to the city's zoning rules facilitated renovations. Changes came at the behest of West Rogers Park Alderman Bernie Stone, who, along with community leaders, saw zoning reform, like the establishment of the *eruv*, as an accommodation for the Jewish community, keeping them in the neighborhood. Reforms to the building codes permitted expansion up and out. Real estate development attorney Robert Matanky—and West Rogers Park resident—reported that homeowners could build up, adding a second floor to a one-story house, and out, pushing particularly to the back. Variants from even generous building codes were granted when homeowners cited family size as a pressing need. Matanky modified his own three-bedroom house through a two-story addition, which added two bedrooms and two bathrooms upstairs and expanded the living space and kitchen downstairs.[79]

No Deer Park house is unchanged, and alterations came quickly after the houses were completed in 1947. Before the second owners of the Wenstrand house bought it in 1949, the first owners had already added a rear extension that created a primary suite: bedroom, bathroom, and multiple closets.[80] The Finks screened in a rear porch (they slept there on hot nights before they got air conditioning in 1956) and added a small glassed/screened porch to the originally unprotected front door. They removed the cumbersome pillar in the center of the two-car garage, created a wall of bookcases that blocked a north-facing window in the living room, and finished the basement (adding a Polynesian scene mural).[81] The first owners of the Myhrum house probably were the ones who added a family room and large screened back porch; those were there in 1968 when the Weisbergs moved in.[82] The Kosdons screened in their back porch, too.[83]

More substantial renovations came later. Arthur Sackville-West's very popular and very modest two-bedroom, one-story house at 2844 West Pratt was one of the smallest in the competition, coming in at less than 1,000 square feet. It was the only two-bedroom house among the ten. Owners have enclosed the small porch, expanded the first floor and added a carport, and attached a second floor.

This house likely has more bathrooms and bedrooms than the original, and bigger living space, too. Thies's modest problem one house is nearly unrecognizable as the original. Unlike most renovations, which add on to

Sackville-West's modest, 900-square-foot house has been expanded up and out. On the top, an early picture of the house as built in Palatine. On the bottom, the Deer Park house after extensive remodeling. (*Prize Homes*, 5; contemporary photo courtesy of Scott McDougall and Lake Forest College.)

Walter Thies's problem one design was built in reverse. Renovations have drastically changed the front façade, for the two-story modification pushes the house to the front. What was once a protruding garage is now flush with the street-facing side. (*Prize Homes*, 11; contemporary photo courtesy of Scott McDougall and Lake Forest College.)

the back of the house, the owners have pushed out the front, bringing the entire house, first and second floor, flush with the protruding garage.

Interviews with former and current residents indicate that they mostly admired their homes, regardless of whether they knew that their houses were architecturally special. The Webers knew, vaguely, that their home had won a prize, but they did not know from whom or why.[84] The Smedley family had no idea their Wheaton house was special, but Eleanor Smedley saved the painting given to her by her real estate agent when she sold the house. The Bryants had no knowledge that their Lombard house was important, either, but they saved their picture, too, painted by their

A painting of W. R. Burns's Lombard house, made when the Bryants occupied the house. It was painted by local artist Vivian Chevillion, who lived in the Woolford and Peterson house across the street. (Photo by Kathy Bryant.)

neighbor, Vivian Chevillion, who lived in the other Prize Homes house across the street.

The Chevillions did know of their home's special provenance, for they passed along to current owners the original open house flyers. Those current owners are excellent custodians of the house's history, having acquired not only a Chevillion painting but also the *Prize Homes* book.[85]

Conclusion
A Competition Like No Other

House design competitions are not relics of a past age; they continue to this day. Sponsors use competitions to promote their visions of what communities and households need: buildings able to withstand flooding from hurricanes and climate change; energy efficiency; small, tiny, and even micro houses; sustainability; renewable materials; and communal living. But in the history of house design competitions, the *Tribune*'s Chicagoland Prize Homes is distinctive. First, the jury's sensibility, and that of whoever included the additional non-winners in the *Prize Homes* book, led them to feature modern houses styled in such a way as to provide something for everyone. If on the inside all the houses had relatively similar interior layouts and amenities, that interior could be clad with a traditional, colonial-style exterior or a somewhat modern exterior. House competitions sponsored by architectural publications generally favored ultra-modern houses, of the kind an architect might want to live in. The Prize Homes competition, however, catered more to middlebrow tastes for a cautious, somewhat conservative house-buying public.

Second, and related, the endeavor was not an "ideas competition" but moved ideas on paper into reality when houses were built, although the number of houses built amounted to more than a handful. Other than *Arts & Architecture*'s Case Study houses—which were quite modern, site specific, and expensive—no other contemporaneous architectural competition bore such fruit, and the Case Study project was not even a competition. Other house competitions throughout the century certainly resulted in built houses, but they are nearly impossible to track. It is the *Tribune*'s own attention to the results of its competition that makes some of the houses traceable. Although the building project was, in the end, quite limited, both in the number of houses and their affordability for the average household, the story of those houses bears witness to the century's vernacular houses and the ordinary families who lived in them.

The competition occurred just at the same time the National Association of Home Builders (NAHB) was founded; today, the organization remains a major advocate for new house construction and a repository of data and other historical evidence about house construction. As the nation began its house-building enterprise in significant numbers through the suburban subdevelopments stereotypical of the postwar building boom, the NAHB conducted the first of many residential showcases through its Parade of Homes in 1948, a festival of model houses that became popular throughout the country in the following years. That first Parade of Homes, according to Samuel Dodd, "included furnished model houses . . . and crowd-drawing publicity stunts," a sales method meant to tantalize American consumers into buying a first home or, by the 1950s, to trade up, swapping the first house for a second, larger one.[1] Dodd's description of the first parade looks a lot like the Prize Homes month-long open houses in the Deer Park neighborhood, where Chicagoans could tour fully furnished Prize Homes houses.

If *Pencil Points* and *Architectural Forum* could supply cutting-edge design, they rarely could bring design to fruition, especially for the middle-income home buyer. The *Tribune* could. The paper had plenty of resources: column inches, colored ink, reporters, a radio station to broadcast publicity, a long-standing partnership with a premier local art museum to help display designs, relationships with builders who could move design to reality, connections to public officials—including the mayor of Chicago and the governor of Illinois—who lent their support by their presence at public groundbreaking events. The *Tribune* could put house plans before the eyes of the viewing public: through the paper, the many exhibitions that traveled for years, and the *Prize Homes* book, which exists today in many library and archive collections, although it is long out of print. The millions of people who saw the competition designs must have been millions more than the regular readers of highbrow architectural publications. In 1948, Briggsville Electric Shop advertised in the *Portage Daily Register and Democrat*, in Wisconsin, that it had kitchen sinks and cabinets "used in Chicago Tribune prize homes," suggesting not only the competition's prestige but also its geographical reach.[2]

At least two dozen houses were built from winning designs, and, although altered, most of those houses still exist. Original owners moved into a prize-winning house, excited to have a distinctive home and to participate in a project sponsored by the *Chicago Tribune*. Harry Scheckerman's daughter is sure her father's decision to purchase 2900 Pratt was in part because it was an award-winning design, though he was not the original owner.[3] Front yard signs, put up during construction and declaring the house to be a Chicagoland Prize Home, would have been fulfilling to buyers. The competition carried enough prestige that even proximity to a winning house was noted: a vacant lot for sale in Blue Island advertised it was the corner lot across from the "Tribune prize house," while another home seller identified the property as "one block from Tribune prize home."[4] When selling the Burch-designed house in Deer Park, the Wassermans made a point of conveying its status as a prize-winning home; buyer Avrum Weinfeld thought they did so to obtain a better price.[5]

First owners knew the provenance of their houses and perhaps identified with being among the small, fortunate group of original owners. In 1953, the women residents of Farwell Avenue put on their finest clothes for a luncheon organized by Esther Kosdon. The neighbors were a tight-knit bunch, "an outgrowth of a good neighbor policy by Mrs. Kosdon and her husband. . . . They were the first pioneers in the Deer Park subdivision." The neighborhood, five years later, had developed as hoped for: "a neighborhood of friendly folks who sometimes pool their lawn mowers and trade off baby sitting."[6] Perhaps subsequent house buyers knew they lived in special houses; occasionally a house-for-sale advertisement would mention the distinction. A 1964 advertisement for a Deer Park house told readers "Tribune Prize Home can be yours. In a nation-wide competition just 16 years ago, this design was one of the top award winners," although the date is wrong.[7] Likely due to the cluster, residents of the Deer Park houses preserved the neighborhood's history better than those elsewhere. Between 1948 and 1970, at least seven real estate ads in the *Chicago Tribune* indicated the house for sale was a Tribune prizewinner.

Over the years, however, the Chicagoland Prize Homes competition and its results fell out of view. As demonstrated earlier, between the first and third editions of the *Book of Small Home Designs*, which featured three of the winners, the designation of having won a prize disappeared. Anyone buying one the three house plans by Wenstrand, Sackville-West, or Taylor would have had no indication that their houses were anything special. Kathy Halper moved to a Uebelhack house when she was four months old, discovering only late in life (she is not sure how) that the house was a winner. When apprised of more of the Prize Homes history, she expressed regret that her late father, who did not much care for the house and always aspired to something "better" yet lived there for more than forty years, never knew the backstory of how the house came to be.[8] Many of the people interviewed for this project had no idea their homes had any special history.

When it came time to sell the houses, classified ads in the *Chicago Tribune* or other newspapers might remind would-be buyers of the house's status as stock there. City revitalization can be cause for celebration, but the subsequent increase in the cost of housing reduces affordability for the working poor and even middle classes. San Francisco and Manhattan, for example, have become largely unaffordable except for the very rich or the very poor. The blue-collar workers who sustain those urban areas are forced to live farther away from them.

Chicago's residential exclusivity has been noted. Some neighborhoods within the city have historically been White, as is true of its suburbs. This is due to various factors, but racially restrictive covenants, redlining, and outright discrimination contribute significantly. Across the country, suburbs and formerly White areas are more diverse. The familiar pattern—that Whites in the 1950s and 1960s left urban areas for suburbs, ceding urban neighborhoods to Black, Latino, and immigrant residents who could not afford or be welcomed in suburbs—has given way to another. Affluent White residents moving either back to cities or even farther out, to exurbs, have left the suburbs to the former urban populations. Towns and neighborhoods that once were exclusively or almost exclusively White have shifted; 2020 census data for Illinois cities and neighborhoods measure the changes. Prize Homes houses went up in White communities, and today, Highland Park, Deerfield, Lombard, and Palatine, for example, remain overwhelmingly White. Kankakee today, however, is over 40 percent Black and 20 percent Hispanic, with non-Hispanic White residents in the minority. Blue Island mimics that, with 47 percent of its population Hispanic, 31 percent Black, and 21 percent White. Bensenville is 43 percent White and 48 percent Hispanic. The Portage Park neighborhood, where the Charles Schroeder house was built, is 51 percent Black and 39 percent Hispanic.[15] As covered in the previous chapter, West Rogers Park's racial demographics have changed considerably. While every original owner of known Prize Homes houses was most certainly White, that is not true of current owners.

The recent global pandemic confined people to their homes for schooling and work, but the modern house, with an open floor plan throughout the shared areas, is designed for people to leave it during the day. Residents who need a house to be a workplace and schoolroom as well may look for more walls and doors. American children play outside less than they used to, altering the need for a grassy lawn as recreation area, although backyard entertaining grows in popularity. Family constellations are ever changing: the number of people who elect to not have children is rising, and the birth rate is down. At the same time, Americans want plenty of room, especially bathrooms.

Despite those potential changes, expect Americans to do what they have always done: look for a home that is comfortable, convenient, and affordable.

The single-family house is yet a part of the American aspiration. Neighborhoods of single-family houses—in the suburbs or not—provide proximity to many good things: high-quality schools, parks and green spaces, religious institutions, stable home prices, and friendly neighbors. Even in an urban setting, a single-family home provides a venue for self-expression, privacy, comfort, and autonomy. We want to be hospitable, sharing our homes with guests, and if that is no longer a formal dinner for eight in our dining rooms with fine china and crystal, now it might be a casual outdoor meal or watching a sporting event in our recreational space. Americans buy houses, move in, either alone or with others, perhaps bring children and/or have children, paint and hang pictures, celebrate holidays, host sleepovers, entertain in the backyard and, eventually, sell the house to another family, which begins the cycle again.

Known Entries to the Prize Homes Competition

Known submitting architects to the Chicagoland Prize Homes competition (some architects submitted multiple entries):

Kazumi Adachi
Stephen J. Alling
James H. Anderson Jr.
(submitting as Anderson &
Simonds)
Robert S. Arnold
Elmer Babb
O. J. Baker (with F. D. Miles)
Charles K. Berg
Curtis Wray Besinger
Robert William Blachmik
William Boedefeld
R. P. Boehm
Frank Boemerman
Bernard H. Bradley
Marcel Breuer
Walter T. Brooks
Madge G. Buckley
Ernst Budke
Edward H. Bugge
Edward L. Burch
W. R. Burns
Carl Cederstrand
C. N. Chau
Victor Chiljean (with Carl
H. Fricke)
Charles Kenneth Clinton

John C. Close
Raymond E. Clouse
Hugh Crawford (with Henry
Fliess)
John W. Davis
Marion A. Denmark
(with Edwin Hill, Jack
Evans, James Evans, and
H. B. Tucker, submitting as
Heidt Associates)
G. Kenneth Duprey
Edward A. Dwyer
David Weston Dykeman Jr.
Winston Elting (with Paul
Schweikher)
Mel C. Ensign
Jack Evans (with Marion
Denmark, Edwin Hill, James
Evans, and H. B. Tucker,
submitting as Heidt
Associates)
James Evans (with Marion
Denmark, Edwin Hill, Jack
Evans, and H. B. Tucker,
submitting as Heidt
Associates)

Eben D. Finney (with
E. H. Glidden Jr.)
Henry Fliess (with Hugh
Crawford)
Merwin H. Freeman
Carl H. Fricke (and Victor
Chiljean)
W. Sanford Full
William B. Fyfe
Patrick Gallaugher (with
Bernard James Slater)
Raymond W. Garbe
Hugh M. G. Garden
Robert A. Genchek
E. H. Glidden Jr. (with Eben
D. Finney)
Millie Goldsholl
Joseph C. Gora
Marion Mahony Griffin
Charles T. Hagerstrom
A. William Hajjar
Edward W. Hanson
Herbert C. Hanson (with
Henry Martorano)
Earle Heritage
Edwin Hill (with Marion
Denmark, Jack Evans, James
Evans, and H. B. Tucker,
submitting as Heidt
Associates)
Charles R. Hogan
Carl F. Huboi
James Bennett Hughes
Miriam S. Hurford
Leon Hyzen
V. E. Jeppsen
Harold E. Jessen
Lester J. Jorge
John F. Kausal
Paul A. Kilp
George Klinkhardt
Charles W. Koch
Herman H. Lackner
Oliver Lundquist

Robert Major
Y. Tom Makino
R. Charles Martini
Henry Martorano (with
Herbert C. Hanson)
Lucille McKirahan
Lee Mielke (with Lawrence
L. Smith)
F. D. Miles (with O. J. Baker)
Richard Y. Mine
Jango Mishimine
Arthur R. Myhrum
Elisabeth Kimball Nedved
(with Rudolph J. Nedved)
Rudolph J. Nedved (with
Elisabeth Kimball Nedved)
Dietrich A. Neyland
Tohzo Nishiseki
Eileen Pei (with I. M. Pei)
I. M. Pei (with Eileen Pei)
Ralph DeLos Peterson Jr. (with
Curtis Woolford)
William G. Pfeufer
Robert F. Pierce
Vsevelod A. Prisadsky
Joseph Prisant
Olen L. Puckett
Ralph Rapson (with John Van
der Meulen)
Nolan Roads
D. C. Robinson
DeWitt C. Robinson
Arthur "Jack" Sackville-West
Charles Schroeder
Fred Schurect (with Laurence
Schwall)
Laurence Schwall (with Fred
Schurect)
Paul Schweikher (with
Winston Elting)
Robert M. Shields
George Patton Simonds
(submitting as Anderson &
Simonds)

Prize Homes Competition Winners and the Designs Known to Be Built

Prize Homes competition winners and known built houses (all cities are in Illinois unless otherwise noted)

#1   R. Coder Taylor (built in Highland Park)
#2   Arthur (Jack) Sackville-West (built in Chicago, Palatine, and Kankakee, possibly in Franklin Park and Park Ridge)
#3   Charles Schroeder (built in Chicago)
#4   Walter Thies (built in Chicago)
#5   Curtis Woolford and Ralph DeLos Peterson (built in Lombard)
#6   J. Floyd Yewell
#7   George Klinkardt
#8   Ray Stuermer
#9   Henry Martorano and Herbert Hanson (built in Chicago, possibly again in Northbrook and Chicago)
#10 Eric Wenstrand (built in Chicago, Blue Island, Highland Park, Deerfield, and Whiting, Indiana)
#11 Carl Cederstrand (built in Chicago, possibly in Beverly Hills)
#12 Frederick Sloan (built in Chicago, possibly in Barrington)
#13 Eben D. Finney and E. H. Glidden
#14 Lucille McKirahan
#15 Marion A. Denmark, Edwin Hill, Jack Evans, James Evans, and H. B. Tucker, submitting as Heidt Associates
#16 W. R. Burns (built in Chicago and Lombard)
#17 Arthur Myhrum (built in Chicago)
#18 Howard Uebelhack (built in Highland Park and Wheaton, and probably in Bensonville)
#19 Raymond Garbe (built in Chicago)

#20 Edward W. Hanson
#21 Edward L. Burch (built in Chicago)
#22 Joseph Gora
#23 Merwin H. Freeman
#24 Ray Stuermer

Notes

Introduction

1. This claim may well be a myth, but it is certainly repeated often. See Joseph C. Bigott, *From Cottage to Bungalow: Houses and the Working Class in Metropolitan Chicago, 1899–1929* (Chicago: University of Chicago Press, 2001), 19.

2. Thomas Hubka, *How the Working-Class Home Became Modern, 1900–1940* (Minneapolis: University of Minnesota Press, 2020).

3. Lipstadt reviews American architectural competitions between 1922 and 1960, including a few small house competitions. She devotes half of one paragraph to the Prize Homes contest. Her source, however, is neither the *Chicago Tribune* nor the *Prize Homes* book but a 1946 *Architectural Forum* article about the competition. Hélène Lipstadt, "In the Shadow of the Tribune Tower," in *The Experimental Tradition: Essays on Competitions in Architecture,* ed. Hélène Lipstadt (New York: The Architectural League of New York, 1989), 79–94. Histories of the paper also neglect the event. Wendt's nearly 800-page history of the *Tribune* omits the competition. Lloyd Wendt, *Chicago Tribune: The Rise of a Great American Newspaper* (Chicago: Rand McNally & Co., 1979). Reiff's thorough history of house plan books excludes *Prize Homes*. Daniel Reiff, *Houses from Books: Treatises, Pattern Books, and Catalogs in American Architecture, 1738–1950* (University Park: The Pennsylvania State University Press, 2000). Benjamin and Sabatino's 2020 book, devoted to midcentury modern houses in Chicago and its suburbs, details the building and history of the owners and architects of fifty-three houses, but the houses are custom-built and expensive, and none originated from the competition. Susan Benjamin and Michelangelo Sabatino, *Modern in the Middle: Chicago Houses, 1929–1975* (New York: The Monicelli Press, 2020). Chicago histories neglect this chapter. The digital Encyclopedia of Chicago, supported by the Chicago History Museum website, has no record of it. http://www.encyclopedia.chicagohistory.org. Accessed May 11, 2021.

Chapter 1. Shortages

1. Herbert Hoover's 1932 Presidential Conference on Home Building and Home Ownership generated multiple reports on inadequate housing in the United States. See also Richard Eddy, "Chicago Housing at Low Rental Levels in 1932" (MA thesis, University of Chicago, 1934).

2. Editors of the Architectural Forum, *The 1936 Book of Small Houses* (New York: Simon and Schuster, 1936); Editors of the Architectural Forum, *The 1938 Book of Small Houses* (New York: Simon and Schuster, 1938).

3. The G. I. Bill benefit propelled a significant number of White people into the middle class through higher education and home ownership. Black veterans, however, were widely excluded from the mortgage benefit. Louis Lee Woods, II, "Almost 'No Negro Veteran . . . Could Get a Loan': African Americans, the GI Bill, and the NAACP Campaign against Residential Segregation, 1917–1960," *The Journal of African American History*, Vol. 98, No. 3 (2013), 392–417. Housing discrimination exacerbated the already inadequate housing for Black Chicagoans; see Richard Eddy, "Chicago Housing at Low Rental Levels in 1932" (MA thesis, University of Chicago, 1934). Indigenous Americans, as well, saw significant barriers to receiving G. I. Bill benefits; see Kasey Keeler, "Putting People Where They Belong: American Indian Housing Policy in the Mid-Twentieth Century," *Native American and Indigenous Studies*, Vol. 3, No. 2 (2016), 70–104.

4. See Clifford Clark, *The American Family Home: 1800–1960* (Chapel Hill: University of North Carolina Press, 1986), chapter 7.

5. John Archer, "The Resilience of Myth: The Politics of the American Dream," *Traditional Dwellings and Settlements Review* (Spring 2014), 7–21, 7.

6. Jan Van Bavel and David S. Reher, "The Baby Boom and Its Causes: What We Know and What We Need to Know," *Population and Development Review*, Vol. 39, No. 2 (June 2013), 257–288, 257.

7. Richard O. Davies, *Housing Reform during the Truman Administration* (Columbia: University of Missouri Press, 1966), 25.

8. Associated Press, "Predict Vast Post-War Needs of Housing and Furnishing," *Chicago Tribune*, January 15, 1943, 25.

9. Louise Bargelt, "Experts Vision Million Homes after the War," *Chicago Tribune*, November 28, 1943, SW9; "Post-War Home Surveys Show Building Trend," *Chicago Tribune*, January 30, 1944, N6; "Lot Buyer Has an Investment in the Future," *Chicago Tribune*, September 24, 1944, W6; "Planning the Post-War Home!" *Chicago Tribune*, January 21, 1945, C1, 9; "Storage Space Planning Vital for New Home," *Chicago Tribune*, February 25, 1945, N3; "Built-In Units to Ease Work in Post-War Home," *Chicago Tribune*, August 5, 1945, N7.

10. Louise Bargelt, "Experts Vision Million Homes after the War," *Chicago Tribune*, November 28, 1943, SW9; Al Chase, "Business Told to Plan Homes Now for Peace," *Chicago Tribune*, April 30, 1944, A7; Al Chase, "Post-War Home Boom

Predicted in Chicago Area," *Chicago Tribune*, September 3, 1944, A6; "Urge Annual Home building of 1¼ Million," *Chicago Tribune*, August 2, 1945, 25; "Prospects for Home building Are Best in Central States," *Chicago Tribune*, September 16, 1945, A5.

11. Shanken has well documented how architects and architectural publications anticipated, during the war, what might come after the war's end. Andrew M. Shanken, *194X: Architecture, Planning, and Consumer Culture on the American Home Front* (Minneapolis: University of Minnesota Press, 2009).

12. "A House for Cheerful Living," *Pencil Points*, December 1944, 58–61, 59.

13. Kenneth Reid, "Don't Fence Us In," *Progressive Architecture*, January 1945, 3.

14. *Progressive Architecture*, August 1945, 23, 38, 159, 41.

15. *Progressive Architecture*, 46, 108, 130, 156, 163.

16. *Progressive Architecture*, 151.

17. A sample: "Looking Ahead in Air Conditioning," *Architectural Record*, May 1943, 14; "Will Construction Furnish the Post-War 'Cushion'?" *Pencil Points*, December 1943, 2; "From the House on the Hill to Smaller Homes Post War," *Architectural Record*, February 1944, 16; "Screen Test (South Pacific)," *Architectural Forum*, September 1944, 40; "Can You Build a Fireproof Wall at Low Cost?" *Architectural Forum*, January 1945, 90.

18. National Conference on Postwar Housing, Committee on Housing, Inc., *Proceedings of the National Conference on Postwar Housing Chicago, March 8–9–10, 1944* (New York: Moak Printing Company, 1944).

19. Chicago Plan Commission, *Housing Goals for Chicago* (Chicago Plan Commission 1946).

20. Chicago Plan Commission, *Housing Goals for Chicago*, chapter V.

21. Chicago Plan Commission, chapter V.

22. Chicago Plan Commission, 76.

23. Chicago Plan Commission, 192.

24. "News," *Architectural Forum*, February 1946, 5.

25. Jean-Pierre Chupin, Carmela Cucizella, and Bechara Helal, "A World of Possibilities," in *Architectural Competitions and the Production of Culture, Quality and Knowledge: An International Inquiry*, ed. Jean-Pierre Chupin, Carmela Cucuzella, and Bechara Helal (Montreal: Potential Architecture Books, 2015), 11–23.

26. Susanna Sirefman's review of American competitions includes the *Chicago Tribune* Tribune Tower contest but neither of its house contests. She mentions "four important contests" in the midcentury: art centers for the College of William and Mary and Wheaton College, a Goucher College redesign in 1938, and a Smithsonian Institution call for a new museum building in 1939. None of the house design contests from the same years warrants her attention. Susanna Sirefman, "American Competitions and Decision-Making," in *Architectural Competitions and the Production of Culture, Quality and Knowledge: An International Inquiry*, ed. Jean-Pierre Chupin, Carmela Cucuzella, and Bechara Helal (Montreal: Potential Architecture Books, 2015), 217–229.

27. Daniel Reiff, *Houses from Books: Treatises, Pattern Books, and Catalogs in American Architecture, 1738–1950* (University Park: The Pennsylvania State University Press, 2000), 35.

28. Stanley Tigerman, *Tribune Tower Competition* (New York: Rizzoli, 1980), 3.

29. For contemporaneous criticism of the jury's favoring the Hood and Howells design over Saarinen's, see Louis Sullivan, "The Chicago Tribune Competition," *Architectural Record*, February 1923, 151–157.

30. A collaboration between A. N. Rebori and Edgar Miller won second prize, John Miller won third prize, and twenty-one more designs earned honorable mentions. James O'Donnell Bennett, "Chicagoan Wins W-G-N Theater Design Contest," *Chicago Tribune*, November 25, 1934, 1.

31. "Best 25 Designs in W-G-N Theater Contest on View," *Chicago Tribune*, December 9, 1934, 22.

32. William Clark and Frederick Adams shared the prize money. Second prize went to Dinion & Merritt, and third to Joseph Gemmi, with fifteen honorable mentions. Larry Wolters, "Two Win $5,000 with Design for W-G-N Theater," *Chicago Tribune*, February 4, 1945, 22.

33. Jan Jennings, *Cheap and Tasteful Dwellings: Design Competitions and the Convenient Interior, 1879–1909* (Knoxville: University of Tennessee Press, 2005).

34. Paul Spreiregen, *Design Competitions* (New York: McGraw Hill, 1979), 119–120.

35. Judith Strong, *Winning by Design: Architectural Competitions* (Oxford: Butterworth Architecture, 1996), 26.

36. Hélène Lipstadt, "In the Shadow of the Tribune Tower," in *The Experimental Tradition: Essays on Competitions in Architecture,* ed. Hélène Lipstadt (New York: The Architectural League of New York, 1989), 79–94, 85.

37. Sarah Bradford Landau, "Coming to Terms: Architecture Competitions in America and the Emerging Profession, 1789 to 1922," in *The Experimental Tradition: Essays on Competitions in Architecture,* ed. Hélène Lipstadt (New York: The Architectural League of New York, 1989), 53–78.

38. Nineteen winning designs plus eighty other house plans from the 1926 contest were published as *Chicago Tribune Book of Homes* (Chicago: Chicago Tribune, 1927). This volume was reprinted as *Elegant Small Homes of the Twenties: 99 Designs from a Competition* (Mineola, NY: Dover Publications, 2008).

39. Bureau of Labor Statistics inflation calculator. www.bls.gov/data/inflation_calculator.htm.

40. A General Electric–sponsored competition in 1935 received more than 2,000 submissions. "Here, There, This & That," *Pencil Points*, April 1935, 18.

41. Janet Hutchinson, "The Cure for Domestic Neglect: Better Homes in America, 1922–1935," *Perspectives in Vernacular Architecture*, Vol. 2(1986), 168–178.

42. Kristina Borrman, "One Standardized House for All: America's Little House," *Buildings and Landscapes*, Fall 2017, 37–57.

43. It is unclear whether the houses' removal was an original plan or came up during the fair. Rebecca Holland, "George Fred Keck's House of Tomorrow from World's Fair Seeks Restoration," *Architectural* Digest.com, February 27, 2019.

44. *Fireproof Homes of Period Design* (The United States Gypsum Company, 1925).

45. *Prize Winning Designs in Bloomingdale's Architectural Competition: "Suburban Houses for New Yorkers"* (New York, 1947).

46. Kathryn Dethier, "The Spirit of Progressive Reform: The Ladies' Home Journal House Plans, 1900–1902," *Journal of Design History*, Vol. 6, No. 4 (1993), 247–261, 249. See also Leland M. Roth, "Getting the Houses to the People: Edward Bok, the Ladies' Home Journal, and the Ideal House," *Perspectives in Vernacular Architecture*, Vol. 4 (1991), 187–196; Sheila Webb, "The Consumer-Citizen: 'Life' Magazine's Construction of a Middle-Class Lifestyle through Consumption Scenarios," *Studies in Popular Culture* (Spring 2012), 23–47.

47. Daniel Reiff, *Houses from Books: Treatises, Pattern Books, and Catalogs in American Architecture, 1738–1950.* (University Park: The Pennsylvania State University Press, 2000).

48. John Morris Dixon, Introduction, xviii, in *Pencil Points Reader: A Journal for the Drafting Room, 1920–1943,* ed. George E. Hartman and Jan Cigliano Hartman (Princeton, NJ: Princeton Architectural Press, 2004).

49. Andrew Shanken, "Breaking the Taboo: Architects and Advertising in Depression and War," *Journal of the Society of Architectural Historians*, Vol. 69, No. 3 (September 2010), 406–429. Shanken does not address competitions.

50. Christine Chapman, *Archetype, Hybrid, and Prototype: Modernism in* House Beautiful's *Small House Competition, 1928–1942* (MS thesis, University of North Carolina at Greensboro, 2007).

51. "Oral History of Ambrose M. Richardson," transcript of an oral history conducted by Betty J. Blum, Chicago Architects Oral History Project, Art Institute of Chicago, 1990, 158.

52. From the Burch, Burch and Burch architectural firm website. http://burchburchandburch.com. Accessed July 29, 2020. Confirmed in a conversation between the author and Burch's son, Brian Burch, January 26, 2021.

Chapter 2. To the Rescue

1. Reprinted as *House Design Competitions Book 11-Drawings: The Detroit Free Press Better Homes Competition-1928* (Altoona, FL: Wilkerson & Hughes, 2015). The foreword indicates the competition included nearly 200 entries.

2. "The Pulse of Public Tastes," *American Architect and Architecture*, April 1935, 53.

3. Nineteen winning designs plus eighty other house plans from the 1926 contest were published as *Chicago Tribune Book of Homes*, 1927. This volume was reprinted as *Elegant Small Homes of the Twenties: 99 Designs from a Competition* (Mineola, NY: Dover Publications, 2008).

4. "Introduction to the Dover Edition," by Daniel Reiff, in *Elegant Small Homes of the Twenties: 99 Designs from a Competition* (Mineola, NY: Dover Publications, 2008).

5. "Introduction to the 1927 Edition," by Louise Bartgelt, in *Elegant Small Homes of the Twenties: 99 Designs from a Competition* (Mineola, NY: Dover Publications, 2008).

6. The Architects' Small House Service Bureau was particularly active during the 1920s. See Daniel Reiff, *Houses from Books: Treatises, Pattern Books, and Catalogs in American Architecture, 1738–1950* (University Park: Pennsylvania State University Press, 2000), Appendix I.

7. "Bond Prizes Offered for Home Designs," *Chicago Tribune*, September 3, 1944, A6.

8. "Home Builders' Convention Stresses Plans for Postwar," *Architectural Record*, February 1945, 60–62.

9. Despite the title "Pittsburgh," the competition did not specify houses for a particular region. "For the Design of a House for Cheerful Living," *Pencil Points: Progressive Architecture*, December 1944, 58–61.

10. "Progressive Architecture-Rich's, Inc. Architectural Competition," *Progressive Architecture: Pencil Points*, October 1945, 37–40.

11. "The Chicago Tribune Announces the $24,000.00 Chicagoland Prize Homes Competition," *Chicago Tribune*, September 30, 1945, 21.

12. Harry S. Truman, "Special Message to the Congress Presenting a 21-Point Program for the Reconversion Period," National Archives, Harry S. Truman Library Museum. https://www.trumanlibrary.gov/library/public-papers/128/special-message-congress-presenting-21-point-program-reconversion-period. Accessed June 7, 2021.

13. "The Chicago Tribune Announces the $24,000.00 Chicagoland Prize Homes Competition," *Chicago Tribune*, September 30, 1945, 21.

14. "Boyd Hill, 66, Dies: 40 Years an Architect," *Chicago Tribune*, January 7, 1964, A6; "Describes Plan for Swainwood Homes Project," *Chicago Tribune*, June 9, 1946, NWB.

15. "Hundreds Visit New Tribune Classified Advertising Office," *Chicago Tribune*, July 27, 1949; "Better Rooms Designers Get New Stimulant," *Chicago Tribune*, February 6, 1949, 29; "Living-Dining Room Designs Lead in Number," *Chicago Tribune*, March 5, 1960, 6; "Better Rooms Contest Judges Pick 52 Winners," *Chicago Tribune*, March 2, 1952, 22.

16. "Paul Gerhardt Found Dead of Suffocation: Architect for Chicago for 37 Years," *Chicago Tribune*, October 12, 1966, B10.

17. "John Merrill Sr., Architect, Dead," *New York Times*, June 13, 1975, 40.

18. James O'Donnell Bennett, "Howells Wins in Contest for Tribune Tower," *Chicago Tribune*, December 3, 1922, 1.

19. "Andrew N. Rebori, Architect, Is Dead," *Chicago Tribune*, June 1, 1966, 1.

20. "John Park, 91, Ex-Tribune Production Manager Dies," *Chicago Tribune*, February 23, 1979, B7.

21. "Irvin Blietz, Home Builder, Is Dead at 72," *Chicago Tribune*, November 17, 1968, A14.

22. Al Chase, "Outlines Plan to Increase GI Home Building," *Chicago Tribune*, May 20, 1945, 20.

23. "The Chicago Tribune Announces the $24,000.00 Chicagoland Prize Homes Competition," *Chicago Tribune*, September 30, 1945, 21.

24. "Jury in $24,000 Tribune Housing Contest Chosen," *Chicago Tribune*, September 20, 1945, 22.

25. "$24,000 for Small Home Designs," *Chicago Tribune*, October 3, 1945, 12. The coupon reappeared on October 6 by itself.

26. "$24,000 for Small Home Designs," *Chicago Tribune*, October 7, 1945, 25.

27. "3,000 Will Get Tribune Rules on Prize Homes," *Chicago Tribune*, October 7, 1945, 25.

28. "$24,000 for Small Home Designs," *Chicago Tribune*, October 8, 1945, 11; October 11, 11; October 15, 14; October 16, 15.

29. "1st Entries Arrive in Tribune's Prize Home Competition," *Chicago Tribune*, November 18, 1945, 28.

30. The headline erroneously listed the total prize money as $25,000 instead of $24,000. "Readers Draft Dream Homes in $25,000 [*sic*] Contest," *Chicago Tribune*, November 25, 1945, 27.

31. "Tribune's Home Contest Will End Tomorrow," *Chicago Tribune*, December 9, 1945, 1.

32. To reduce confusion, the rules booklet will be referred to as *The Chicagoland Prize Homes Competition Program*. Breuer's copy is twelve pages; Rapson's copy contains pages 13 and 14. Marcel Breuer Papers, Special Collections Research Center, Syracuse University Libraries; Cranbrook Archives.

33. *The Chicagoland Prize Homes Competition Program*; Letter from Boyd Hill to All Registrants, October 30, 1945; Letter from Boyd Hill to All Registrants, November 1, 1945.

34. "Oral History of Coder Taylor," transcript of an oral history conducted by Betty J. Blum, Chicago Architects Oral History Project, Art Institute of Chicago, 1989, 63.

35. "Home Designs for Small Lots Lead in Contest," *Chicago Tribune*, December 27, 1945, 2.

36. Chicago Plan Commission, *Housing Goals for Chicago* (Chicago Plan Commission, 1946), 26.

37. James R. Wetzel, "American Families: 75 Years of Change," *Monthly Labor Review* (March 1990), 4–13, 8.

38. See Siobhan Moroney, "Rooms of Their Own: Child Experts, House Design, and the Rise of the Child's Private Bedroom," *Journal of Family History* (April 2019), 119–144.

39. Judy Fink Essek, interview by author, June 28, 2022.

40. "Oral History of Coder Taylor," transcript of an oral history conducted by Betty J. Blum, Chicago Architects Oral History Project, Art Institute of Chicago, 1989, 58.

41. "Home Designs for Small Lots Lead in Contest," *Chicago Tribune*, December 27, 1945, 2.

42. See Gail Radford, *Modern Housing for America: Policy Struggles in the New Deal Era* (Chicago: University of Chicago Press, 1996), 25; Joseph C. Bigott, *From Cottage to Bungalow: Houses and the Working Class in Metropolitan Chicago, 1899–1929* (Chicago: University of Chicago Press, 2001), 44.

43. *Prize Homes* (Chicago: Tribune Company, 1948), 4. An April 1946 *Architectural Forum* article highlighting the competition indicated 1,943 entries. The number, off

by a thousand, lacks any other substantiation. "Ten Prize-Winning Houses," *Architectural Forum*, April 1946, 112–116, 112.

44. "Chicagoland Competition Awards," *Journal of the American Institute of Architects* (February 1946), 72.

45. Stanley Tigerman, *Chicago Tribune Tower Competition* (New York: Rizzoli, 1980), 6.

46. "Announcing the $24,000.00 Chicagoland Prize Home Competition," *Architectural Forum*, October 1945, 206.

47. "Announcements: Competitions," *Architectural Forum*, November 1945, 174; "Competitions," *Journal of the American Institute of Architects*, November 1945, 212; "Competitions Announced," *Architectural Record*, November 1945, 156.

48. "Chicagoland Prize Homes Competition," *FAA Bulletin*, Vol. 7, No. 5 (October 1945), 2.

49. "Oral History of Ambrose M. Richardson," transcript of an oral history conducted by Betty J. Blum, Chicago Architects Oral History Project, Art Institute of Chicago, 1990, 158.

50. "Announcing the Chicago Tribune Small Homes Competition," *Chicago Tribune*, September 12, 1926, B5.

51. Louise Bargelt, "Tribune Small Home Competition Closes; 841 Plans Received," *Chicago Tribune*, December 12, 1926, B1. The *Tribune* did not, apparently, see any conflict between Bargelt both reporting on and judging the competition.

52. "Tribune Prize Home under Construction at Mount Prospect," *Chicago Tribune*, May 15, 1927, B2; "A Prize Winner," *Chicago Tribune*, July 24, 1927, H2; "Tribune Prize Homes Open for Inspection," *The Highland Park Press*, September 15, 1927, 1. Although beyond the scope of this research, the 1927 ten-house project in Highland Park is a clear precursor to the 1946 Deer Park enterprise. Several of those houses still stand.

53. Mine's entry is digitized at the Art Institute of Chicago. https://www.artic.edu/artworks/239449/chicago-tribune-chicagoland-prize-homes-competition-multiple-views. Accessed June 7, 2021.

54. Papers of Robert Arnold, Highland Park Historical Society.

55. Papers of Curtis Wray Besinger, University of Kansas.

56. "Here, There, This & That," *Pencil Points*, April 1935, 18; "Report of the Jury Award: Pencil Points 1936 Architectural Competition," *Pencil Points*, April 1936, 165.

57. "Small House Competition," *Architectural Forum*, October 1938, 275.

58. "Report of the Jury," *Pencil Points*, May 1945, 4.

59. Pamela Hill, "Marion Mahony Griffin: The Chicago Years," in *Chicago Architecture: Histories, Revisions, Alternatives*, ed. Charles Waldheim and Katerina Ruedi Ray (Chicago: University of Chicago Press, 2005), 143–162.

60. Breuer's digitized archive contains important ephemera: twelve of fourteen pages of *The Chicagoland Prize Homes Program* sent to potential applicants, two letters sent to registered applicants from Boyd Hill, invitations to Art Institute events, correspondence about display, and eventual publication of the designs in book form. Marcel Breuer Papers, Special Collections Research Center, Syracuse University Libraries.

61. "Homes for All Displayed at Tribune Show," *Chicago Tribune*, February 10, 1946, 23.

62. "Burket Graf's Design in Chicago Exhibition," *Beatrice Daily Sun*, February 22, 1946, 1; "Home Designs of Shreveporter on Display at Chicago," *Shreveport Journal*, February 22, 1946, 2.

63. *The Chicagoland Prize Homes Program*.

64. "Readers Draft Dream Homes in $25,000 [*sic*] Contest," *Chicago Tribune*, November 25, 1945, 27.

65. *The Chicagoland Prize Homes Program*.

66. "Brief Sketches of Winners of Tribune Prizes," *Chicago Tribune*, January 6, 1946, 4.

67. John M'Cutcheon, "Dentist Turns First Spade at His Prize Home," *Chicago Tribune*, June 16, 1946, SW2.

68. "Report of the Jury Award: Pencil Points-'Suntile' Architectural Competition," *Pencil Points*, August 1937, 475.

69. Bugge's architecture degree was from the University of Washington, which has biographical information and some of his student work. University of Washington Library Collection. https://digitalcollections.lib.washington.edu/digital/collection /ac/id/1838. Accessed June 15, 2021.

70. Daniel Reiff, *Houses from Books: Treatises, Pattern Books, and Catalogs in American Architecture, 1738–1950: A History and Guide* (University Park: Pennsylvania State Press, 2000), 149.

71. *The Chicagoland Prize Homes Program*.

72. Slater's address—Dept. of Agriculture—may have been an error, as he was more likely at the Department of Architecture.

73. *Prize Homes*, 27.

74. Andrew Shanken, *194X: Architecture, Planning, and Consumer Culture on the American Home Front* (Minneapolis: University of Minnesota Press, 2009), 5.

75. "Pick Winners of $24,000 for Prize Homes," *Chicago Tribune*, January 6, 1946, 1, 4.

76. "Navy Man's Home Plans Exhibited," (Minneapolis) *Star Tribune*, January 23, 1946, 33.

77. "Oral History of Coder Taylor," transcript of an oral history conducted by Betty J. Blum, Chicago Architects Oral History Project, Art Institute of Chicago, 1989, 51.

78. "Oral History of Coder Taylor," 51.

79. Pamela Hill, "Marion Mahony Griffin: The Chicago Years," in *Chicago Architecture: Histories, Revisions, Alternatives*, ed. Charles Waldheim and Katerina Ruedi Ray (Chicago: University of Chicago Press, 2005), 143–162, 158.

80. "Report of the Jury," *Pencil Points*, May 1945, 54.

81. Kenneth Reid, "Two Competitions," *Progressive Architecture: Pencil Points*, April 1945, 51.

82. "The Chicago Tribune Announces the $24,000.00 Chicagoland Prize Homes Competition," *Chicago Tribune*, September 30, 1945, 21; *The Chicagoland Prize Homes Competition Program*, 1.

83. *Chicago Tribune Book of Small Homes* (Chicago: Chicago Tribune, 1927). Ripley & Boutillier, Pierre & Wright, and George F. Axt and Clarence B. MacKay submitted in both categories.

84. "Report of the Jury of Award," *Pencil Points*, April 1936, 165–216. A northern house design from George Conner and Robert Loney took second place; two of their houses earned a mention in the southern house group, 169, 199–200.

85. Frank Weiss earned two mentions in 1945: "Report of the Jury," *Pencil Points*, May 1945, 87–88. Lyle Reynolds Wheeler did likewise; *Pencil Points*, 1946, 94–95.

86. "Oral History of Bertrand Goldberg," transcript of an oral history conducted by Betty J. Blum, Chicago Architects Oral History Project, Art Institute of Chicago, 1992, 154.

87. "Oral History of L. Morgan Yost," transcript of an oral history conducted by Betty J. Blum, Chicago Architects Oral History Project, Art Institute of Chicago, 1986, 26.

88. This list is not exhaustive but includes some of the major competitions.

89. "Report of the Jury," *Pencil Points/Progressive Architecture*, May 1945, 61.

90. "Glass and More Glass in This House," *Chicago Tribune*, September 22, 1946, C8. Quite a number of architects repeatedly submitted to other contests. George Connor, Owen Lau Gowman, John Hironimus, Amadeo Leone, and Royal Barry Wills entered at least three each. I. M. Pei and co-designer Frederick G. Roth took second place in the Pittsburgh competition, a Pei design earned a mention in the Georgia contest, and Barry featured his *Tribune* submission, a modern, two-bedroom house, designed by Eileen and I. M. Pei, among his non-winning favorites.

91. *Chicago Tribune Book of Homes* (Chicago: Chicago Tribune, 1927), 21.

92. "Best 25 Designs in W-G-N Theater Contest on View," *Chicago Tribune*, December 9, 1934, 22; Larry Wolters, "Two Win $5,000 with Design for W-G-N Theater," *Chicago Tribune*, February 4, 1945, 22.

93. White Pine Bureau, *An Architectural Monograph on a Suburban House and Garage* (St. Paul, MN: White Pine Bureau, 1916), 8–9.

94. Henry Smith, *The Books of a Thousand Homes*, Volume I (New York: Home Owners Service Institute, 1923), 7; Daniel Reiff, *Houses from Books: Treatises, Pattern Books, and Catalogs in American Architecture, 1738–1950: A History and Guide* (University Park: The Pennsylvania State Press, 2000), 220–222.

95. *Home Builder's Plan Book* (New York: Building Plan Holding Corporation, 1921).

96. *Prize Winning Designs in Bloomingdale's Architectural Competition: Suburban Houses for New Yorkers* (New York, 1947). All eighteen winners have New York addresses, suggesting the competition restricted entrants to New York residents.

97. "Brief Sketches of Winners of Tribune Prizes," *Chicago Tribune*, January 6, 1946, 4.

98. Rapson's papers are housed at the Cranbrook Archives, where he was a student. The archive contains submission information to thirty-four competitions, most but not all of them for residential buildings. https://archives.cranbrook.edu/repositories/2/archival_objects/1227. Accessed June 15, 2021.

99. "Report of the Jury Award," *Pencil Points*, April 1936, 165.

100. "Brief Sketches of Winners of Tribune Prizes," *Chicago Tribune*, January 6, 1946, 4.

101. "Report of the Jury of Award," *Pencil Points*, April 1936, 165.

102. *Prize Homes*, 100, 57.

103. *Prize Homes*, 21, 49.

104. Daniel Reiff, *Houses from Books: Treatises, Pattern Books, and Catalogs in American Architecture, 1738–1950: A History and Guide* (University Park: Pennsylvania State Press, 2000), 220.

105. Rapson wrote at the top of a copy of the Barry article featuring the house. Thanks to Cranbook archivist Laura MacNewman for assistance in deciphering Rapson's handwriting.

106. Lisa Marie Tucker, "The Small House Problem in the United States, 1918–1945: The American Institute of Architects and the Architects' Small House Service Bureau," *Journal of Design History*, Vol. 23, No. 1 (2010), 43–59.

107. "Report of the Jury," *Pencil Points/Progressive Architecture*, May 1945, 54–92.

108. "Home Builders," *Architectural Record*, February 1945, 60–63.

109. "Progressive Architecture-Rich's Inc. Architectural Competition: A Realistic House for A Family in Georgia," *Progressive Architecture*, April 1946, 96.

110. "Winning Designs," *Arts and Architecture*, February 1945, 10.

111. "Fourth Prize, National," *Architectural Forum*, March 1951, 120.

112. "Oral History of William Keck," transcript of an oral history conducted by Betty J. Blum, Chicago Architects Oral History Project, Art Institute of Chicago, 1991, 281.

113. The exhibit displayed the twelve of twenty-four winners from the Chicago area. "Homes for All Displayed at Tribune Show," *Chicago Tribune*, February 10, 1946, 23. The *Tribune*'s publicity about the exhibit also listed forty-five additional names of local designers included in the show.

114. *Prize Homes*, 4.

115. *Prize Homes*, 67.

116. Nereya Otieno, "Paul R. Williams: Behind the Mastery of the Master Architect," *Architectural Digest*, February 11, 2021. https://www.architecturaldigest.com /story/paul-williams-behind-mastery-master-architect.

117. Lois Wilson Worley won a $200 prize in the Architectural Forum American Gas Association contest in 1939. Architectural Forum, *The 1940 Book of Small Houses* (New York: Simon and Schuster, 1939), 211. Phyllis Hoffzimer earned a mention in the 1946 Georgia competition: "A Realistic House for a Family in Georgia," *Progressive Architecture*, April 1946, 81; Lucille B. Raport earned honorable mention for kitchen planning in the Architectural Forum Small House competition in 1951; "Special Prizes," *Architectural Forum*, March 1951, 143. Many winning and mentioned architects are identified only by initials, and they may well have been women, too.

118. *The Tulean Dispatch*, Saturday, June 20, 1942, 1.

Chapter 3. Spreading the News

1. "The Winners," *Architectural Record*, February 1946, 60; "The Winners," *Architectural Forum*, February 1946, 152.

2. "Winners Announced," *Architectural Record*, March 1946, 142.

3. "Aid to Housing," *Chicago Tribune*, January 10, 1946, 9.

4. A nearly identical piece appeared the following day, again reminding readers to save the designs. "Coming Sunday! The First Showing of the $24,000.00 Prize Homes Designs," *Chicago Tribune,* February 1, 1946, 1.

5. "Winning Designs in the Tribune's Prize Homes Competition," *Chicago Tribune*, February 3, 1946, C1–3; "More Winning Designs in the Chicago Tribune Prize Homes Contest," *Chicago Tribune*, February 10, 1946, C1–2; "More Winning Designs in the Chicago Tribune Prize Homes Contest," February 17, 1946, C1–2; "4th Group of Winning Designs in the Chicago Tribune Prize Homes Contest," *Chicago Tribune,* February 24, 1946, C1–2; "Final Group of Winning Designs in the Chicago Tribune Prize Home Contest," *Chicago Tribune*, March 3, 1946, C1–2.

6. "Oral History of Coder Taylor," transcript of an oral history conducted by Betty J. Blum, Chicago Architects Oral History Project, Art Institute of Chicago, 1989, 65.

7. Lloyd Wendt, *Chicago Tribune: The Rise of a Great American Newspaper* (Chicago: Rand McNally & Co., 1979), 615.

8. "Ten Prize-Winning Houses," *Architectural Forum*, April 1946, 112.

9. Edward Barry, "Winning Designs," *Chicago Tribune*, February 3, 1946, C1–2.

10. "Prize Homes," *Chicago Tribune*, February 10, 1946, C2.

11. Edward Barry, "More Winning Designs," *Chicago Tribune*, February 17, 1946, C1–2.

12. One of his paintings is owned by the National Gallery of Art. https://www.nga.gov/collection/art-object-page.145075.html. Accessed June 15, 2021.

13. The National Gallery of Art owns twenty-five lithographs, although they are not on display. https://www.nga.gov/collection/artist-info.5308.html?artobj _artistId=5308&pageNumber=2. Accessed June 15, 2021.

14. Edward Barry, "4th Group of Winning Designs," *Chicago Tribune,* February 24, 1946, C1, 8.

15. The entry is from J. H. Raftery. Chicago Tribune, *Elegant Small Homes of the Twenties: 99 Designs from a Competition* (Mineola, NY: Dover Publications, 2008), 72.

16. Edward Barry, "Final Group of Winning Designs," *Chicago Tribune*, March 3, 1946, C1, 10.

17. "Homes for All Displayed at Tribune Show," *Chicago Tribune*, February 10, 1946, 23.

18. "Oral History of Coder Taylor," transcript of an oral history conducted by Betty J. Blum, Chicago Architects Oral History Project, Art Institute of Chicago, 1989, 68–69.

19. The seven paintings were exhibited at least once, at the Graham Foundation, in a month-long exhibit in 1985: The Postwar American Dream. Graham Foundation, *Architecture in Context: The Postwar American Dream*, Chicago, 1985. Exhibit catalog.

20. Art Institute of Chicago, Prize House #12, Chicago Tribune Chicagoland Prize Homes Competition, Presentation Drawing. https://www.artic.edu/artworks

/248763/prize-house-12-chicago-tribune-chicagoland-prize-homes-competition -presentation-drawing. Accessed June 29, 2019.

21. Art Institute of Chicago. https://www.artic.edu/collection?q=chicagoland%20 prize%20homes. Accessed June 15, 2021.

22. The Art Institute's digitized archive of its collection shows beautiful paintings, with vibrant colors; they are more colorful than their appearance in the *Prize Homes* book. Visit the Art Institute archive: https://www.artic.edu/collection ?q=chicagoland%20prize%20homes.

23. The two presentation renderings were available for purchase in summer of 2021, through a web-based company that sells the prints with a variety of framing options. https://museumprints.myshopify.com.

24. Edward Barry, "Break Ground Tomorrow for Prize Dwelling," *Chicago Tribune*, June 9, 1946, SW1.

25. "Palatine Is Site of Sixth Prize Home for Vet," *Chicago Tribune*, June 30, 1946, NW1, 20.

26. Art Institute records of this exhibit include two photos of unidentified Governor Dwight Green (who is identified in a *Tribune* photo); a photo of unidentified Boyd Hill, Daniel Catton Rich (Art Institute Director of Fine Arts), and Mayor Edward J. Kelly (they are identified in the same photo in the *Tribune*); a press release announcing free admission on Washington's Birthday and listing the Prize Home exhibit among others on view.

27. "Prize Exhibit," *Chicago Tribune*, February 3, 1946, C2.

28. The invitation indicates 167 houses would be displayed, not the 172 number that was later repeated. This is likely due to the addition of new designs as the month-long exhibit went on.

29. The Palmer House occupies a celebrated spot in Chicago history, and it even has its own museum. It does not have any records of the cocktail party, however. For its history, see https://www.palmerhousehiltonhotel.com/about-our-hotel. Accessed July 27, 2021.

30. "Homes Exhibit to Open Today at Art Institute," *Chicago Tribune*, February 9, 1946, 15.

31. "Art Institute's Leader Praises Homes Exhibit," *Chicago Tribune*, February 27, 1946, 23.

32. "Tribune Prize Homes Display at Institute Will Wind up Today," *Chicago Tribune*, March 8, 1946, 3.

33. "Homes Exhibit to Open Today at Art Institute," *Chicago Tribune*, February 9, 1946, 15.

34. Edward Barry, "Five Prize Houses That Won the Readers' Vote," *Chicago Tribune*, April 7, 1946, F5.

35. Barry, "Five Prize Houses That Won the Readers' Vote," F5.

36. "Tribune House Designs in Home Builders' Show," *Chicago Tribune*, February 25, 1946, 15.

37. "Display Tribune House Plans in Midland, Michigan," *Chicago Tribune*, March 29, 1946, 11.

38. "Evanston Sees 10 Prize Homes Designs Exhibit," *Chicago Tribune*, August 25, 1946, N4.

39. Boyd Hill to Marcel Breuer, Cambridge, Massachusetts, March 21, 1946. Marcel Breuer Papers, Special Collections Research Center, Syracuse University Libraries.

40. "J. L. Hudson Slates Home Plan Show," *Detroit Free Press*, June 16, 1946, 15; "Indianapolis Will View Winning Homes Designs," *Chicago Tribune*, May 6, 1946, 18.

41. "Fair Exhibits Home Designs: Tribune Prize Winners to Be Displayed Aug. 27–Sept. 1," *Escanaba Daily Press*, August 8, 1946, 5.

42. "People and Events," *Chicago Tribune*, March 21, 1947, 31.

43. "Tribune Home Designs on Show in Milwaukee," *Chicago Tribune*, March 10, 1948, 10.

44. "Chicagoland Home Designs on Exhibit in City," *Blue Island Sun-Standard*, February 16, 1950, 1; "Tribune Prize Home Designs to Be Shown," *Chicago Tribune*, March 12, 1950, NW1; "Harvey Firm to Display 42 Tribune Home Designs," *Chicago Tribune*, July 2, 1950, SW1; "42 Tribune Prize Homes Are Displayed in Area," *Chicago Tribune*, August 20, 1950, SW9.

45. "Art Exhibition to Open at CMA Gallery, Nov. 17," *The Culver Citizen*, November 14, 1951, 13.

46. "Prize-Winning Designs Shown," *Los Angeles Times*, August 24, 1952, 119.

47. "Home Show Exhibits to Include Designs of Better Rooms," *Freeport Journal-Standard*, March 9, 1953, 4.

48. Lloyd Wendt, *Chicago Tribune: The Rise of a Great American Newspaper* (Chicago: Rand McNally & Co., 1979), 673.

49. "$26,250.00 'Better Rooms for Better Living' Competition," *Chicago Tribune*, December 15, 1946, G16.

50. Edward Barry, "$26,250 Contest for Decorating of Homes Opens," *Chicago Tribune*, December 8, 1946, 2.

51. "Tribune 'Better Rooms' Will Be at Art Institute," *Chicago Tribune*, June 9, 1947, 33.

52. Rita Fitzpatrick, "Stores Create Live Reality in Tribune Rooms," *Chicago Tribune*, September 16, 1947, 2.

53. "Prize Winners in Home Design Contest Listed," *Chicago Tribune*, April 13, 1947, 7.

54. "Tribune Rooms Sketches Seen in 22 States," *Chicago Tribune*, April 15, 1951, SW, B3.

Chapter 4. A More Permanent Legacy

1. W. J. Byrnes to Marcel Breuer, Cambridge, Massachusetts, April 23, 1946. Marcel Breuer Papers, Special Collections Research Center, Syracuse University Libraries.

2. Williamson designed many Wilcox & Follett books, among them Luther Gable, *The Miracle of Television*, 1949; Eugenia Stone, *Page Boy for King Arthur*, 1949; Lee de Forest, *Father of Radio: The Autobiography of Lee de Forest*; Benjamin Lipsner, *The*

33. *Prize Homes,* 25.

34. See Siobhan Moroney, "Master Bedrooms and Master Suites: Modern Marriage and the Architecture of American Homes," *Journal of Family History* (January 2016), 81–94.

35. *Prize Homes,* 54, 65, 88.

36. *Prize Homes,* 10, 102.

37. *Prize Homes,* 15.

38. *Prize Homes,* 63.

39. Amy Ogata, *Designing the Creative Child: Playthings and Places in Midcentury America* (Minneapolis: University of Minnesota Press, 2013). See especially chapter 3.

40. *Prize Homes,* 20, 70, 71.

41. Judy Fink Essek, interview by author, June 28, 2022.

42. *Prize Homes,* 70.

43. Diane Harris, *Little White Houses: How the Postwar Home Constructed Race in America* (Minneapolis: University of Minnesota Press, 2013), 106.

44. *Prize Homes,* 25, 90, 70.

45. *Prize Homes,* 82.

46. *Prize Homes,* 94.

47. *Prize Homes,* 29, 53.

48. *Prize Homes,* 34.

49. *Prize Homes,* 95.

50. Two are in problem one and one is in problem two, and all three are very modern designs. *Prize Homes,* 22, 31, 61.

51. *Prize Homes,* 65, 89, 97.

52. *Prize Homes,* 91.

53. Garage expansion arose not only because of the affordability of multiple cars but also for storage that could not be easily accommodated within the house, such as for bicycles and seasonal outdoor furniture and equipment. See Steven Morris, "Garages: Driving Force in Residential Designs," *Chicago Tribune,* May 11, 1985, https://www.chicagotribune.com/news/ct-xpm-1985-05-11-8501290735-story.html.

54. *Prize Homes,* 68.

55. *Prize Homes,* 23.

56. Isenstadt indicates that even interior decorators advised using paint, wallpaper, mirrors, furniture, and furniture placement to increase perceptions of spaciousness in small rooms. Sandy Isenstadt, *The Modern American House: Spaciousness and Middle-Class Identity* (Cambridge: Cambridge University Press, 2006), chapter 3.

57. Gwendolyn Wright, *Moralism and the Modern Home: Domestic Architecture and Cultural Conflict in Chicago, 1873–1913* (Chicago: University of Chicago Press, 1980), 234–235, 244–246. Wright also makes the point that as the home was no longer a source of production (for canning and quilting, for example), it needed less space. Gwendolyn Wright, *Building the Dream: A Social History of Housing in America* (New York: Pantheon Books, 1981), 171.

58. Jacobs includes a page from a house plan catalog from the teens or twenties, suggesting a "plaster arch . . . [is] . . . purposely wide entering the dining room to give

you full use of the two rooms together for entertaining." James A. Jacobs, *Detached America: Building Houses in Postwar Suburbia* (Charlottesville: University of Virginia Press, 2015), 102.

59. Kathleen and Terry Shiel, interview by author, June 19, 2022.

60. Kathy Bryant, interview by author, May 18, 2022.

61. Thomas Hubka, *How the Working-Class Home Became Modern, 1900–1940* (Minneapolis: University of Minnesota, 2020), 100–106.

62. Elizabeth Collins Cromley, *The Food Axis: Cooking, Eating, and the Architecture of American Houses* (Charlottesville and London: University of Virginia Press, 2010), especially chapter 5.

63. *Prize Homes,* 81, 88.

64. *Prize Homes,* 54.

65. Edward Barry, "Living-Dining Room Designs Lead Contest," *Chicago Tribune*, March 30, 1947, F11.

66. Ann Moran, interview by author, January 26, 2021.

67. Sara Belkov, interview by author, June 30, 2022.

68. An internet search on whether houses still need dining rooms and dining tables turns up a resounding no. One review finds the "American dining room dying a slow death." Melinda Fakuade, "What Is the Dining Table Really For?" Vox.com, March 26, 2021.

69. *Prize Homes,* 12, 47.

70. Strasser quotes a woman who called laundry "the great domestic dread of the household." See her chapter on laundry, "Blue Monday." Susan Strasser, *Never Done: A History of American Housework* (New York: Pantheon Books, 1982).

71. *Prize Homes,* 22, 28, 29, 65, 68, 74.

72. *Prize Homes,* 53.

73. *Prize Homes,* 81.

74. "Boston Architect's Prize-Winning House: Joseph C. Gora's Plan Eliminates Both the Cellar and Attic," *The Boston Globe*, January 12, 1946, 32.

75. *Prize Homes,* 16, 35, 89.

76. Kathy Bryant, interview by author, June 20, 2022.

77. *Prize Homes,* 49, 92.

78. *Prize Homes,* 37, 60, 21.

79. *Prize Homes,* 71.

80. *Prize Homes,* 51.

81. Sara Belkov, interview by author, June 30, 2022.

82. Ursula O'Hayer and Peter Wendt, interview by author, July 3, 2022.

83. *Prize Homes,* 29.

84. Ann Moran, interview by author, January 26, 2021.

85. *Prize Homes,* 88.

86. *Prize Homes,* 11.

87. *Prize Homes,* 74, 69, 70.

88. *Prize Homes,* 79.

89. *Prize Homes,* 102.

90. *Prize Homes,* 54.

91. See Sandy Isenstadt, *The Modern American House: Spaciousness and Middle-Class Identity* (Cambridge: Cambridge University Press, 2006), chapter 8.

92. *Prize Homes,* 56.

93. Susan Weber Postma, interview by author, September 20, 2022.

94. *Prize Homes,* 11.

95. *Prize Homes,* 85.

96. *Prize Homes,* 10, 19, 28, 60, 62, 69, 83.

97. Bill and Valerie Kanter, interview by author, June 12, 2022.

98. *Prize Homes,* 25.

99. *Prize Homes,* 51.

100. *Prize Homes,* 59.

101. *Prize Homes,* 65.

102. *Prize Homes,* 95.

103. *Prize Homes,* 97.

104. Barbara Kelly, *Expanding the American Dream: Building and Rebuilding Levittown* (Albany, NY: SUNY Press, 1993), 68.

105. Kristina Borrman, "One Standardized House for All: America's Little House," *Buildings and Landscapes,* Fall 2017, 37–57, 41.

106. Spigel traces the question of where to place the television in the house, a problem she argues was "formulated and reformulated, solved and recast." Lynn Spigel, *Make Room for TV: Television and the Family Ideal in Postwar America* (Chicago: University of Chicago Press, 1992), 37.

107. Rita Fitzpatrick, "2 Better Rooms Show City How to Live with TV," *Chicago Tribune,* April 25, 1952, B2.

Chapter 6. Modernism Skepticism

1. Thomas Hubka, *How the Working-Class Home Became Modern, 1900–1940* (Minneapolis: University of Minnesota, 2020), xxii, xxiii, 182–186.

2. Hubka, *How the Working-Class Home Became Modern,* xxiii.

3. James Ford and Katherine Morrow Ford, *The Modern House in America* (New York: Architectural Book Publishing Co., 1940), 8, 10.

4. For the evolution of the garage in conjunction with the house, see J. B. Jackson, "The Domestication of the Garage," in *The Necessity for Ruins and Other Topics* (Amherst: University of Massachusetts Press, 1980), 103–111; and Kenneth T. Jackson, *Crabgrass Frontier: The Suburbanization of the United States* (New York: Oxford University Press, 1985), 251–253.

5. David Smiley, "Making the Modified Modern," *Perspecta,* Vol. 32 (2001), 38–54, 42.

6. Wright asserts that postwar home buyers wanted a house no one had ever lived in before. Gwendolyn Wright, *Building the Dream: A Social History of Housing in America* (New York: Pantheon Books, 1981), 253–254.

7. Al Chase, "Hope of Magic Home May Cut Building Rate," *Chicago Tribune,* January 11, 1944, 19. For more on how the building industry attempted to moderate buyers' expectations, see Timothy Mennel, "'Miracle House Hoop-La': Corporate

Rhetoric and the Construction of the Postwar American House," *Journal of the Society of Architectural Historians* (September 2005), 340–361.

8. Edith Weigle, "Design Experts Take a Look at the Home of the Future," *Chicago Tribune*, January 19, 1944, 19.

9. Edith Weigle, "Experts Voice Sane Ideas on Home of Future," *Chicago Tribune*, January 23, 1944, E9.

10. Louise Bargelt, "Planning the Post-War Home!" *Chicago Tribune*, January 21, 1945, C1. See also Louise Bargelt, "Post-War Home Surveys Show Building Trend: No Fantasy in Ideas for New Houses," *Chicago Tribune*, January 30, 1944, N6.

11. *Fireproof Homes of Period Design: Seventy-Two Designs for Fireproof Homes from a National Competition among Architects, Draftsmen and Architectural Students* (The United States Gypsum Company, 1925).

12. Lewis Storrs, *The Key to Your New Home: A Primer of Liveable and Practical Houses* (New York: McGraw-Hill Book Company, 1938). (This publication date is wrong; on page six of the preface, he refers to the "termination of the Second World War.") See pages 105, 81, 94.

13. Susan Benjamin and Michelangelo Sabatino, *Modern in the Middle: Chicago Houses, 1929–1975* (New York: Monicelli Press, 2020), 35.

14. *Prize Homes*, 32.

15. George Nelson and Henry Wright, *Tomorrow's House: How to Plan Your Post-War Home Now* (New York: Simon and Schuster, 1945), 34.

16. Sandy Isenstadt, *The Modern American House: Spaciousness and Middle-Class Identity* (Cambridge: Cambridge University Press, 2006), 150–156.

17. "Report of the Jury Award," *Pencil Points*, April 1936, 164–216.

18. Volz makes this point. Candace M. Volz, "The Modern Look of the Early-Twentieth-Century House: A Mirror of Changing Lifestyles," in *Home Life, 1880–1930: A Social History of Spaces and Services,* eds. Jessica H. Foy and Thomas J. Schlereth (Knoxville: University of Tennessee Press, 1992), 25–48, 30.

19. Bill and Valerie Kanter, interview by author, June 12, 2022.

20. *Prize Homes*, 21.

21. *Prize Homes*, 49.

22. *Prize Homes*, 65.

23. *Prize Homes*, 57, 37.

24. *The Chicagoland Prize Homes Competition Program*, 4.

25. 5523 Sunnyside in Chicago and 1603 Warwick in Whiting, Indiana.

26. Salomon's research on driveways notes their standardization in the postwar period but does not address lot size. David Salomon, "Research Notes: Toward a History of the Suburban Driveway," *Buildings & Landscapes: Journal of the Vernacular Architectural Forum*, Vol. 24, No. 2 (Fall 2017), 85–99.

27. *Prize Homes*, 52, 88.

28. *Prize Homes*, 16.

29. *Prize Homes*, 45.

30. *Prize Homes*, 81, 38.

31. *Prize Homes*, 102, 62.

32. *Prize Homes,* 28, 99.

33. *Prize Homes,* 74.

34. Ursula O'Hayer and Peter Wendt, interview by author, July 3, 2022. Audrey Hellinger, interview by author, July 15, 2022.

35. "Second of Series of 14 Model Houses Now on Display," *The Highland Park Press,* August 7, 1947, 1.

36. Thomas Hubka, *Houses without Names: Architectural Nomenclature and the Classification of America's Common Houses* (Knoxville: University of Tennessee Press, 2013).

37. *Prize Homes,* 23.

38. *Prize Homes,* 35.

39. *Prize Homes,* 36.

40. *Prize Homes,* 44.

41. *Prize Homes,* 18, 41, 45, 82, 102.

42. *Prize Homes,* 29, 38.

43. *Prize Homes,* 96.

44. *Prize Homes,* 45.

45. *Prize Homes,* 35.

46. *Prize Homes,* 64.

47. *Prize Homes,* 23.

48. *Prize Homes,* 35.

49. *Prize Homes,* 36.

50. *Prize Homes,* 44.

51. *Prize Homes,* 56.

52. *Prize Homes,* 57.

53. *Prize Homes,* 19.

54. *Prize Homes,* 74.

55. Ursula O'Hayer and Peter Wendt, interview by author, July 3, 2022.

56. Shimon Langer, interview by author, June 19, 2022.

57. *Prize Homes,* 11.

58. *Prize Homes,* 15.

59. *Prize Homes,* 61, 95.

60. Edward Barry, "Two Story Home That Avoids Monotony," *Chicago Tribune,* March 24, 1946, C4.

61. "Ten Prize-Winning Houses," *Architectural Forum,* April 1946, 112–116.

62. Thomas Hubka, *Houses without Names: Architectural Nomenclature and the Classification of America's Common Houses* (Knoxville: University of Tennessee Press, 2013), 34.

63. *Prize Homes,* 19, 21, 49, 61.

64. David Smiley, "Making the Modified Modern," *Perspecta,* Vol. 32 (2001), 38–54.

65. Edward Barry, "Five Prize Houses That Won the Readers' Vote Presented as a Model Community of Homes," *Chicago Tribune,* April 7, 1946, F5.

66. "Spiegel: Stores for the Home," *Chicago Tribune,* March 10, 1946, 17.

67. "Interior Designs for Chicagoland Homes," *Chicago Tribune,* July 21, 1946, 1.

68. "Interior Decorating Schemes for Tribune Prize Homes," *Chicago Tribune*, August 11, 1946, C1.

69. Sears publicity poster, courtesy of Bill and Valerie Kanter.

70. Edward Barry, "A Three Level Home," *Chicago Tribune*, March 17, 1946, C9.

71. Edward Barry, "A House of Unusual Windows," *Chicago Tribune*, May 19, 1946, D8.

Chapter 7. Competing Visions

1. Haight explores the tension between artistically modern and commercially popular traditional houses in her research on Canadian house competitions in the 1930s. Susan Haight, "Machines in Suburban Gardens: The 1936 T. Eaton Company Architectural Competition for House Designs," *Material Culture Review*, vol. 44, no. 1 (June 1996).

2. This issue of *Architectural Forum* is not digitized at USModernist, an exhaustive archive on which I have frequently relied. Publisher Harcourt, Brace & Company published as an individual book, however, what looks like most of the April 1935 issue (there are no advertisements), under the title *The House for Modern Living*. Architectural Forum, *The House for Modern Living* (New York: Harcourt, Brace & Co., 1935). Subsequent citations refer to the original, not the reprint.

3. "The House for Modern Living," *Architectural Forum*, April 1935, 275.

4. "The House for Modern Living," 275–276.

5. "Competition Week," *Architectural Forum*, April 1935, 280.

6. *Architectural Forum*, April 1935, 375.

7. *Architectural Forum*, April 1935, 358, 397.

8. "1875," *Architectural Forum*, April 1935, 274.

9. "81 New Houses," *Architectural Forum,* April 1941, 217.

10. "81 New Houses," 273.

11. The author is grateful to Nancy Webster, Highland Park Library archivist, who researched this issue when the library was closed due to a public health emergency.

12. A 1949 college textbook gently assures house planners that "it is usually best to select houses not radically different from those prevailing in a community." Deane G. Carter and Keith H. Hinchcliff, *Family Housing* (John Wiley & Sons, 1949), 103.

13. "Report of the Jury," *Pencil Points*, May 1945, 54–92.

14. Kenneth Reid, "Two Competitions," *Progressive Architecture*, April 1946, 51.

15. "Progressive Architecture-Rich's, Inc.: Architectural Competition; A Realistic House for a Family in Georgia," *Progressive Architecture*, April 1946, 38.

16. "Progressive Architecture-Rich's, Inc.: Architectural Competition: A Realistic House for a Family in Georgia," *Progressive Architecture*, April 1946, 62.

17. "Progressive Architecture-Rich's, Inc.: Architectural Competition," *Progressive Architecture*, October 1945, 37.

18. "Progressive Architecture-Rich's, Inc.: Architectural Competition: A Realistic House for a Family in Georgia," *Progressive Architecture*, April 1945, 63.

19. "Progressive Architecture-Rich's, Inc.: Architectural Competition: A Realistic House for a Family in Georgia," *Progressive Architecture*, April 1945, 62.

20. Editor, "Competition: 'Designs for Postwar Living,'" *Arts & Architecture*, April 1943, 35.

21. "'Designs for Postwar Living' Competition Rules," *Arts & Architecture*, April 1943, 67.

22. Editor, "Designs for Postwar Living," *Arts & Architecture*, May 1943, 27.

23. "Designs for Postwar Living: Announcing the Winning Designs in the Architectural Competition Sponsored by California Arts and Architecture," *Arts & Architecture*, August 1943, 22–37.

24. "5 Entries Receiving Honorable Mention," *Arts & Architecture*, September 1943, 19–31. Two of the five mentions went to married couple design teams: Fred and Louis Langhorst, and Susanne and Arnold Wasson-Tucker.

25. "A Fabric House," *Arts & Architecture*, October/November 1943, 22–27.

26. "Art & Architecture's Sceond Annual Competition for the Design of a Small House," *Arts & Architecture*, February 1945, 32.

27. "Arts & Architecture's Second Annual Competition for the Design of a Small House," *Arts & Architecture*, February 1945, 28–41.

28. "Announcing the Case Study Program," *Arts & Architecture*, January 1945, 37–39.

29. "Announcing the Case Study Program," 38.

30. Amelia Jones and Elizabeth A. T. Smith, "The Thirty-Six Case Study Projects," *Blueprints for Modern Living: History and Legacy of the Case Study Houses*, ed. Elizabeth A. T. Smith (Cambridge, MA: MIT Press, 1990), 41–81, 42.

31. "Case Study Houses #8 and #9," *Arts & Architecture*, December 1945, 43–51.

32. "Proposal for Case Study House #4," *Arts & Architecture*, August 1945, 30–34.

33. "Part 2: Proposal for Case Study House #4," *Arts & Architecture*, September 1945, 33–38. The woman watching the baby is the only figure I have ever seen, among hundreds of elevation sketches, whose ethnicity is not immediately readable as White; she may be a Black woman.

34. Edward Barry, "A Three Level Home," *Chicago Tribune*, March 17, 1946, C9.

35. "Case Study House #2," *Arts & Architecture*, April 1945, 25–29.

36. "Case Study House #3," *Arts & Architecture*, June 1945, 26–30.

37. "Case Study House #7," *Arts & Architecture*, November 1945, 38–42.

38. "Case Study Houses #8 and #9," *Arts & Architecture*, December 1945, 43–51.

39. "Competition Report," *Architectural Forum*, March 1951, 105.

40. "$100,000 NAHB Forum House Design Competition," *Architectural Forum*, September 1950, 88a, b.

41. "House Design Competition," *Architectural Forum*, March 1951, 103.

42. "House Design Competition," 103.

43. "How to Acquire Fresh Approach to Small House Design," *Architectural Forum*, January 1951, 250.

44. "House Design Competition," *Architectural Forum*, March 1951, 108.

45. "House Design Competition," 111–114.

46. "House Design Competition," 115–117.

47. "House Design Competition," 118–119.

48. "House Design Competition," 120–121.

49. Alysa Slay, interview by author, June 9, 2022.

50. Christine Chapman, *Archetype, Hybrid, and Prototype: Modernism in* House Beautiful's *Small House Competition, 1928–1942* (MS thesis, University of North Carolina at Greensboro, 2007).

51. "Small House Competition, Sponsored by Ladies Home Journal," *Architectural Forum*, October 1938, 275.

52. Paul Cret, "The Pencil Points Competition for an Eight-Room Residence," *Pencil Points*, July 1930, 513.

53. Paul R. Williams, *The Small Home of Tomorrow* (Santa Monica, CA: Hennessey + Ingalls, 2009).

54. Williams, *The Small Home of Tomorrow*, 12, 30, 92.

55. Williams, 7, 8.

56. Williams, 66, 60.

57. Williams, 70.

58. Williams, 12.

59. Williams, 24.

60. Williams, 72.

61. Bloomingdale's, *Prize Winning Designs in Bloomingdale's Architectural Competition*, 1947, 15.

62. Louis La Beaume, "Report of the Jury Award," *Pencil Points*, July 1934, 309–339.

63. "Report of the Jury Award," *Pencil Points*, April 1936, 164–216.

64. "Report of the Jury Award," 165.

65. "Report of the Jury Award," *Pencil Points*, August 1937, 475–518.

66. Brian Burch, interview by author, January 26, 2021.

67. "Letters," *Architectural Forum*, February 1946, 38.

68. "Letters," 38.

69. Wright found a similar architectural conservatism in the 1920s with the influential Architects' Small House Service Bureau. Gwendolyn Wright, *Building the Dream: A Social History of Housing in America* (New York: Pantheon Books, 1981), 200.

70. Joseph B. Mason, *History of Housing in the U.S.: 1930–1980* (Houston, TX: Gulf Publishing Company, 1982), chapter 1.

71. Marc A. Weiss, *The Rise of the Community Builders: The American Real Estate Industry and Urban Land Planning* (New York: Columbia University Press, 1987), 151.

72. Miles Colean, *American Housing: Problems and Prospects* (New York: The Twentieth Century Fund, 1944), 120–129.

73. Gwendolyn Wright, *Building the Dream: A Social History of Housing in America* (New York: Pantheon Books, 1981), 251.

74. See Miles Colean, *American Housing: Problems and Prospects* (New York: The Twentieth Century Fund, 1944), chapter 10; and Avi Friedman, "The Evolution

of Design Characteristics during the Post-Second World War Housing Boom: The US Experience," *Journal of Design History*, Vol. 9, No. 2 (1995), 131–146, 131. Greer documents the reach of FHA regulations: "sub-soil and soil conditions, set back from the street, minimal lot size, requirements for a separate kitchen and living room, the number of bedrooms, number of windows per room, requirements for all basic utilities including plumbing, sewer, and electrical systems, neighborhood amenities including the provision of shopping, public parks and open space, access to metropolitan transportation systems as well as public and cultural facilities, dictates on the economic future of the community both within the metropolitan area and the likely future of the community, and the social, ethnic, and racial makeup of the neighborhood." James L. Greer, "Historic Home Mortgage Redlining in Chicago, *Journal of the Illinois State Historical Society*, Vol. 107, No. 2 (Summer 2014), 204–233, 109–10.

75. George Nelson and Henry Wright, *Tomorrow's House: How to Plan Your Post-War Home Now* (New York: Simon and Schuster, 1945), 202–203.

76. Sunny Balsam, interview by author, July 22, 2021.

77. U.S. President's Commission on Veterans' Pensions, *A Report on Veterans Benefits in the United States*. Staff Report No 1x-c. Washington, D.C.: U.S. Government Printing Office, 1956, 5–19, in *Federal Housing Policy & Programs: Past and Present*, ed. J. Paul Mitchell (New Brunswick, NJ: Rutgers University Press, 1985), chapter 6.

78. Avi Friedman and David Krawitz, *Peeking through the Keyhole: The Evolution of North American Homes* (Montreal: McGill-Queens University Press, 2005), 131.

79. "81 New Houses," *Architectural Forum*, April 1941, 217.

80. Special thanks to Alejandro Saldana Perales for alerting me to this filmstrip. American Plan Service, *APS Home Plans: 40 Plans for 1, 2 and 3 Bedroom Homes Suitable for Building Anywhere in U.S.A.*, 1946.

81. American Builder, *Buyer-Approved Homes of Known Cost* (Chicago: Simmons-Boardman Publishing). No publication date is given, but references to 1939 suggest it was published in 1941, before the United States entered World War II.

82. American Builder, *Buyer-Approved Homes of Known Cost*, 5.

83. American Builder, 50.

84. American Builder, 103–104.

85. American Builder, 86–89.

86. Samuel Glaser, *Designs for 60 Small Homes: From $2,000 to $10,000* (New York: Coward-McCann, Inc., 1939).

87. Glaser, *Designs for 60 Small Homes*, foreword.

88. For the influence of the Architects' Small House Service Bureau on mass-building projects, see Lisa Tucker, *American Architects and the Single-Family Home: Lessons Learned from the Architects' Small House Service Bureau* (New York: Routledge, 2015).

89. The Architects' Small House Service Bureau, Inc., *Two Story Homes: Seventy-Three Small Homes Prepared by a National Association of Architects* (The Architects' Small House Service Bureau, 1941). Tucker indicates this was the last of the twenty-five

house plan books the bureau published between 1919 and 1941. Lisa Tucker, *American Architects and the Single-Family Home: Lessons Learned from the Architects' Small House Service Bureau* (New York: Routledge, 2015), 19.

90. The Architects' Small House Service Bureau, Inc., *Two Story Homes: Seventy-Three Small Homes Prepared by a National Association of Architects* (The Architects' Small House Service Bureau, 1941); sewing rooms: 9, 10, 15, 27, 59, 62, 68; study: 30.

91. The Architects' Small House Service Bureau, Inc., *Two Story Homes*, owners' bathrooms: 25, 40, 41, 45, 47, 59, 60; lavatories: 29, 48, 51, 55, 61.

92. The Architects' Small House Service Bureau, Inc., 61.

93. The Architects' Small House Service Bureau, Inc., 6, 31, 43, 44, 64.

94. The Architects' Small House Service Bureau, Inc., 28, 35, 69.

95. The Architects' Small House Service Bureau, Inc., 28, 29, 38.

96. The Architects' Small House Service Bureau, Inc., 37, 38, 41, 42, 45 53, 59, 61, 71.

97. The Architects' Small House Service Bureau, Inc., 26.

98. The Architects' Small House Service Bureau, Inc., 18.

99. The Architects' Small House Service Bureau, Inc., 67.

100. The Architects' Small House Service Bureau, Inc., 28.

101. The Architects' Small House Service Bureau, Inc., modern house on 69; compare to Georgian on 47.

102. The Architects' Small House Service Bureau, Inc., 74.

103. The Architects' Small House Service Bureau, Inc., 75.

104. Harold E. Group, *Small Houses of the Forties, with Illustrations and Floor Plans* (Mineola, NY: Dover Publications, 2007); originally published as *House-of-the-Month Book of Small Houses* (Garden City, NY: Garden City Publishing Co, 1946), 4.

105. Group, *Small Houses of the Forties*, 43.

106. Group, 75.

107. Group, 79.

108. Group, 9.

109. Group, 9–10.

110. Group, 13.

111. Group, 41.

112. Group, 33, 37, 39, 45, 47, 89, 100.

113. Group, 51.

114. Group, 31.

115. Group, 31.

116. American Builder Magazine, *Blueprint Plans from American Builder Magazine* (Chicago: American Builder/A Simmons-Boardman Publication, 1946), 4.

117. American Builder Magazine, *Blueprint Plans from American Builder Magazine*, 12.

118. American Builder Magazine, 13.

119. American Builder Magazine, 14.

120. American Builder Magazine, 28.

121. American Builder Magazine, 18.

122. They used a sketch of an uncredited Randolph Evans house found in Group's book, criticizing background depictions of "majestic surrounds of wooded glens or rolling hills," when in reality, houses would be on ordinary streets. John P. Dean and Simon Breines, *The Book of Houses* (New York: Crown Publishers, 1946), 45. See Group, 41.

123. John P. Dean and Simon Breines, *The Book of Houses* (New York: Crown Publishers, 1946), 34.

124. In a more academic treatment of home buying, Dean exhaustively covers all that might go wrong with home ownership, including concerns about "[c]hanging fashions in home designs" that will render a house purchase obsolete. John P. Dean, *Home Ownership: Is It Sound?* (New York: Harper & Brothers, 1945), 113.

125. John P. Dean and Simon Breines, *The Book of Houses* (New York: Crown Publishers, 1946), vii.

126. Dean and Breines, *The Book of Houses*, vii.

127. Dean and Breines, 29.

128. Dean and Breines, 85.

129. Dean and Breines, 90.

130. Dean and Breines, 88.

131. Dean and Breines, 98.

132. Dean and Breines, 104.

133. Dean H. Robinson, *Book of Small Home Designs* (Detroit: The Scale Model Home Planning Co., 1948), preface.

134. Arguably the best-known house plan catalogs came from Sears, Roebuck & Co., which offered buyers inexpensive plans and/or full building kits between 1908 and 1940. Sears's architects were "adept followers—rather than leaders—of fashion," according to Stevenson and Jandl, who attribute Sears's success to that attentiveness. Katherine Cole Stevenson and H. Ward Jandl, *Houses by Mail: A Guide to Houses from Sears, Roebuck and Company* (Washington, D.C.: Preservation Press, 1986), 32.

135. Jurors complained about the lack of sloping roofs, as such roofs provide insulation in hot climates.

136. *Prize Homes*, 84.

137. *Prize Homes*, 23, 52.

138. *Prize Homes*, 42, 52, 76, 77, 84, 101.

139. *Prize Homes*, 101, 102.

140. *Prize Homes*, 19, 102.

141. *Mr. Blandings Builds His Dream House*, RKO Studios, 1948. For publicity, RKO studio built seventy-three dream houses throughout the country, raffling off many, and some Blandings houses still stand. Upon completion of several of the houses, appliance manufacturers and department stores combined to furnish the houses, and promoters arranged to open the furnished homes to visitors. If the studio had not relied on one single design, their house-building project might rival, if not surpass, many contemporary architectural competitions and architectural and design journals. See Catherine Jurca, "Hollywood, the Dream House Factory," *Cinema Journal*, Summer 1998, 19–36, 29–30.

142. Esther McCoy, "Arts & Architecture Case Study Houses," *Blueprints for Modern Living: History and Legacy of the Case Study Houses,* ed. Elizabeth A. T. Smith (Cambridge, MA: MIT Press, 1990), 15–39, 18.

143. Margaret Ruth Little, "Getting the American Dream for Themselves: Postwar Modern Subdivisions for African Americans in Raleigh, North Carolina," *Buildings & Landscapes*, Vol. 19, No. 1 (Spring 2012), 73–86.

144. Edward Barry, "Five Prize Houses That Won the Readers' Vote," *Chicago Tribune*, April 1, 1946, F5.

145. Edith Farnsworth and Mies Van Der Rohe fought over many things during their "partnership" in the building of the infamous Farnsworth house, and furniture was one of them. Alex Beam, *Broken Glass: Mies Van Der Rohe, Edith Farnsworth, and the Fight over a Modernist Masterpiece* (New York: Random House, 2020).

146. Edward Barry, "Winning Designs," *Chicago Tribune*, February 3, 1946, C1.

147. Edward Barry, "92 Home Designs from Entries in the Tribune Contest," *Chicago Tribune*, May 2, 1948, B8.

Chapter 8. Breaking Ground

1. "The Chicago Tribune Announces," *Chicago Tribune*, September 30, 1945, 21.

2. Gregory Randall briefly summarized that episode in *America's Original GI Town: Park Forest, Illinois* (Baltimore: Johns Hopkins University Press, 2000), 170–172.

3. Thomas Buck, "Prefab Housing Industry Seeks Faith of Public," *Chicago Tribune*, January 1, 1947, 59. Lane recounts the bankruptcy of a postwar Chicago firm, Smith and Hill, which had bet on prefabrication but lost when the houses did not sell. Barbara Miller Lane, *Houses for a New World: Builders and Buyers in American Suburbs, 1945–1965* (Princeton, NJ: Princeton University Press, 2015), 157.

4. Robert Young, "Wyatt Resigns Job as Housing Administrator," *Chicago Tribune*, December 5, 1945, 8; Robert Young, "Truman Names Chicagoan to Succeed Wyatt," *Chicago Tribune*, December 6, 1946, 19. Davies's history of housing policies during the Truman administration nicely recounts the story. Richard O. Davies, *Housing Reform during the Truman Administration* (Columbia: University of Missouri Press, 1966), 52–57.

5. Richard O. Davies, *Housing Reform during the Truman Administration* (Columbia: University of Missouri Press, 1966), 41.

6. "Veteran Finds House, Then His Luck Gives Out," *Chicago Tribune*, October 6, 1946, 12.

7. "Need Home Today," *Chicago Tribune*, November 10, 1946, 45.

8. "Vet 'Squatters' Warned: Move or Be Evicted," *Chicago Tribune*, November 7, 1946, 29.

9. Robert Cromie, "'Squatters' Hop 25,000 in Line, CHA Charges," *Chicago Tribune*, November 8, 1946, 9.

10. "CHA Forestalls More Housing Unit Seizures," *Chicago Tribune*, November 11, 1946, 21.

11. "50 Vets Lease Flats Seized by Squatters," *Chicago Tribune*, November 10, 1946, 1.

12. "Lawyers in Vet Home Grab Fail to Compromise," *Chicago Tribune*, November 14, 1946, 25; "Vet Squatters Give up Project Homes for Other Veterans," *Chicago Tribune*, December 1, 1946, 4.

13. Venice T. Spraggs, "2 Million New Homes Not 'for White Only,'" *The Chicago Defender*, February 23, 1946, 1.

14. "Takes up Flat Left by Vet in Row at Project," *Chicago Tribune*, November 18, 1946, 15.

15. "Rocks Injure 8 in Disturbance at Vets' Homes: Crowd Makes Protest as Negroes Move In," *Chicago Tribune*, December 6, 1946, 11.

16. "Mayor Assures Vet Protection: Hits Race Violence in Chicago Housing," *Chicago Defender*, November 30, 1946, 5; "Arrest 217 in Housing Fight," *Chicago Defender*, August 23, 1947, 1; "The Housing Bottleneck and Racial Tension," *Chicago Defender*, August 23, 1947, 14.

17. "Truman Signs Vets' Housing Bill into Law," *Chicago Tribune*, May 23, 1946, 8.

18. "Order Emergency Housing Posted 'Hold for Veterans,'" *Chicago Tribune*, September 1, 1946, SWA.

19. "Work Is Started on $389,000 Project for Veterans' Homes," *Chicago Tribune*, December 1, 1946, SWA; "Plans 60 Homes for Veterans Near Wheaton," *Chicago Tribune*, September 22, 1946, NWA; "Work Started on Three New Flat Buildings," *Chicago Tribune*, November 10, 1946, 43; "78 Homes Near Completion by McIntosh Firm," *Chicago Tribune*, November 3, 1946, 42.

20. Al Chase, "Big Vet Housing Projects Begun in Chicago Area," *Chicago Tribune*, June 2, 1946, SB; Thomas Furlong, "Plan 70 Acres of South Side Homes: Insurance Co. Would Invest 5–10 Millions," *Chicago Tribune*, April 4, 1946, 1; "Announce Plan for 1,650 Homes at Bensenville," *Chicago Tribune*, September 15, 1946, NA.

21. Anton Reminih, "Review of '46 Traces Hopes for New Year: Housing, or Lack of It, a Big Issue," *Chicago Tribune*, December 29, 1946, NW1.

22. *The Chicagoland Prize Homes Competition Program*.

23. Boyd Hill to All Registrants, October 30, 1945. Marcel Breuer Papers, Special Collections Research Center, Syracuse University Libraries.

24. Larry Wolters, "Plan Ceremony of Spade Work on Prize Home," *Chicago Tribune*, June 1, 1946, 8; Edward Barry, "Break Ground Today on Prize Tribune Home: Navy Vet Turns 1st Shovel for Own Abode," *Chicago Tribune*, June 2, 1946, 7; "Third Prize Home for a Veteran," *Chicago Tribune*, June 16, 1946, 8; John M'Cutcheon, "Dentist Turns First Spade at his Prize Home," *Chicago Tribune*, June 16, 1945, SW2.

25. Edward Barry, "Break Ground Today on Prize Tribune Home: Navy Vet Turns 1st Shovel for Own Abode," *Chicago Tribune*, June 2, 1946, 7.

26. Edward Barry, "Vet Starts Dream Home at Ceremony," *Chicago Tribune*, June 3, 1946, 32.

27. "New Developments," *Arts and Architecture*, June 1946, 43; "First Home Nears Completion in the Chicago Tribune's Home Building Program," *Gas Appliance Merchandising*, Vol. 19, 1947, 4, 33.

28. Edward Barry, "Break Ground Today on Prize Tribune Home: Navy Vet Turns 1st Shovel for Own Abode," *Chicago Tribune*, June 2, 1946, 7.

29. Edward Barry, "Vet Starts Dream Home at Ceremony," *Chicago Tribune*, June 3, 1946, 32.

30. Edward Barry, "Break Ground Tomorrow for Prize Dwelling," *Chicago Tribune*, June 9, 1946, SW1.

31. Larry Wolters, "W-G-N to Carry Start of Work on Prize Home," *Chicago Tribune*, June 15, 1946, 23.

32. "Vet Looks over His New Home Site," *Chicago Tribune*, June 20, 1946, W7.

33. "Ground Broken for Vet Home on North Side," *Chicago Tribune*, June 25, 1946, 16.

34. "Palatine Is Site of Sixth Prize Home for Vet," *Chicago Tribune*, June 30, 1946, NW1.

35. "Tribune Prize Home in Lombard in Process of Construction," *Chicago Tribune*, July 28, 1946, W6.

36. Edward Barry, "Veteran Builds Tribune Home," *Chicago Tribune*, November 17, 1946, B12.

37. "Veteran Breaks Soil to Start Work on Home," *Chicago Tribune*, June 17, 1946, 12; "Ground Broken for Third Prize Home for a Veteran," *Chicago Tribune*, June 17, 1946, 38.

38. "Highland Park Day: Briargate Villas," *The Highland Park Press*, September 15, 1927, 5. A half-dozen of those 1927 houses survive.

39. City of Chicago FOIA requests for 2900, 2908, and 2914 West Pratt. Received May 4, 2021.

40. "Vets Will Get Ten Tribune Prize Homes," *Chicago Tribune*, November 24, 1946, 7.

41. City of Chicago FOIA requests for 2900, 2908, and 2914 West Pratt. Received May 4, 2021.

42. Edward Barry, "Neighborhood of Prize Homes," *Chicago Tribune*, June 22, 1947, G14, 17.

43. James A. Jacobs, *Detached America: Building Houses in Postwar Suburbia* (Charlottesville: University of Virginia Press, 2015), 41–47.

44. Greer Braun, interview by author, June 15, 2022.

45. "Open 10 Tribune Prize Homes to Public Inspection Tomorrow—$400,000 Experiment in Finer Living," *Chicago Tribune*, October 11, 1947, 34.

46. Spiegel ads in the *Chicago Tribune*: March 10, 1946, 17; March 17, 1946, 17.

47. "On Display Sunday, October 19," *Kankakee Daily Journal*, October 18, 1947.

48. Ward Walker, "Prize Homes on N. W. Side Get Preview," *Chicago Tribune*, October 11, 1947, 1.

49. "Popular Home's House of Everlasting Style," *Popular Home*, Early Fall, 1949, 2.

50. Edward Barry, "Tribune Prize Home for a Veteran," *Chicago Tribune*, December 29, 1946, D10.

51. Edward Barry, "Interiors for Prize Homes," *Chicago Tribune*, July 21, 1946, G1, G8.

52. Edward Barry, "Interiors for Prize Homes," *Chicago Tribune*, August 11, 1946, C1, C4; Edward Barry, "Interiors for Prize Homes," *Chicago Tribune*, September 15, 1946, F1, F11.

53. "Top Flight Automatic Heating," *Chicago Tribune*, October 11, 1947, 5.

54. "Record Cabinet of the Month," *Chicago Tribune*, October 12, 1947, 3.

55. "Presenting a Prize Home," *Chicago Tribune*, October 12, 1947, NW5, W6, part 3-page 4.

56. "Wonderful News: Precedent Is Back at Colby's," *Chicago Tribune*, May 5, 1948, 11.

57. Bill and Valerie Kanter, interview by author, June 12, 2022.

58. Sears publicity poster, courtesy of Bill and Valerie Kanter.

59. James A. Jacobs, *Detached America: Building Houses in Postwar Suburbia* (Charlottesville: University of Virginia Press, 2015), 49.

60. "Public to View 1st of Tribune Model Homes," *Chicago Tribune*, July 12, 1947, 1.

61. "Thousands See Tribune Prize Home Opening," *Chicago Tribune*, July 14, 1947, 3.

62. "A Dream Come True! That's [*sic*] Tribune House," *Chicago Tribune*, July 18, 1947, 3.

63. "Thousands Visit Tribune's Prize Home in Suburb," *Chicago Tribune*, July 20, 1947, N2.

64. "2d of Tribune Prize Homes Ready to Show," *Chicago Tribune*, August 2, 1947, 1.

65. "40,000 See First 2 of 19 Tribune Prize Homes," *Chicago Tribune*, August 29, 1947, 7; "Wheaton Prize House Will Be Open to Public," *Chicago Tribune*, September 6, 1947, 3.

66. "'Perfect Home,' Visitors Say of Tribune House," *Chicago Tribune*, September 8, 1947, 2.

67. "2 More Tribune Prize Homes to Go on Display," *Chicago Tribune*, October 4, 1947, 7.

68. Gladys Priddy, "Found: The Home of Our Dreams, Women Agree," *Chicago Tribune*, September 14, 1947, W6.

69. "Prize Winning Home Inspires Praise of 3,000," *Chicago Tribune*, September 29, 1947, 3.

70. Agnes Lynch, "Club Members Heap Praise on Lombard House," *Chicago Tribune*, October 12, 1947, W8.

71. "51 Leyden High Girls Inspect Tribune Homes, *Chicago Tribune*, October 22, 1947, 20.

72. Michael Mech, interview by author, May 23, 2022.

73. Jo-Ellen Black, interview by author, June 8, 2022.

74. Jacobs shows how the National Home Week "Parade of Homes" encouraged massing display houses on a single block and creating special events around those openings, but his narrative suggests those practices began in the 1950s. James A. Jacobs, *Detached America: Building Houses in Postwar Suburbia* (Charlottesville: University of Virginia Press, 2015), 49–52. Dodd's history of the Parade of Homes indicates builders added more and more publicity-generating stunts to the parades: female models, often in bathing suits, and at least once, a girl in a bathtub; food cooking in the kitchens to create homey aromas; and nightclothes laid out on the bed. Like Jacobs, Dodd shows such activities began in the 1950s. Samuel Dodd, "Parade

of Homes: Salesmanship and the Post-War American Housing Industry," *Journal of Design History*, Vol. 28, No. 4 (2015), 385–404.

75. "Tribune Homes Exhibit Closes; Seen by 215,000," *Chicago Tribune*, November 10, 1947, 10.

76. Bill and Valerie Kanter, interview by author, June 12, 2022; Judy Fink Essek, interview by author, June 28, 2022.

77. Bill and Valerie Kanter, interview by author, June 12, 2022. Jacobs notes that theft of small items brought an additional cost to open houses with many visitors. James Jacobs, *Detached America: Building Houses in Postwar Suburbia* (Charlottesville: University of Virginia Press, 2015), 45.

78. City of Chicago FOIA requests for 2900, 2908, and 2914 West Pratt. Received May 4, 2021.

79. Ward Walker, "Prize Homes on N.W. Side Get Preview," *Chicago Tribune*, October 11, 1947, 1.

80. "Crowds Larger at Display of Tribune Homes," *Chicago Tribune*, October 16, 1947, 6.

81. "Crowds Larger at Display of Tribune Homes," *Chicago Tribune*, October 16, 1947, 6.

82. Sears publicity poster, courtesy of Bill and Valerie Kanter.

83. "Home Exhibit Televised," *Broadcasting*, November 10, 1947, 68.

84. Larry Wolters, "Television Wins Fans at Tribune Homes Exhibit," *Chicago Tribune*, October 26, 1947, NW12. See *WGN: A Pictorial History*, no publisher, 1961, 80.

85. Special thanks to Marilyn Domsky, who gave me one of her copies of this flyer.

86. Special thanks to Donna Scheckerman Orlove, who shared this and other documents.

87. Ward Walker, "Tribune's Ten Prize Houses on View Today," *Chicago Tribune*, October 12, 1947, 1.

88. Ward Walker, "51,819 Inspect 10 Tribune Prize Homes!" *Chicago Tribune*, October 13, 1947, 1; "51,819 Visit 10 Tribune Homes on Opening Day," *Chicago Tribune*, October 13, 1947, back page.

89. "Thousands See Tribune Homes on Second Day," *Chicago Tribune*, October 14, 1947, 15.

90. "Tribune Homes Are Studied by 5,000 Visitors," *Chicago Tribune*, October 15, 1947, 2.

91. "Crowds Larger at Display of Tribune Homes," *Chicago Tribune*, October 16, 1947, 6.

92. "200,000 Inspect Tribune's Prize Winning Homes," *Chicago Tribune*, October 19, 1947, 8.

93. "See Them Today: This Entire Community of Ten New Chicago Tribune Prize Homes," *Chicago Tribune*, October 21, 1947, 21.

94. "Tribune Homes Exhibit Closes; Seen by 215,000," *Chicago Tribune*, November 10, 1947, 10.

95. Sylvia Zimmerman told the story to the subsequent owners. Bill and Valerie Kanter, interview by author, June 12, 2022.

26. Bigott notes this in his history of Polish immigrants to Chicago. Joseph C. Bigott, *From Cottage to Bungalow: Houses and the Working Class in Metropolitan Chicago, 1899–1929* (Chicago: University of Chicago Press, 2001), 111.

27. See Davarian Baldwin, *Chicago's New Negroes: Modernity, the Great Migration, and Black Urban Life* (Chapel Hill: University of North Carolina Press, 2007), passim chapter 2. Greer documents redlining in Chicago: James L. Greer, "Historic Home Mortgage Redlining in Chicago," *Journal of the Illinois State Historical Society*, Vol. 107, No. 2 (Summer 2014), 204–233. Freund demonstrates that discrimination resulted from racialized federal policies. David Freund, *Colored Property: State Policy and White Racial Politics in Suburban America* (Chicago: University of Chicago Press, 2007), especially chapter 3.

28. *Proceedings of National Conference on Postwar Housing*, 8.

29. "Home Builders' Convention Stresses Plans for Postwar," *Architectural Forum*, February 1945, 60–63, 60–61.

30. Neal Samors and Michael Williams, *Neighborhoods within Neighborhoods: Twentieth Century Life on Chicago's Far North Side* (Rogers Park/West Ridge Historical Society, 2002), 164.

31. "2 Bungalow Districts Make History: West Ridge, South Shore Join Ranks of National Register," *Chicago Tribune*, March 13, 2009, SSW-B10.

32. Irving Cutler, *The Jews of Chicago: From Shtetl to Suburb* (Urbana: University of Illinois Press, 2009), 209–210.

33. Cutler, *The Jews of Chicago*, 193.

34. Cutler, 119.

35. Beverly Siegel Productions, "Driving West Rogers Park: Chicago's Once and Future Jewish Neighborhood," dir. Beverly Siegel. 2017; updated 2020. www.jndcchicago.org.

36. Beverly Siegel Productions, "Driving West Rogers Park."

37. Marilyn Domsky, interview by author, July 7, 2022.

38. Donna Scheckerman Orlove, correspondence with author, July 15, 2022.

39. Neal Samors and Michael Williams, *Neighborhoods within Neighborhoods: Twentieth Century Life on Chicago's Far North Side* (Rogers Park/West Ridge Historical Society, 2002), 164.

40. Joel Scheckerman, interview by author, June 14, 2022.

41. Sara Belkov, interview by author, June 30, 2022.

42. Rogers Park/West Ridge Historical Society, "House Tour, June 10, 2012." Deer Park, A Community of Prize-Winning Homes, Booklet, 6.

43. Al Chase, "Leasehold Land to Be Used for Homes Project," *Chicago Tribune*, December 15, 1946, WA.

44. Rogers Park/West Ridge Historical Society, "House Tour, June 10, 2012." Deer Park, A Community of Prize-Winning Homes, Booklet, 4.

45. Donna Scheckerman Orlove, interview by author, July 14, 2022.

46. U.S. Census, 1950, 103–4960, 24, 29, 30, 34.

47. "25 Acre Homes Tract Is Opened in Rogers Park," *Chicago Tribune*, March 31, 1946, 26.

48. Beverly Siegel Productions, "Driving West Rogers Park: Chicago's Once and Future Jewish Neighborhood," dir. Beverly Siegel. 2017; updated 2020. www .jndcchicago.org.

49. U.S. Census, 1950, 103–4960, 24, 29, 30, 24.

50. Irving Cutler, *The Jews of Chicago: From Shtetl to Suburb* (Urbana: University of Illinois Press, 2009), 244.

51. See Dominic A. Pacyga and Ellen Skerrett, *Chicago: City of Neighborhoods* (Chicago: Loyola University Press, 1986), chapter 4; Neal Samors and Michael Williams, *Neighborhoods within Neighborhoods: Twentieth Century Life on Chicago's Far North Side* (Rogers Park/West Ridge Historical Society, 2002).

52. Kathy Halper, interview by author, May 16, 2022; Sunny Balsam, interview by author, July 22, 2021.

53. Irving Cutler, *The Jews of Chicago: From Shtetl to Suburb* (Urbana: University of Illinois Press, 2009), 255.

54. Bill and Valerie Kanter, interview by author, June 12, 2022.

55. Kathleen and Terry Shiel, interview by author, June 19, 2022; Rita Horovicz, interview by author, July 17, 2022.

56. Jewish United Fund, "Jewish History of West Rogers Park Explored in New Documentary," https://www.juf.org/news/arts.aspx?id=444787. Accessed April 28, 2021.

57. Ben Sales, "The Rise, Fall and Rise Again of a Historically Jewish Chicago Neighborhood," Jewish Telegraphic Agency, December 19, 2019. https://www.jta .org/2019/12/19/united-states/the-rise-fall-and-rise-again-of-a-historically-jewish -chicago-neighborhood.

58. See Irving Cutler, *The Jews of Chicago: From Shtetl to Suburb* (Urbana: University of Chicago Press, 1996), passim chapter 5.

59. Javonte Anderson, "23 Chicago-Area Roman Catholic Parishes to Close, Merge in Latest Round of Restructuring," *Chicago Tribune*, February 7, 2020.

60. TRD Staff, "Jewish Elementary School Buys Former St. Timothy Parish in Chicago's West Ridge," *The Real Deal: Chicago Real Estate News*, April 12, 2022. https:// therealdeal.com/chicago/2022/04/12/jewish-elementary-school-buys-former-st -timothy-parish-in-chicagos-west-ridge.

61. Kathleen and Terry Shiel, interview by author, June 19, 2022.

62. Ben Sales, "The Rise, Fall and Rise Again of a Historically Jewish Chicago Neighborhood," Jewish Telegraphic Agency, December 19, 2019. https://www.jta .org/2019/12/19/united-states/the-rise-fall-and-rise-again-of-a-historically-jewish -chicago-neighborhood.

63. "Our Story," Patel Brothers. https://www.patelbros.com/our-mission.

64. CMAP Community Data Snapshot, West Ridge, Chicago Community Area, June 2020 release.

65. Ursula O'Hayer, interview by author, July 3, 2022; Kathleen and Terry Shiel, interview by author, June 19, 2022; Jeremy Goerner, "Lottery Winner's Cyanide Poisoning Death Remains Unsolved Five Years Later," *Chicago Tribune*, July 25, 2017.

66. Rita Horovicz, interview by author, June 17, 2022.

67. Judy Fink Essek, interview by author, June 28, 2022.

68. U.S. Census, 1950, 103–4960, 24, 29, 30, 34.

69. A 2020 Pew study affirms that while the average birth rate for all Americans is 2.3 children, the average for Orthodox Jews is 3.3. Pew Research Center, Jewish Americans in 2020 (May 11, 2021). https://www.pewresearch.org/religion/2021/05/11 /jewish-demographics/#:~:text=Orthodox%20Jewish%20adults%20report%20 having,among%20non%2DOrthodox%20Jews. Accessed July 20, 2022.

70. Ben Zeller, interview by author, June 2, 2021.

71. Bill and Valerie Kanter, interview by author, June 12, 2022.

72. Marilyn Domsky, interview by author, July 7, 2022.

73. Bill and Valerie Kanter, interview by author, June 12, 2022.

74. Beverly Siegel, interview by author, May 3, 2021.

75. Bill and Valerie Kanter, interview by author, June 12, 2022.

76. Robert Matanky, interview by author, May 3, 2021.

77. Jeffrey Steele, "West Ridge: 'Around the World in 80 Blocks,'" *Chicago Tribune*, March 9, 2003, O1–2.

78. Steele, "West Ridge: 'Around the World in 80 Blocks,'" O2.

79. Robert Matanky, interview by author, May 3, 2021.

80. Joel Scheckerman, interview by author, June 14, 2022.

81. Sara Belkov, interview by author, June 30, 2022; Judy Fink Essek, interview by author, June 28, 2022.

82. Audrey Hellinger, interview by author, July 15, 2022.

83. Greer Braun, interview by author, July 24, 2022.

84. Susan Weber Postma, interview by author, September 20, 2022.

85. Rich Schneider, interview by author, July 16, 2022.

Conclusion

1. Samuel Dodd, "Parade of Homes: Salesmanship and the Post-War American Housing Industry," *Journal of Design History*, Vol. 28, No. 4 (2015), 385–404, 385.

2. "Geneva Modern Kitchens," *Portage Daily Register and Democrat*, August 7, 1948, 5.

3. Donna Scheckerman Orlove, interview by author, July 14, 2022.

4. "Real Estate for Sale," *Blue Island Sun Standard*, October 16, 1947, 26; "For Sale—Palanois Park," *Arlington Heights Herald*, June 4, 1948, 12.

5. Avrum Weinfeld, interview by author, July 24, 2022.

6. Ruth Moss, "22 in Tribune Homes Hold a Neighbor Fete," *Chicago Tribune*, October 8, 1953, C8.

7. "Tribune Prize Home Can Be Yours," *Chicago Tribune,* September 12, 1964, 34.

8. Kathy Halper, interview by author, May 16, 2022.

9. Edith Weigle, "Decorating Ingenuity Makes Small Apartment Spacious," *Chicago Tribune*, September 15, 1948, 31.

10. Rogers Park/West Ridge Historical Society, "House Tour, June 10, 2012." Deer Park, A Community of Prize-Winning Homes.

11. Philip Berger, ed., *Highland Park: American Suburb at Its Best, an Architectural and Historical Survey* (Highland Park: The Highland Park Landmark Preservation Committee, 1982).

12. Alysa Slay, interview by author, June 9, 2022.

13. Rachel and Hester Balsam, interview by author, July 19, 2021; Sunny Balsam, interview by author, July 22, 2021.

14. The author's post on a Facebook group, "You Know You're From Wheaton If . . ." identified the Smedleys and their memories of the house.

15. https://censusreporter.org/locate.

Index

SIOBHAN MORONEY is an associate professor of
politics and the chair of American Studies
at Lake Forest College.

The University of Illinois Press
is a founding member of the
Association of University Presses.

_____

Composed in 10.5/13 Minion Pro
with Avenir LT Std display
by Kirsten Dennison
at the University of Illinois Press
Manufactured by Sheridan Books, Inc.

University of Illinois Press
1325 South Oak Street
Champaign, IL 61820-6903
www.press.uillinois.edu